First World War
and Army of Occupation
War Diary
France, Belgium and Germany

36 DIVISION
Divisional Troops
150 Field Company Royal Engineers
5 October 1915 - 28 February 1919

WO95/2497/3

The Naval & Military Press Ltd
www.nmarchive.com
Published in association with The National Archives

Published by

The Naval & Military Press Ltd

Unit 10 Ridgewood Industrial Park,

Uckfield, East Sussex,

TN22 5QE England

Tel: +44 (0) 1825 749494

www.naval-military-press.com

www.nmarchive.com

This diary has been reprinted in facsimile from the original. Any imperfections are inevitably reproduced and the quality may fall short of modern type and cartographic standards.

© Crown Copyright
Images reproduced by permission of The National Archives, London, England, 2015.

Contents

Document type	Place/Title	Date From	Date To
Heading	WO95/2497/3 150 Field Company Royal Engineers		
Heading	36th Division 150th Field Coy. R.E. Oct 1915-Feb 1919		
Heading	36th Division 150th Coy R.E. Vol I. Oct. 15		
War Diary	Bordon	05/10/1915	05/10/1915
War Diary	Havre	06/10/1915	06/10/1915
War Diary	Bertangles	07/10/1915	12/10/1915
War Diary	Bertangle to Arqueves	12/10/1915	12/10/1915
War Diary	Arqueves	13/10/1915	31/10/1915
Heading	36th Division 150th F.C.R.E. Vol. 2 Nov 15		
War Diary	Arqueves	01/11/1915	16/11/1915
War Diary	Englebelmer	17/11/1915	23/11/1915
War Diary	Arquerves	24/11/1915	27/11/1915
War Diary	Bernaville	28/11/1915	28/11/1915
War Diary	Domqueur	29/11/1915	30/11/1915
Heading	36th Division 150th F.C.R.E. Vol : 3. Dec. 15		
War Diary	Domqueur	01/12/1915	28/12/1915
War Diary	Doullens	29/12/1915	31/12/1915
Heading	36th Div. Jan 1916. 150th F.C.R.E. Vol 4		
Heading	War Diary of 150th Field Coy R.E. From Jany 1/1916 To Jany 31/1916		
War Diary	Doullens	01/01/1916	31/01/1916
Miscellaneous			
Heading	150 Coy. R.E. 36th Div. Vol 5		
Heading	War Diary of 150th Field Co. R.E. February 1916		
War Diary	Doullens	01/02/1916	04/02/1916
War Diary	Mailley-Maillet	05/02/1916	29/02/1916
Heading	150th Field Coy R.E. War Diary March 1916. Vol 6		
War Diary	Mailley Maillet	01/03/1916	05/03/1916
War Diary	Mailly-Maillet. Acheux	06/03/1916	17/03/1916
War Diary	Mailly-Maillet Martinsart	18/03/1916	23/03/1916
War Diary	Martinsart	24/03/1916	31/03/1916
Heading	War Diary of 150th Field Coy. R.E. April, 1916. Vol 67		
War Diary	Martinsart	01/04/1916	30/04/1916
Heading	War Diary of 150th Field Coy. R.E. May 1916. Vol 8		
War Diary	Martinsart	01/05/1916	31/05/1916
Heading	36th Divisional Engineers 150th Field Company R.E. June 1916		
War Diary	Forceville	01/06/1916	30/06/1916
Heading	36th Divisional Engineers 150th Field Company R.E. July 1916		
War Diary	Thiepval Wood	01/07/1916	02/07/1916
War Diary	Martinsart	02/07/1916	02/07/1916
War Diary	Forceville	03/07/1916	04/07/1916
War Diary	Aveluy	05/07/1916	09/07/1916
War Diary	Beauval	10/07/1916	10/07/1916
War Diary	Beaumetz	11/07/1916	11/07/1916
War Diary	Berguette	12/07/1916	12/07/1916
War Diary	Campagne	12/07/1916	12/07/1916
War Diary	Serques	13/07/1916	21/07/1916

War Diary	Ledringham	22/07/1916	23/07/1916
War Diary	Croix De Poperinghe	24/07/1916	24/07/1916
War Diary	Ledon	25/07/1916	31/07/1916
Heading	War Diary of 150th Field Coy R.E. August, 1916. Vol 11		
War Diary	Le Don	01/08/1916	31/08/1916
War Diary	War Diary of 150th Field Coy. R.E. September 1916. Vol 12		
War Diary	Le Don	01/09/1916	04/09/1916
War Diary	M.35.b.5.1	05/09/1916	30/09/1916
War Diary	War Diary of 150th Field Coy R.E. October 1916. Vol 13		
War Diary	Dranoutre	01/10/1916	31/10/1916
War Diary	War Diary of 150th Field Coy R.E. November 1916. Vol 14		
War Diary	Dranoutre	01/11/1916	30/11/1916
War Diary	War Diary of 150th Field Coy R.E. December 1916. Vol 15		
War Diary	Dranoutre M.35.b.4.4	01/12/1916	23/12/1916
War Diary	T.23.d.7.9	23/12/1916	31/12/1916
War Diary	War Diary of 150th Field Coy. R.E. January 1917. Vol 16		
War Diary		01/01/1917	31/01/1917
War Diary	War Diary of 150th Field Coy. R.E. February 1917. Vol 17		
War Diary		01/02/1917	28/02/1917
War Diary	War Diary of 150th Field Coy. R.E. March 1917. Vol 18		
War Diary	Camp	01/03/1917	10/03/1917
War Diary	Monmouth Camp Dranoutre	11/03/1917	26/03/1917
War Diary	Monmouth Camp	28/03/1917	31/03/1917
Heading	War Diary of 150th Field Coy. R.E. April, 1917. Vol 19		
War Diary	In The Field	01/04/1917	22/04/1917
War Diary	Dranoutre	23/04/1917	30/04/1917
Miscellaneous	Appendix "A".		
Heading	War Diary of 150th Field Coy. R.E. May 1917. Vol 20		
War Diary	Dranoutre	01/05/1917	31/07/1917
Heading	War Diary of 150th Field Coy. R.E. June, 1917. Vol 21		
War Diary	Dranoutre	01/06/1917	07/06/1917
War Diary	In The Field	07/06/1917	30/06/1917
War Diary	War Diary of 150th Field Coy. R.E. July, 1917. Vol 22		
War Diary		01/07/1917	06/07/1917
War Diary	Merckeghem	07/07/1917	14/07/1917
War Diary	Sheet 27. c.30.b.2.5	15/07/1917	29/07/1917
War Diary	Sheet 27. L.16 Central	30/07/1917	30/07/1917
War Diary	Sheet 27. L.16a Central	31/07/1917	31/07/1917
War Diary	War Diary of 150th Field Coy. R.E. August, 1917. Vol 23		
War Diary	Belgium & France Sheet 27. L.16.a.2.4	01/08/1917	03/08/1917
War Diary	Sheet 27. L.16.a.24	04/08/1917	04/08/1917
War Diary	Sheet 28. H.8.a.5.9. & I.1.b.6.0.0	05/08/1917	14/08/1917
War Diary	Forward Billet I.1.B.6-0	15/08/1917	16/08/1917
War Diary	Capricorn Trench C.18.d.2.1	16/08/1917	16/08/1917
War Diary	H.8.a.5.9. & I.1.B.6.0	17/08/1917	17/08/1917
War Diary	Sheet 27. J.6.a.1.7	18/08/1917	23/08/1917
War Diary	France Sheet 57.C	24/08/1917	24/08/1917

War Diary	O.10.c.1.6	25/08/1917	29/08/1917
War Diary	Bertincourt Hermies (57C P7604 & J 23 d 50)	29/08/1917	29/08/1917
War Diary	57.C.P.7.b.6.4. J.23.d.5.0	30/08/1917	31/08/1917
Map			
Miscellaneous	No. 6. Track (Wheeled). Red.		
Heading	War Diary of 150th Field Coy. R.E. September 1917. Vol 24		
War Diary	Sheet 57.c Back Billet P.7.b.6.4	01/09/1917	01/09/1917
War Diary	Hermies J.23.d.50. Forward Biller	01/09/1917	01/09/1917
War Diary	57c P.7.b.6.4. J.23.d.5.0	02/09/1917	13/09/1917
War Diary	As Before	13/09/1917	21/09/1917
War Diary	Sheet 57c Forward Billet (J.23.d.5.0 Hermies) Back Billet P.7.b.6.4. (Bertincourt)	22/09/1917	24/09/1917
War Diary	As Before	25/09/1917	30/09/1917
Map			
Heading	War Diary of 150th Field Coy R.E. October 1917. Vol 25		
War Diary	Bertincourt & Hermies P.7.b.6.7. K.23.D.5.0	01/10/1917	31/10/1917
Heading	War Diary of O.C. 150th Field Coy R.E. for November 1917. Vol 26		
War Diary	Bertincourt & Hermies	01/11/1917	30/11/1917
Heading	War Diary 150th Field Coy. R.E. November 1917		
Heading	War Diary of 150th Field Coy. R.E. December, 1917. Vol 27		
War Diary	Field	01/12/1917	31/12/1917
Heading	War Diary of 150th Field Coy R.E. January 1918. Vol 28		
Miscellaneous			
War Diary	Domart	01/01/1918	06/01/1918
War Diary	Domart Fresnoy	07/01/1918	07/01/1918
War Diary	Fresnoy	08/01/1918	08/01/1918
War Diary	Fresnoy Billancourt	09/01/1918	09/01/1918
War Diary	Billancourt	10/01/1918	10/01/1918
War Diary	B-Ollezy	11/01/1918	13/01/1918
War Diary	Out Side Gd-Seraucourt G.8.a.30.35	14/01/1918	16/01/1918
War Diary	Gd Seraucourt G.6.a.77	17/01/1918	27/01/1918
War Diary	Back Area Gd Seraucourt	28/01/1918	28/01/1918
War Diary	Billets G.9.c.1.4.-Forward Area Billet 2 Sec S. G.6.a.7.7	29/01/1918	31/01/1918
Miscellaneous			
Heading	War Diary of 150th Field Coy R.E. February 1918 Vol 29		
War Diary	Gd. Seraucourt G.9.c.1.4. Forward Billet G.6.a.7.7	01/02/1918	01/02/1918
War Diary	Gd. Seraucourt.	02/02/1918	18/02/1918
War Diary	Field	19/02/1918	28/02/1918
Heading	36th Divisional Engineers 150th Field Company R.E. March 1918		
Heading	War Diary of 150th Field Coy R.E. March. 1918 Vol 30		
War Diary	Field	01/03/1918	22/03/1918
War Diary	Golancourt	23/03/1918	31/03/1918
Heading	36th Divisional Engineers 150th Field Company R.E. April 1918		
Heading	War Diary of O.C. 150th Field Company R.E. for Month of April, 1918 Vol 31		
War Diary	Embreville	01/04/1918	04/04/1918
War Diary	Ypres Salient	05/04/1918	16/04/1918

War Diary	Canal Bank Ypres	17/04/1918	30/04/1918
Heading	War Diary of 150th Field Coy. R.E. From April to April 30/1918		
Heading	War Diary of 150th Field Coy R.E. From May 1st to May 31st 1918 Vol. 32		
War Diary	Forward Billet for 2 Sections Canal Bank Ypres C.25.a.8.2 Wagon Lines And Two Sections Hurst Camp A.10 A.02	01/05/1918	30/05/1918
War Diary	Ypres Salient as Before	31/05/1918	31/05/1918
Heading	War Diary of 150th Field Coy R.E. June, 1918 Vol 33		
War Diary	Back Billet Approx 2 Sections Wayon Lines Hirst Camp A.10 A.0.2 Forward Billet 2 Sections Canal Bank Dugouts Ypres c.25 A.8.2	01/06/1918	05/06/1918
War Diary	Ball Camp	06/06/1918	13/06/1918
War Diary	Proven	14/06/1918	26/06/1918
War Diary	Proven	14/06/1918	30/06/1918
Heading	War Diary of 150th Field Coy R.E. July 1918 Vol34		
War Diary	Proven	01/07/1918	01/07/1918
War Diary	St Jan Ter Biezen	02/07/1918	02/07/1918
War Diary	Sheet 127 O 26 c 4.2.	03/07/1918	06/07/1918
War Diary	Eecke	07/07/1918	31/07/1918
Heading	War Diary of 150th Field Coy R.E. August 1918 Vol 35		
War Diary	Field	01/08/1918	09/08/1918
War Diary	Eecke	10/08/1918	31/08/1918
Heading	War Diary of 150th Field Coy. R.E. September 1918 Vol 36		
War Diary		01/09/1918	22/09/1918
War Diary	Pesel Hoek	23/09/1918	30/09/1918
Heading	War Diary of 150th Field Coy. R.E. April, 1918		
War Diary	West Hoek	01/10/1918	01/10/1918
War Diary	Becelaere	02/10/1918	14/10/1918
War Diary	Field	14/10/1918	14/10/1918
War Diary	Cohen House	15/10/1918	16/10/1918
War Diary	Ledeghem	17/10/1918	18/10/1918
War Diary	Absul 29/ B15a	19/10/1918	20/10/1918
War Diary	19/c 13 c53	21/10/1918	26/10/1918
War Diary	Lendelede	27/10/1918	28/10/1918
War Diary	St Annes	29/10/1918	31/10/1918
Miscellaneous	Narrative of Operations by 150th Field Coy., R.E., 15th Oct.- 1st Oct.1918	23/10/1918	23/10/1918
Heading	War Diary of 150th Field Company R.E. November. 1918 Vol 38		
War Diary	St Annes Sheet 29	01/11/1918	09/11/1918
War Diary	Mouscron	10/11/1918	12/11/1918
War Diary	Escanaffles	13/11/1918	18/11/1918
War Diary	Roncq	19/11/1918	30/11/1918
Heading	War Diary of 150th Field Coy R.E. December, 1918 Vol 39		
War Diary	Roncq	01/12/1918	31/12/1918
Heading	War Diary of 150th Field Coy R.E. January 1919 Vol 40		
War Diary	Roncq	01/01/1919	31/01/1919
Heading	War Diary of 150th Field Coy R.E. February 1919 Vol 41		
War Diary	Roncq	01/02/1919	28/02/1919

mo/a5/a4a7/3

150 Field Company Royal Engineers

36TH DIVISION

150TH FIELD COY. R.E.
OCT 1915 - FEB 1919.

36TH DIVISION

121/7437

36th Division

150th by R.E.
Vol I

Oct 15

Army Form C. 2118.

WAR DIARY
or
INTELLIGENCE SUMMARY
(Erase heading not required.)

Instructions regarding War Diaries and Intelligence
Summaries are contained in F.S. Regs., Part II.
and the Staff Manual respectively. Title pages
will be prepared in manuscript.

Place	Date	Hour	Summary of Events and Information	Remarks and references to Appendices
Bordon	5/10/15	10 A.M.	Left Bordon - arrived Southampton 1 A.M. left for Havre 4.35 p.m.	
Havre	6/10/15		Arrived 7 A.M. - Remained in No 5 Rest Camp - left Havre	
			10 midnight	
Berdoogh	7/10/15		Arrived 4.30 p.m. - went into Billets	
"	8 Oct		Cleaning up billets - Sheets etc -	
"	9 Oct		Section Drill - made straw mats - Search light instruction	
"	10		Section Drill. Not Sect. Rent mask.	
"	11		Sect. 1 & 3 making temporary range. No 2 - Cutting posts	
			for telegraph wire. No 4 Fatigues & rucker, filled	
			in sp 6 - 11.2. Major present highest visible with	
	12		Left Approved heavy. left Berdough 6 a.m. & marched to Bergminn	
Berdough to Bergminn			arrived Bergminn. left Bergminn 9 p.m. approx 3.30 p.m.	

WAR DIARY
or
INTELLIGENCE SUMMARY.
(Erase heading not required.)

Army Form C. 2118.

Place	Date	Hour	Summary of Events and Information	Remarks and references to Appendices
Arqueves	13 Oct		Cleaning up billets. Analysing latrines. Breaking up & making out defences works at heath Hill	
	14		Sect 1, 2, 3 & 4 working do	
	15		do do	
	16		do do 96 Pioneers working on front line	
	17		Church Parade. C.R.E. inspect R.E.S. 156 Pioneers working	
	18		Sections 2 at Central new defences VII. 150 Pioneers working	
			Sect 4 at No VIII setting out	
			Sect 3 at No IX " "	
			Sect 1 at No X " "	
	19		Sect 1, 2, 3 & 4 @ Defences No X, IX, VIII, VII respects	
			150 Pioneers working at No VII	

Oct 19ᵃ 1915

J C Boyle
Major R.E.

WAR DIARY
or
INTELLIGENCE SUMMARY.
(Erase heading not required.)

Army Form C. 2118.

Place	Date	Hour	Summary of Events and Information	Remarks and references to Appendices
Arqueves	21st Oct.		Sections 1.2.3.4. Setting our defence works & digging 100 Pioneer digging on defence VII. & 4.5 making hurdles	
"	2/10th		Sects: 1.2.3.4. Setting out palisades. defences VII. VIII. IX. X.	
			7. Pioneers digging in No VII.	
			Cost men on transport fatigue	
"	22nd		Sects 1.2.3.4. Setting out & digging defences VII. VIII.	further that part 22
			IX & X. Pioneers working on defence No VII.	
			Seph fut T.G. about 70. 19 Corporals Armr Class ditto	
"	23rd		defence No VII.	
	24		Church Parade — washing clothes &c —	
"	25		Sect2 working on No VII defence tos 10 Platoon bathed & washed	
			VIII " 104	
			IX " 12.0 — Pioneer 16.P.A.R squad	
			X " 80	
			4 Capt Clayton Bournequith to No 4 Clearing Station	

Army Form C. 2118.

WAR DIARY
or
INTELLIGENCE SUMMARY.
(Erase heading not required.)

Instructions regarding War Diaries and Intelligence Summaries are contained in F. S. Regs., Part II. and the Staff Manual respectively. Title pages will be prepared in manuscript.

Place	Date	Hour	Summary of Events and Information	Remarks and references to Appendices
Anzac	26/10/15		Sect I Setting out revetting Sepum IX fg Pioneers digging " II " " " Sepum VII 115 Latrine Buffer digging " III " " " Sepum IXI 170 Pioneers digging " IV " " VIII fg Latrine Bath digging	
"	27/10/15		Sect I Setting out revetting Sepum X 92 Pioneers working Culvert trenches " II do Sepum VII 85 Latrine hut works " III " " IX 16 Pioneers digging " IV " " VIII 80 Latrine Bath digging	
"	28/10/15		Sect I Revetting Sepum X 96 Pioneers working " II " " VII 87 Latrine Baths " III " " IX 123 Pioneers working " IV " " VIII 33 Latrine Bath working	

Army Form C. 2118.

WAR DIARY
or
INTELLIGENCE SUMMARY.

(Erase heading not required.)

Instructions regarding War Diaries and Intelligence Summaries are contained in F. S. Regs., Part II. and the Staff Manual respectively. Title pages will be prepared in manuscript.

Place	Date	Hour	Summary of Events and Information	Remarks and references to Appendices
Argoeuvres	29/4/15		Sect. 1 Buildings th' dugout X. 94 Pioneer working	
			" 2. " " " VII 130 Luton hollow working	
			" 3. " " " IX 147 Pioneers working	
			" 4. " " " VIII 33 Labour batt'n ditto	
			2 Comm. breast work trenches	
			around — gateway to dugout VIII.	
			Sect 1 — Buildings th' dugout X —	
			" 2 " " " VII 93 Lamoncelle working	
			" 3 " " " IX 123 Pioneers working	
			" 4 " " " VIII 51 — Labour batt'n working	
			Further supply tank trench will be very troublesome to	
			being cut near trenches for use to keep trench far away to hide	
			trench. Trench allotted for 2.0 truck away. —	
	30/4			
		3.15pm	Church Service. Cleaning up generally. Working	
			parties.	
			J Corpley Major R.E.	

36th Kurwin

150 £ 7 C R E
Fol. 2

15.
Nov. 37

121/7631

WAR DIARY
or
INTELLIGENCE SUMMARY

Army Form C. 2118

Place	Date	Hour	Summary of Events and Information	Remarks and references to Appendices
APQ4EVR53	Nov 1		Sect 1. Revetting & preparing trenches for Defence VII X — Defence VII	Infantry staff 4 Pioneer Coy SLI
			2. " " "	1/4 Loyal N Lancs/ptes
			3. Digging +c Defence IX X	3. Pioneers, Inf Rein
			4. Revetting Defence X	31 La man Butts Coys
			No trucks available for No 3 Section hence undertipped all morn =	
	2.		Sect 1. Revetting Defence X	
			2. Revetting & preparing trenches for Defence VII	5 No 2 alarm Butts working
			3. " " Defence IX	10 " " "
			4. " VIII	
			Very wet. Knocked off work at one p.m.	
	3		Sect 1. Revetting & Defence X	
			2. Revetting " VII IX	67 Pioneers working
			3. Revetting " XII	114 Labour Bn to "
			4. " "	and 38 Kohn Bulls

Army Form C. 2118.

WAR DIARY
or
INTELLIGENCE SUMMARY.
(Erase heading not required.)

Instructions regarding War Diaries and Intelligence Summaries are contained in F.S. Regs., Part II. and the Staff Manual respectively. Title pages will be prepared in manuscript.

Place	Date	Hour	Summary of Events and Information	Remarks and references to Appendices
Ypres	Nov 4		Sect 1. Brethn etc before XI	
			" " " " VII	83 Poperinghe hutting
				116 Zuidschoote
		3.	Clearing trenches etc IX	
		4.	Brethn etc - hutting huts out VIII	37 Zillebeke huts
	Nov 5	Sec. 1.	Brethn to Reserve x	83 Pioneers
		2.	" " " VII	107 Lecture But. huts
		3.	" " " IX	and
		4.	" " " VIII	50 "
	6th	Sec 1	" " " X	75 Pioneers hutting
		2	" " " VII	Labour Batt.
		3	" " " IX	104 "
		4	" " " VIII	50 Labour Batt.
	7.		The Company is billetted in barns as Sh- we have been forced	
			here has $\frac{+N_0}{+N_0}$ newspapers given to the them in particular	
			applied for them. New that the carry are such few	

WAR DIARY
INTELLIGENCE SUMMARY

Army Form C. 2118.

Place	Date	Hour	Summary of Events and Information	Remarks and references to Appendices
Acquino	8/11/15		Sect 1. Entrenching works Defence X.	
			Sect 2. Entrenching works at " VII.	9 O & other ranks now working
			Sect 3. " " " IX.	
			" " " " VIII	4 O & other ranks —
			The 1st & 2nd Field Cos to prepare defence North
			Khaka XI & the 11/2/3 2d Co to prepare
			works South of Defence VII. Some signallers
			are making defences of the Village of Acquino.
	9/11/15		Sect 1. Entrenching works Defence X.	23 Pioneers working
			" 2. " " " VII.	100 Labour Battn
			" 3. " " " IX.	46 Pioneers
			" 4. " " " VIII.	37 Labour Battn

WAR DIARY or INTELLIGENCE SUMMARY

Army Form C. 2118.

Refers once to a Veterinary Officer for the [unit] — When units get there 11. The unites [units] will be fit in much Smaller [stronger] but some Cobm supplied by the latter better & one tenten[?] have saved[?] trouble.

At present pen tenten is being drawn by Motor transport about 20 miles — The teeth have been but still the hosts feed — Men have not yet had water here it a chance of going to see the health of the men will suffer. The rations are good. The men satisfied with them. This dirt like the tea long hours (no cnt) — many of the men had. Their teeth pulled before leaving England & have not been supplied with false ones. Consequently many men are suffering. Not been one unable to masticate their food & feau [are] being invalided with suffer[ing with] their health —

WAR DIARY
or
INTELLIGENCE SUMMARY.

Army Form C. 2118

Place	Date	Hour	Summary of Events and Information	Remarks and references to Appendices
10/4/15 Aupem	10/4/15		Marched out to our huts at Aupeme work arry frequency rain	
	11/4/15		Sect. 1 Entrenching St. Defence 2 - 3 - 4 - X 25 Pioneers working VII 90 Labour Battn IX 30 Pioneers VIII 59 Labour Battn.	
	12/4/15		Sect. 1 Entrenching &c Defence 2 - 3 - 4 - X 33 Pioneers working VII 86 Labour Battn IX 30 Pioneers VIII 60 Labour Battn.	
	13/4/15		Church Parade Ankemtomme Sect 1 Entrenching &c defence 2 - 3 - X VII } wet morning no Pioneers IX } not Labour Battn men VIII } turned up at work	

Army Form C. 2118

WAR DIARY
or
INTELLIGENCE SUMMARY.
(Erase heading not required.)

Instructions regarding War Diaries and Intelligence Summaries are contained in F. S. Regs., Part II. and the Staff Manual respectively. Title pages will be prepared in manuscript.

Place	Date	Hour	Summary of Events and Information	Remarks and references to Appendices
Orgueves	14/11/15		Church Parade: Company washing	
	15/11/15		Section 1 Entrenching etc Dickens X	
			2 — VII	
			3 — IX	
			4 — VIII (ENGELBELMER)	
	16/11/15		Sections 1 & 4 to Engelbelmer — Marched in WVth	
			2 — " " in charge of	
			3 — " "	
			— 2 & 3 to (MESNIL) MEINIL	
			Headquarters Section could not move owing to the state of the roads caused by fall of snow	
Engelbelmer	17/11/15		Headquarters moved to (ENGELBELMER) ENGEBELMER, Sections 1 working on 2nd line trenches with gun-pits by R.E.	
			(Stationed in Billets)	2. Road making main in Joint West Lane R.E.
				3. Fatigues in German line

2353 Wt. W2544/1454 700,000 5/15 D. D. & L. A.D.S.S./Forms/C. 2118.

Army Form C. 2118.

WAR DIARY
or
INTELLIGENCE SUMMARY.

(Erase heading not required.)

Place	Date	Hour	Summary of Events and Information	Remarks and references to Appendices
ENGLEBELMER	Nov '18		Sections No 1 } working in 2nd line trenches with 9th FIELD Co. R.E. 4	
			2. Road making and mines in MESNIL village } with WEST LANCS. R.E.	
			3. Dugouts in Second line trenches	
"	19		Sections No 1 } working in 2nd line trenches with 9th FIELD Co. R.E. 4	
			2. Road making & mines in MESNIL village } with WEST LANCS. R.E.	
			3. Dugouts in Second line trenches	
"	20		Sections No 1 } working in Second line trenches with 9th FIELD Co. R.E. 4 (One man Rct. Pal. H.) Injured by 3.80 Sap. with ?	
			2. Road making & mines in MESNIL village } with WEST LANCS. R.E.	
			3. Dugouts in Second line trenches	
"	21		Sections 1 } Parties on the works. Rct. Foot inspection by the officers 4	
			2. Road making & mines in MESNIL village } with WEST LANCS. R.E.	
			3. Dugouts in Second line trenches	

WAR DIARY or INTELLIGENCE SUMMARY

Army Form C. 2118.

Place	Date	Hour	Summary of Events and Information	Remarks and references to Appendices
ENGLEBELMER	Nov 22		Sections 1) Wiring in second line trenches with 9th FIELD Co. R.E.	
			2) Road making and mining in N. ESNIL village	
			3) Dugout in Search line trenches	
			"Moore" Mine (G=360 Coy. R.E. 5 Km.) drain. The body was buried at 6 o'clock pm on the 23rd	
	23		At the Dugout Cemetery near E. MAILLY at 6 o'clock pm on the 23rd	
			The 15 oth. Field Company moved to JRQUEVES	
ARQUEVES	24		Sections 1 Entrenching 6th Pioneers X 14 Pioneers	Pioneers from 9am working with
			2 " VII 40 Labour Bn	
			3 " IX 33 Pioneers	working with
			4 " VIII 55 Labour Bn	Rest day
	25		Sections 1 Entrenching 6th Pioneers X 25 Pioneers	working with
			2 " VII 12 Labour Bn	Coy
			3 " IX 32 Pioneers	
			4 " VIII 50 Labour Bn	
	26		Company having been handed over 9 lines works VII VIII to O.C.122 n.73 Coy. R.E. and N.T.K. to Pioneer Bn a.m.	

Army Form C. 2118.

WAR DIARY
or
INTELLIGENCE SUMMARY.
(Erase heading not required.)

Instructions regarding War Diaries and Intelligence Summaries are contained in F. S. Regs., Part II. and the Staff Manual respectively. Title pages will be prepared in manuscript.

Place	Date	Hour	Summary of Events and Information	Remarks and references to Appendices
ARQUEVES	Nov 27		The Company moved Codages from ARQUEVES to BERNAVILLE where they stopped in Billets for the night.	
BERNAVILLE	28		The Company moved Codages from BERNAVILLE to DOMQUEUR	
DOMQUEUR	29		The Company occupied Billets. The Company engaged in repairing Billets and in cleaning up the Billeting area.	
DOMQUEUR	30		The Company engaged on repairing roads etc in the Billeting area. Sitting together by their Potato Workshop. Repaired at Starting point 10 minute late owing to difficulty in getting horses on that push in will started 10 minute late made a forced march till our guide lost us into a ploughed field with no road at. he lost our position thought we was closely by man handling it I got on a good road again after a round march. Our guide disappears when we find in the Hough's field! J. Boyle Lieut OC 152 Coy Pl

150th F.C.RE.
fol. 3

15/7795

36th Kitchener

Keep 15

Army Form C. 21

WAR DIARY
or
INTELLIGENCE SUMMARY.
(Erase heading not required.)

Place	Date	Hour	Summary of Events and Information	Remarks and references to Appendices
DONQUEUR	Dec 1		The Company took over an Engineering Dump on the LE PLOUY Road at N'DONQUEUR. This Dump is being used by the Company for the manufacture of fittings for the Brigade Baths for the 109th Brigade, and for necessary Engineering work generally. The R.E. Park was moved from CANDAS to HAPPY-le-haut-COCHER by the 3rd Bridging Train (one N.C.O. and a party of two Sappers in charge temporarily). The Company engaged on miscellaneous works in Brigade Baths for 109th Brigade. Resuming Roads in Billeting Area. Trench Scheme commenced for 109th Brigade at ERGNIES.	
"	2		Company at miscellaneous works viz. laying out trenches at ERGNIES for 109th Brigade; making fittings for Brigade Bath in workroom; Experimental work on machine gun (that one newly in service) for machine gun section of Musketry Building; Quarrying Chalk at DONQUEUR for huts standings.	

WAR DIARY
or
INTELLIGENCE SUMMARY.
(Erase heading not required.)

Army Form C. 2118

Place	Date	Hour	Summary of Events and Information	Remarks and references to Appendices
DONQUEUR	Dec 3		Miscellaneous works viz making fittings for Brigade Bath in workshop. Cleaning manure out of billets. Repairing room in billeting area. Commenced horse standings at LONGVILLERS to hold 1/150000 ARTILLERY Brigade Territorial Force.	
"	4		Misc works viz making fittings for Brigade Bath in workshop. Cleaning manure out of billets. Repairing roads in Billeting area. Working at horse standings at LONGVILLERS for 1/150 H.A Brigade	
"	5		Artillery Brigade Territorial Force. Church Parade: Pay Parade: Fatigues	
"	6		Miscellaneous works viz Continuing Brigade Baths 100th Brigade at DONQUEUR. Working on horse standings at LONGVILLERS for the 1 London Artillery Brigade Territorial Forces. Quarrying stone at DONQUEUR for horse standings. Pontoning equipment to the Bs. sent to SAUVILLE in charge of 1210. Field Coy R.E. for Pontooning Course.	

WAR DIARY
or
INTELLIGENCE SUMMARY.
(Erase heading not required.)

Army Form C. 21

Place	Date	Hour	Summary of Events and Information	Remarks and references to Appendices
DONQUEUR	7		Modelling was continuing. Congratulating Amended 2 R.E.s at DONQUEUR. Horse Standings at LONGVILLERS for 14 London Field Coy R.E. Reasoning Roads in Billeting area, traning remounts etc. A visit from Lieut Tannage Remount Brigade Major R.F.A. to discuss Horse Standings at C.C.D. + Q. VILLIERS. Lieut Peacock appointed Enquiry Officer on arrival of 2nd Bn H. DONQUEUR to investigate claims for alleged damage to property of inhabitants.	
	8		2 Garrison and twenty men from R.E. on charge a saw mill at FONTAINE to saw the use of Infantry Brigade purposes. An N.C.O. sent to assist at Buissons (5449) to take charge of wood cutting parties of 9th Batt South Lancs. Regt. and 5 Lancs Fusiliers. arrived in Brigade Baths at DONQUEUR. Lieut Standing was in attendance on the 5. 7. Lucy Bond McDONQUEUR at LONGVILLERS and in attendance on the 5. 7. Lucy Bond McDONQUEUR	

WAR DIARY or INTELLIGENCE SUMMARY

Place	Date	Hour	Summary of Events and Information	Remarks and references to Appendices
DONQUEUR	8	Cont.d	Parties repairing billets and carting manure out of billets. Division parade put up as car tracks in previous roads in the Divisional area.	
"	9		Lt Cameron and fatigue Cameron worked at Saw mill at PONDRIN. Work cont.d on Brigade baths at DONQUEUR on lines standing at LONGVILLERS and in Brigade workshops at DONQUEUR. Lt Armstrong visited 158C field Ambulance at ST ALEYIA. H.H. Coy ASC at SURCHAMPS to consult with regard to state standings. Cast goods admitted to 10th High.L and Canadians Highland Casualty Clearing station. Some left. Work continued on Brigade baths at DONQUEUR. These baths are now working and bathing parades are taking place every day. Bathing parade for men of this Coy to-day. Work continued on Brigade workshops DONQUEUR.	
"	10		Lt Armstrong visited 1/2 London Brigade R.F.A at BRANKINGH	

WAR DIARY
or
INTELLIGENCE SUMMARY.

Army Form C. 2118

Place	Date	Hour	Summary of Events and Information	Remarks and references to Appendices
DOULENS	11		With Companies at Parades at 7.30 9.11 & 2.P. Work Continued as Before. Instruction in Machine gun fire, inspection of rifles - Musketry, Bayonet fighting, box respirator - one each of Lewis guns to Company. Bath, Bomb Throwers. Rifle & Bayonet Company drill. Bathing parade. Game with 15th London Regiment met at Dulgens for 11 A.H. Gordon Brigade. 7 Frank & 15 LR squads for training match R.F.H. St Gauburn and 9.40% working in conjunction with 5th on P.T. at DOULLENS and at the Saw mill at FONTAINE	
	12		Church Parade: Bathing parade: Dental Inspection. Cleaning Billets	

WAR DIARY
or
INTELLIGENCE SUMMARY.

(Erase heading not required.)

Army Form C. 21

Place	Date	Hour	Summary of Events and Information	Remarks and references to Appendices
DOMQUEUR	13		Work continued at Brigade batho DOMQUEUR, fitting rifle work. Work in Brigade workshop — overhauling wagons; rifle work for batho; sheet metal work for Field oven for 9th Inniskilling Fusiliers; iron troughs for R.F.A. Lieut. Jamieson R.E. and party marking tree standings for 154 Bde. R.F.A. at BOUCHON, COCQUEREL, MOUFLER, L'ÉTOILE, VAUCHELLES, and working saw mill at FONTAINE. Lieut. Armstrong R.E. and party setting out tranches at ERGNIES for 109th Brigade. Lieut. Smyth R.E. visited LONGVILLERS to buy timber, and LES MASURES to buy bricks. Party repairing billets for 9th Inniskilling Fusiliers DOMQUEUR.	
"	14		Lieut. Jamieson R.E. and party making tree standings for R.F.A at BOUCHON, COCQUEREL, MOUFLER, L'ÉTOILE, VAUCHELLES, and working saw mill at FONTAINE. Lieut. Armstrong R.E. and party cutting timber at LA FOLIE AUBERE for tree standings. Work continued at Brigade batho DOMQUEUR, fitting rifle work. Work in Brigade workshop — making billets and fitting for batho; tables for 9th Inniskilling Fusiliers canteen; iron new gun flash covers to fit machine gun stocks 9th Inniskilling Fusiliers; bomb thrower aiming stick. Party marring shaft at DOMQUEUR for tree standings. Party at ribbon work.	

Army Form C. 2118

WAR DIARY
or
INTELLIGENCE SUMMARY.
(Erase heading not required.)

Instructions regarding War Diaries and Intelligence Summaries are contained in F.S. Regs., Part II. and the Staff Manual respectively. Title pages will be prepared in manuscript.

Place	Date	Hour	Summary of Events and Information	Remarks and references to Appendices
DOMQUEUR	15		Work continued at Brigade Baths DOMQUEUR fitting pipe work. Work in Brigade Workshop — making tools and fitting for baths, making gun flash arrestors for machine gun section 98 Inf Bde, Bomb thrower and shield. Party at section drill. Detention boards erected at various roads in Divisional area. Lieut Jameson R.E. and party making horse standings for R.F.A. at BOUCHON. COCQUEREL, MOUFLER, L'ETOILE, VAUCHELLES, and working saw mill at FONTAINE.	
	16		Work continued at Brigade Baths DOMQUEUR fitting pipe work. Work in Brigade Workshop — making tools and fitting for baths. Party at section drill. Lieut Jameson R.E. and party making horse standings for R.F.A. at BOUCHON, COCQUEREL, MOUFLER, L'ETOILE, VAUCHELLES, and working saw mill at FONTAINE. Lieut Jameson R.E. instructed to hand over horse standings to Lieut Palmer, 1.2.1.st Field Co. R.E. and to withdraw his party to DOMQUEUR. Lieut Smyth R.E. and party at PONTREMY repairing engine for C.R.E.	

Army Form C. 2118

WAR DIARY
or
INTELLIGENCE SUMMARY.
(Erase heading not required.)

Instructions regarding War Diaries and Intelligence Summaries are contained in F. S. Regs., Part II. and the Staff Manual respectively. Title pages will be prepared in manuscript.

Place	Date	Hour	Summary of Events and Information	Remarks and references to Appendices
DOMQUEUR	17		Lt. Jamison R.E. handed over horse standings for R.F.A. to Lieut Palmer R.E. 121st Field Co. R.E. and returned to his unit with his party. Saw Mill at FONTAINE still working. Sawyers and N.C.O. of this Company. Work continued at Brigade Baths DOMQUEUR flooring, fitting. Work at Brigade Workshop — overhauling wagons, manufacturing horse troughs, kit-gear for washhouse. Party at Section Drill.	
	18		Work continued at Brigade Baths flooring, fitting. Work at Brigade workshop — making forks and piping for baths. Party at Section Drill. Party at BRUCAMPS repairing church for Cinema Hall for 11th Inniskilling Fusiliers. Church parade, cleaning billets, pay parade. On the instructions of C.R.E. all parties withdrawn from various works and started on engineering training.	
	19			
	20		One Horsui employed on workshop. Party at engineering training.	
	21		Work continued at Brigade Baths flooring, fitting. Work at Brigade workshop — making boards & piping for baths, repairing machine Gun Pits for 9th Inniskilling Fusiliers.	

2353 Wt. W5344/1454 700,000. 5/15 D. D. & L. A.D.S.S./Forms/C. 2118.

Army Form C. 2118

WAR DIARY
or
INTELLIGENCE SUMMARY.
(Erase heading not required.)

Instructions regarding War Diaries and Intelligence Summaries are contained in F. S. Regs., Part II. and the Staff Manual respectively. Title pages will be prepared in manuscript.

Place	Date	Hour	Summary of Events and Information	Remarks and references to Appendices
DOMQUEUR	22		Company engaged in Engineering training and rifle exercises.	
	23		Party engaged in Engineering training and rifle exercises. Work continued at Brigade Baths - Buses flying. Orders received from the 6th M.R.S. for the Company to move to DOULLENS on the 27th instant.	
	24		Work continued at Brigade Baths - Buses flying. Work at Brigade workshops - making toilet flying tin baths. Party engaged in Engineering training and rifle exercises.	
	25		Christmas Day. Holiday.	
	26		Company packing up preparatory to moving.	
	27		Company moved off from DOMQUEUR at 8.0. a.m. and arrived in DOULLENS at 3.0 p.m. and was billeted in empty house. Five men attached to 154th Bde. R.F.A. to work saw Mill at FONTAINE. Two men at LONGVILLERS to work saw Mill for 9th Dismantling Division. One man at DOMQUEUR to work heating apparatus for Brigade Baths.	
	28		Company engaged in unpacking and issuing tools.	

2353 Wt. W2544/1454 700,000 5/15 D. D. & L. A.D.S.S./Forms/C. 2118.

WAR DIARY
or
INTELLIGENCE SUMMARY.
(Erase heading not required.)

Army Form C. 2118

Place	Date	Hour	Summary of Events and Information	Remarks and references to Appendices
DOULLENS	29		Fixing up billets: making arrangements for refreshing area billets here Standing by - Procuring tools paper Fscap. Ink shifts. - Purchased 126 Poplar trees for sawing up. -	
	30		Drawing materials & ammunition. Making own billets more comfortable	
	31		Drawing material, preparing billeting areas - making Storm standings for artillery. getting workshops started. - This area's been prepared for & held with R.E. - to held Australian Infantry. - a bit of R.A. Stewart turns up every maple & g field corps. billets & available overnight action. Shewan those standings for 400 horses	

O.C. 150th FIELD COY R.E. = 16.

150th F.C.R.E.
Vol: 4

36th Div
Jan 1916

Army Form C. 2118.

WAR DIARY
or
INTELLIGENCE SUMMARY.

(Erase heading not required.)

Confidential

War Diary

of

150th Field Coy. R.E.

From Jany 1/1916. To Jany. 31/1916.

Army Form C. 2118.

WAR DIARY
or
INTELLIGENCE SUMMARY.
(Erase heading not required.)

Place	Date 1916	Hour	Summary of Events and Information	Remarks and references to Appendices
DOULLENS	Jan 1.		Repair billets, making horse standings for 13 Army Corps	
	2.		Sunday.	
	3.		Repairing billets etc — For 13 Army Corps.	
	4.		Repairing billets, making horse standings for 13 Army Corps. weeding saw.	
	5.		Repairing billets, making horse standings for 13 Army Corps.	
	6.		Repairing billets, making horse standings for 13 Army Corps.	
	7.		Repairing billets, making horse standings for 13 Army Corps.	
	8.		Repairing billets, making horse standings for 13 Army Corps.	
	9.		(Sunday) Cleaning up billets, Church Parade.	
	10		Repairing billets, making horse standings for 13 Army Corps.	

Army Form C. 2118.

WAR DIARY
or
INTELLIGENCE SUMMARY.
(Erase heading not required.)

Instructions regarding War Diaries and Intelligence Summaries are contained in F. S. Regs., Part II. and the Staff Manual respectively. Title pages will be prepared in manuscript.

Place	Date	Hour	Summary of Events and Information	Remarks and references to Appendices
DOULLENS	11		Repairing billets, making horse standings for 13th Corps	
	12		Repairing billets, making horse standings for 13th Corps	
	13		Repairing billets, making horse standings for 13th Corps	
	14		Repairing billets, making horse standings for 13th Corps	
	15		Repairing billets, making horse standings for 13th Corps	
	16		(Sunday) cleaning up billets. Church parade.	
	17		Repairing billets, making horse standings for 13th Corps	
	18		Repairing billets, making horse standings for 13th Corps	
	19		Repairing billets, making horse standings for 13th Corps. On this date the Company came under the command of the 14th Corps.	
	20		Repairing billets, making horse standings for 14th Corps.	

Army Form C. 2118.

WAR DIARY
or
INTELLIGENCE SUMMARY.

(Erase heading not required.)

Instructions regarding War Diaries and Intelligence Summaries are contained in F.S. Regs., Part II. and the Staff Manual respectively. Title pages will be prepared in manuscript.

Place	Date	Hour	Summary of Events and Information	Remarks and references to Appendices
DOULLENS	21		Repairing billets, making horse standings for 14th Corps.	
	22		Repairing billets, making horse standings for 14th Corps.	
	23		Repairing billets, making horse standings for 14th Corps.	
	24		Repairing billets, making horse standings for 14th Corps.	
	25		Repairing billets, making horse standings for 14th Corps.	
	26		Repairing billets, making horse standings for 14th Corps.	
	27		Repairing billets, making horse standings for 14th Corps.	
	28		Repairing billets, making horse standings for 14th Corps.	
	29		Repairing billets, making horse standings for 14th Corps.	
	30		(Sunday) Cleaning up billets, Church Parade	
	31		Repairing billets, making horse standings for 14th Corps.	

J.E. Boyle
O.C. 150th Field Coy. R.E.

Army Form C. 2118.

WAR DIARY
or
INTELLIGENCE SUMMARY.

(Erase heading not required.)

Instructions regarding War Diaries and Intelligence Summaries are contained in F. S. Regs., Part II. and the Staff Manual respectively. Title pages will be prepared in manuscript.

Place	Date	Hour	Summary of Events and Information	Remarks and references to Appendices

2353 Wt. W2544/1454 700,000 5/15 D. D. & L. A.D.S.S./Forms/C. 2118.

150. Coy. RE.
36th Div.
Vol. 5.

Confidential

War Diary

of

150th Field Co R.E.

February 1916

Army Form C. 2118.

WAR DIARY
or
INTELLIGENCE SUMMARY.

(Erase heading not required.)

Instructions regarding War Diaries and Intelligence Summaries are contained in F. S. Regs., Part II. and the Staff Manual respectively. Title pages will be prepared in manuscript.

Place	Date 1916	Hour	Summary of Events and Information	Remarks and references to Appendices
DOULLENS	Feb. 1		Repairing billets, making horse standings for 14th Corps.	
	2		Repairing billets, making horse standings for 14th Corps.	
	3		Repairing billets, making horse standings for 14th Corps.	
	4		Company moved from DOULLENS	
			Company arrived at MAILLEY-MAILLET. Company stationed in billets	
MAILLEY-MAILLET	5		Company engaged in unpacking transport and cleaning up billets.	
	6		Parties engaged in repairing trenches and working on and trenchwork	
			First Line trenches and on water supply, one horse killed by aerial bomb.	
	7		Parties engaged in repairing trenches and working in and trenchwork First Line trenches and on water supply	

2353 Wt W2544/1454 700,000 5/15 D. D. & L. A.D.S.S./Forms/C. 2118.

Army Form C. 2118

WAR DIARY
or
INTELLIGENCE SUMMARY

(Erase heading not required.)

Instructions regarding War Diaries and Intelligence Summaries are contained in F. S. Regs., Part II. and the Staff Manual respectively. Title Pages will be prepared in manuscript.

Place	Date	Hour	Summary of Events and Information	Remarks and references to Appendices
	8		Parties engaged in repairing trenches and trenchwork and working in first line trenches, and on Water supply.	
	9		Parties engaged in repairing trenches and trenchwork and working in first line trenches, and on Water supply. Two men wounded in action (No. 57421 Sapper Connor J, (subsequently died in Hospital) No. 64174 Sapper Hagan W.)	
	10		Parties engaged in repairing trenches and trenchwork and working in first line trenches, and on Water supply.	
	11		Parties engaged in repairing trenches and trenchwork and working in first line trenches and on Water supply.	

1875 Wt. W593/826 1,000,000 4/15 J.B.C. & A. A.D.S.S./Forms/C. 2118.

Army Form C. 2118

WAR DIARY
or
INTELLIGENCE SUMMARY
(Erase heading not required.)

Instructions regarding War Diaries and Intelligence Summaries are contained in F. S. Regs., Part II. and the Staff Manual respectively. Title Pages will be prepared in manuscript.

Place	Date	Hour	Summary of Events and Information	Remarks and references to Appendices
	12		No working parties out. Company engaged in cleaning up billets. Saw Mill and Workshop started. Party on water supply and trench work	
	13		Parties engaged in repairing trenches and working in first line trenches, and on water supply. Party engaged on Saw Mill and Workshop.	
	14		Parties engaged in repairing trenches and working in first line trenches, and on water supply. Party engaged on Saw Mill and Workshop. and trench work	
	15		Parties engaged in repairing trenches and working in first line trenches, and on water supply. Party engaged in Workshop. and trench work	
	16		Parties engaged in repairing trenches and working in first line trenches, and on water supply. Party engaged in Workshop.	

Army Form C. 2118

WAR DIARY
or
INTELLIGENCE SUMMARY
(Erase heading not required.)

Instructions regarding War Diaries and Intelligence Summaries are contained in F.S. Regs., Part II. and the Staff Manual respectively. Title Pages will be prepared in manuscript.

Place	Date	Hour	Summary of Events and Information	Remarks and references to Appendices
	17		Parties engaged in repairing trenches and working in front line trenches, and on water supply. Party engaged in workshop.	
	18		Parties engaged in repairing trenches, and working in front line trenches and on water supply. Party engaged in workshop.	
	19		Parties engaged in repairing trench and trench work and working in front line trenches and on water supply. Party engaged in workshop.	
	20		Parties engaged in repairing trench and trench work, and working in front line trenches, and on water supply. Party engaged in workshop.	
	21		Parties engaged in repairing trench and trench work, and working in front line trenches, and on water supply. Party engaged in workshop.	

Army Form C. 2118

WAR DIARY
or
INTELLIGENCE SUMMARY
(Erase heading not required.)

Instructions regarding War Diaries and Intelligence Summaries are contained in F. S. Regs., Part II. and the Staff Manual respectively. Title Pages will be prepared in manuscript.

Place	Date	Hour	Summary of Events and Information	Remarks and references to Appendices
	22		Parties engaged in repairing trench, and trench work, and working in First line trenches, and on Water Supply. Party engaged in Workshop.	
	23		Parties engaged in repairing trench and trench work and working in First line trenches, and on Water Supply. Party engaged in Workshop.	
	24		Parties engaged in repairing trench, and trench work, and working in First Line trenches and on Water Supply. Party engaged in Workshop.	
	25		Parties engaged in repairing trench, and trench work and working in First line trenches, and on Water Supply. Party engaged in Workshop.	
	26		Parties engaged in repairing trench, and trench work, and working in First line trenches, and on Water Supply. Party engaged in Workshop.	

Army Form C. 2118

WAR DIARY
or
INTELLIGENCE SUMMARY
(Erase heading not required.)

Place	Date	Hour	Summary of Events and Information	Remarks and references to Appendices
	27		Parties engaged in repairing trench and trench work, and working in first line trenches, and on water supply. Party engaged in workshop.	
	28		Parties engaged in repairing trench and trench work, and working in first line trenches, and on water supply. Party engaged in workshop.	
	29		Parties engaged in repairing trench and trench work, and working in first line trenches, and on water supply. Party engaged in workshop.	

J.Boyle
Major R.E.

ISOFER
Vol 6

150th Field Arty E.
War Diary
March 1919

Confidential

Army Form C. 2118

WAR DIARY
or
INTELLIGENCE SUMMARY

(Erase heading not required.)

Instructions regarding War Diaries and Intelligence Summaries are contained in F. S. Regs., Part II. and the Staff Manual respectively. Title Pages will be prepared in manuscript.

Place	Date	Hour	Summary of Events and Information	Remarks and references to Appendices
MAILLEY MAILLET	1916 March 1		Company stationed in billets. Parties engaged in repairing trench and trench work and working on first line trenches. Party engaged on water supply and in Workshops.	
	2		Parties engaged in repairing trench and trench work and working in first line trenches. Party engaged on water supply and in Workshops.	
	3		Parties engaged in repairing trench and trench work and working in first line trenches. Party engaged on water supply and in Workshops.	
	4		Parties engaged in repairing trench and trench work and working in first line trenches. Party engaged on water supply and in Workshops.	

Army Form C. 2118

WAR DIARY
or
INTELLIGENCE SUMMARY
(Erase heading not required.)

Instructions regarding War Diaries and Intelligence Summaries are contained in F.S. Regs., Part II. and the Staff Manual respectively. Title Pages will be prepared in manuscript.

Place	Date	Hour	Summary of Events and Information	Remarks and references to Appendices
MAILLY-MAILLET	5		Parties engaged in repairing trenches, and trench work, and working in first line trenches. Party engaged on water supply and in workshops.	
	6		Parties engaged in repairing trenches, and trench work, and working in first line trenches. Party engaged on water supply and in workshops.	
ACHEUX			No 4 section moved to ACHEUX and stationed in billets	
	7		Parties from No. 1, 2, & 3 sections engaged in repairing trenches, and trench work and working in first line trenches. Party engaged on water supply and in tender workshops. No 4 section engaged in general maintenance work at ACHEUX	
	8		Parties from Nos. 1, 2, & 3 sections engaged in repairing trenches, and trench work, and working in first line trenches. Party engaged on water supply and in workshops. No 4 section engaged in general maintenance work at ACHEUX	

Army Form C. 2118

WAR DIARY
or
INTELLIGENCE SUMMARY

(Erase heading not required.)

Instructions regarding War Diaries and Intelligence Summaries are contained in F. S. Regs., Part II. and the Staff Manual respectively. Title Pages will be prepared in manuscript.

Place	Date	Hour	Summary of Events and Information	Remarks and references to Appendices
	9		Parties from Nos 1, 2, & 3 Sections engaged in repairing trenches and trench work, and working in first line trenches. Party engaged on Water supply and in Workshops. No. 4 Section engaged in general maintenance work at ACHEUX.	
	10		Parties from Nos 1, 2 & 3 Sections engaged in repairing trenches and trench work and working in first line trenches. Party engaged on Water supply and in Workshops. No. 4 Section engaged in general maintenance work at ACHEUX.	
	11		Parties from Nos 1, 2, & 3 Sections engaged in repairing trenches and trench work, and working in first line trenches. Party engaged on Water supply and in Workshops. No. 4 Section engaged in general maintenance work at ACHEUX.	
	12		Parties from Nos 1, 2, & 3 Sections engaged in repairing trenches, and trench work, and working on first line trenches. Party engaged on Water supply and in Workshops. No. 4 Section engaged in general maintenance work at ACHEUX.	

Army Form C. 2118

WAR DIARY
or
INTELLIGENCE SUMMARY
(Erase heading not required.)

Instructions regarding War Diaries and Intelligence Summaries are contained in F. S. Regs., Part II. and the Staff Manual respectively. Title Pages will be prepared in manuscript.

Place	Date	Hour	Summary of Events and Information	Remarks and references to Appendices
	13		Parties from Nos 1, 2, & 3 Sections engaged in repairing trenches, and trench work, and working up first line trenches. Party engaged on water supply and in Workshops. No 4 Section engaged in general maintenance work at ACHEUX	
	14		Parties from Nos 1, 2, & 3 Sections engaged in repairing trenches and trench work, and working in first line trenches. Party engaged on water supply and in Workshops. No 4 Section engaged in general maintenance work at ACHEUX	
	15		Parties from Nos 1, 2, & 3 Sections engaged in repairing trenches, and trench work, and working in first line trenches. Party engaged on water supply and in Workshops. No 4 Section engaged in general maintenance work at ACHEUX	
	16		Parties from No. 1, 2 & 3 Sections engaged in repairing trenches, and trench work, and working in first line trenches. Party engaged on water supply and in Workshops. No 4 Section engaged in general maintenance work at ACHEUX	

Army Form C. 2118

WAR DIARY
or
INTELLIGENCE SUMMARY
(Erase heading not required.)

Instructions regarding War Diaries and Intelligence Summaries are contained in F. S. Regs., Part II. and the Staff Manual respectively. Title Pages will be prepared in manuscript.

Place	Date	Hour	Summary of Events and Information	Remarks and references to Appendices
	17		Parties from Nos 1, 2, & 3 Sections engaged in repairing trenches and trench work, and working in first line trenches. Party engaged on Water supply and in Workshops. No. 4 Section engaged on general maintenance work at ACHEUX	
MAILLY-MAILLET MARTINSART	18		Parties from Nos 1 & 3 Sections engaged in repairing trenches, and trench work and working in first line trenches. Party engaged on water supply and in Workshops. No. 2 Section moved from MAILLY-MAILLET to MARTINSART No. 4 Section moved from ACHEUX to MARTINSART for work under O.C. 109th Brigade. Both Sections stationed in Billets.	
	19		Parties from Nos 1 & 3 Sections engaged in repairing trenches and trench work, and working in first line trenches. Party engaged on water supply and in Workshops. Nos. 2 & 4 Sections engaged in general trench work at MARTINSART under O.C. 109th Brigade	

1875 Wt. W593/826 1,000,000 4/15 J.B.C. & A. A.D.S.S./Forms/C. 2118.

Army Form C. 2118

WAR DIARY
or
INTELLIGENCE SUMMARY

(Erase heading not required.)

Instructions regarding War Diaries and Intelligence Summaries are contained in F.S. Regs., Part II. and the Staff Manual respectively. Title Pages will be prepared in manuscript.

Place	Date	Hour	Summary of Events and Information	Remarks and references to Appendices
	20		Parties from Nos 1 & 3 Sections engaged in repairing trenches, and trench work, and working in First line trenches. Party engaged on water supply and in workshops. Nos 2 & 4 sections engaged in general trench work at MARTINSART under G.O.C. 109th Brigade.	
	21		Parties from Nos 1 & 3 Sections engaged in repairing trenches, and trench work, and working in First line trenches. Party engaged on water supply and in workshops. Nos 2 & 4 Sections engaged in general trench work at MARTINSART under G.O.C. 109th Brigade.	
	22		Parties from Nos 1 & 3 Sections engaged in repairing trenches, and trench work, and working in First line trenches. Party engaged on water supply and in workshops. Nos 2 & 4 sections engaged in general trench work at MARTINSART under G.O.C. 109th Brigade.	

Army Form C. 2118

WAR DIARY
or
INTELLIGENCE SUMMARY
(Erase heading not required.)

Instructions regarding War Diaries and Intelligence Summaries are contained in F. S. Regs., Part II. and the Staff Manual respectively. Title Pages will be prepared in manuscript.

Place	Date	Hour	Summary of Events and Information	Remarks and references to Appendices
	23		Parties from Nos 1 & 3 Sections engaged in repairing trenches, and trench work, and working in front line trenches. Party engaged on water supply and in Workshops. Nos 2 & 4 Sections engaged in repairing general trench work at MARTINSART under G.O.C. 109th Brigade.	
MARTINSART	24		Hdqrs. Nos 1 & 3 Sections moved from MAILLY-MAILLET to MARTINSART. Sections stationed in Billets. Nos 2 & 4 Sections moved to Dugouts behind Front Line.	
	25		Nos 1 & 3 Sections engaged in repairing billets. Nos 2 & 4 Sections engaged in general trench work.	
	26		Nos 1 & 3 Sections engaged in repairing billets. Nos 2 & 4 Sections engaged in general trench work.	

Army Form C. 2118

WAR DIARY
or
INTELLIGENCE SUMMARY

(Erase heading not required.)

Instructions regarding War Diaries and Intelligence Summaries are contained in F.S. Regs., Part II. and the Staff Manual respectively. Title Pages will be prepared in manuscript.

Place	Date	Hour	Summary of Events and Information	Remarks and references to Appendices
	27		Nos 1 + 3 Sections engaged in repairing billets	
			Nos 2 + 4 Sections engaged in general trench work	
	28		Nos 1 + 3 Sections engaged in repairing billets	
			Nos 2 + 4 Sections engaged in general trench work	
	29		Nos 1 + 3 Sections engaged in repairing billets	
			Nos 2 + 4 Sections engaged in general trench work	
	30		Nos 1 + 3 Sections engaged in repairing billets	
			Nos 2 + 4 Sections engaged in general trench work	
	31		Nos 1 + 3 Sections engaged in repairing billets	
			Nos 2 + 4 Sections engaged in general trench work	

J L Porter
Major R.E.
O.C. 150th Field Coy R.E.

Confidential

War Diary

of

150th Field Coy. R.E.

April 1916.

Army Form C. 2118

WAR DIARY
or
INTELLIGENCE SUMMARY
(Erase heading not required.)

Instructions regarding War Diaries and Intelligence Summaries are contained in F.S. Regs., Part II. and the Staff Manual respectively. Title Pages will be prepared in manuscript.

Place	Date 1916	Hour	Summary of Events and Information	Remarks and references to Appendices
MARTINSART	April 1		Nos 1 & 3 Sections engaged in repairing billets	
	2		No. 2 & 4 Sections engaged in general trench work	
			No. 3 Section engaged in repairing billets	
			Nos. 1. 2. 4 Sections engaged in general trench work	
	3		No. 3 Section engaged in repairing billets and erecting huts	
			Nos. 1. 2. 4. Sections engaged on general trench work	
	4		No. 3 Section engaged in repairing billets and erecting huts	
			Nos 1. 2. 4. Sections engaged on general trench work	
	5		No. 3. Section engaged in repairing billets and erecting huts	
			Nos 1. 2. 4. Sections engaged on general trench work.	
	6		No. 3. Section engaged in repairing billets and erecting huts	
			Nos. 1. 2. 4. Sections engaged on general trench work	

Army Form C. 2118

WAR DIARY
or
INTELLIGENCE SUMMARY
(Erase heading not required.)

Instructions regarding War Diaries and Intelligence Summaries are contained in F. S. Regs., Part II. and the Staff Manual respectively. Title Pages will be prepared in manuscript.

Place	Date	Hour	Summary of Events and Information	Remarks and references to Appendices
	7		No 3 Section engaged in repairing billets and erecting huts	
	8		Nos 1. 2. 4. Sections engaged in general trench work.	
			No 1. Section moved to Dug-outs behind front line trenches.	
			No 3 Section engaged in repairing billets and erecting huts	
			No. 1. 2. 4. Sections engaged in general trench work	
			Three men wounded in action by shell fire	
			(No. 64293 Sapper Minnelly R. No. 64197 Sapper Gray H.	
			No. 64189 Sapper Henry W.)	
	9		No. 3 Section engaged in repairing billets and erecting huts.	
			Nos 1. 2. 74. Sections engaged in general trench work.	
	10		No 3 Section engaged in erecting huts	
			Nos 1. 2. 74. Sections engaged in general trench work.	
	11		No. 3 Section engaged in erecting huts	
			Nos 1. 2. 4. Sections engaged in general trench work	

WAR DIARY
or
INTELLIGENCE SUMMARY

(Erase heading not required.)

Army Form C. 2118

Place	Date	Hour	Summary of Events and Information	Remarks and references to Appendices
	12		Nos. 1, 2, 3 & 4 sections engaged in general trench work	
	13		Nos. 1, 2, 3 & 4 sections engaged on general trench work	
	14		Nos. 1, 2, 3 & 4 sections engaged in general trench work	
	15		Nos. 1, 2, 3 & 4 sections engaged in general trench work	
	16		Nos. 1, 2, 3 & 4 sections engaged in general trench work	
	17		Nos. 1, 2, 3 & 4 sections engaged in general trench work	
	18		Nos. 1, 2, 3 & 4 sections engaged in general trench work	
	19		Nos. 1, 2, 3 & 4 sections engaged in general trench work	
	20		Nos. 1, 2, 3 & 4 sections engaged in general trench work	
	21		Nos. 1, 2, 3 & 4 sections engaged in general trench work	
	22		Nos. 1, 2, 3 & 4 sections engaged in general trench work. 2nd Lieut Michael Richard Leader Armstrong killed in action by Trench Mortar. The body was buried at AUTHUILLE Cemetery. No. 57596 Sapper Murray R. wounded in action by Trench Mortar. (Shell Shock)	

Army Form C. 2118

WAR DIARY
or
INTELLIGENCE SUMMARY
(Erase heading not required.)

Instructions regarding War Diaries and Intelligence Summaries are contained in F.S. Regs., Part II. and the Staff Manual respectively. Title Pages will be prepared in manuscript.

Place	Date	Hour	Summary of Events and Information	Remarks and references to Appendices
	23		Nos 1. 2. 3. 4 Sections engaged in general trench work	
	24		Nos 1. 2. 3. 4. Sections engaged in general trench work	
	25		Nos 1. 2. 3. 4. Sections engaged in general trench work	
	26		Nos 1. 2. 3. 4 Sections engaged in general trench work	
	27		Nos 1. 2. 3. 4. Sections engaged in general trench work	
	28		Nos 1. 2. 3. 4. Sections engaged in general trench work. No 3 Sections moved to new Dugouts behind front line trenches	
	29		Nos 1. 2. 3. 4. Sections engaged in general trench work	
	30		Nos 1. 2. 3. 4 Sections engaged in general trench work.	

L. C. Boyle
Major R.E.
O.C. 150th Field Coy. R.E.

150 FE RE
Vol 8

XXXVI

Confidential
War Diary
- of -
150th Field bty R.E.
May 1916

Original

Army Form C. 2118

WAR DIARY
or
INTELLIGENCE SUMMARY

(Erase heading not required.)

Instructions regarding War Diaries and Intelligence Summaries are contained in F.S. Regs., Part II. and the Staff Manual respectively. Title Pages will be prepared in manuscript.

Place	Date 1916	Hour	Summary of Events and Information	Remarks and references to Appendices
MARTINSART	May 1		Company engaged in making French Mortar emplacements, Dug-outs, Brigade Bomb Stores, Divisional Bomb Store, Ration Stores, Brigade Headquarters and working in front line Trenches.	
	2		Company engaged in making French Mortar emplacements, Dug-outs, Brigade Bomb Stores, Divisional Bomb Store, Ration Stores, Brigade Headquarters and working in front line Trenches.	
	3		Company engaged in making French Mortar emplacements, Dug-outs, Brigade Bomb Stores, Divisional Bomb Store, Ration Stores, Brigade Headquarters and working in front line Trenches. (No 64393 Sapper Hodgson wounded by Machine Gun fire)	
	4		Company engaged in making French Mortar emplacements, Dug-outs, Brigade Bomb Stores, Divisional Bomb Store, Ration Stores, Brigade Headquarters, and working in front line Trenches.	
	5		Company engaged in making French Mortar emplacements, Dug-outs, Brigade Bomb Stores, Divisional Bomb Store, Ration Stores, Brigade Headquarters, and working in front line Trenches.	

Army Form C. 2118

WAR DIARY
or
INTELLIGENCE SUMMARY
(Erase heading not required.)

Instructions regarding War Diaries and Intelligence Summaries are contained in F.S. Regs., Part II. and the Staff Manual respectively. Title Pages will be prepared in manuscript.

Place	Date	Hour	Summary of Events and Information	Remarks and references to Appendices
	6		Company engaged in making Trench Mortar emplacements, Dug-outs, Brigade Bomb Stores, Divisional Bomb Stores, Ration Stores, Brigade Headquarters and working on Front Line Trenches. New communication trench Dug ENNISKILLEN AVENUE.	
	7		Company engaged in making Trench Mortar emplacements, Dug-outs, Brigade Bomb Stores, Divisional Bomb Stores, Ration Stores, Brigade Headquarters and working on new communication trench and Front Line Trenches.	
	8		Company engaged in making Trench Mortar emplacements, Dug-outs, Brigade Bomb Stores, Divisional Bomb Stores, Ration Stores, Brigade Headquarters and working on new communication Trench and Front Line Trenches.	
	9		Company engaged in making Trench Mortar emplacements, Dug-outs, Brigade Bomb Stores, Divisional Bomb Stores, Ration Stores, Brigade Headquarters and working on new communication Trench and Front Line Trenches.	
	10		Company engaged in making Trench Mortar emplacements, Dug-outs, Brigade Bomb Stores, Divisional Bomb Stores, Ration Stores, Brigade Headquarters and working on new communication Trench and Front Line Trenches.	

Army Form C. 2118

WAR DIARY
or
INTELLIGENCE SUMMARY
(Erase heading not required.)

Instructions regarding War Diaries and Intelligence Summaries are contained in F. S. Regs., Part II. and the Staff Manual respectively. Title Pages will be prepared in manuscript.

Place	Date	Hour	Summary of Events and Information	Remarks and references to Appendices
	11		Company engaged in making French Mortar emplacements, Dug-outs, Brigade Bomb Stores, Divisional Bomb Store, Ration Store, Brigade Headquarters, and working on new communication trench and Front line trenches.	
	12		Company engaged in making French Mortar emplacements, Dug-outs, Brigade Bomb Stores, Divisional Bomb Store, Ration Store, Brigade Headquarters and working on new communication trench and Front line trenches.	
	13		Company engaged in making French Mortar emplacements, Dug-outs, Brigade Bomb Stores, Divisional Bomb Store, Ration Store, Brigade Headquarters, and working on new communication trench and Front line trenches.	
	14		Company engaged in making French Mortar emplacements, Dug-outs, Brigade Bomb Stores, Divisional Bomb Store, Ration Store, Brigade Headquarters, and working on new communication trench and Front line trenches.	

WAR DIARY
or
INTELLIGENCE SUMMARY

(Erase heading not required.)

Army Form C. 2118

Instructions regarding War Diaries and Intelligence Summaries are contained in F.S. Regs., Part II. and the Staff Manual respectively. Title Pages will be prepared in manuscript.

Place	Date	Hour	Summary of Events and Information	Remarks and references to Appendices
	15		Company engaged in making Trench Mortar emplacements, Dug-outs, Brigade Bomb Stores, Divisional Bomb Stores, Ration Stores, Brigade Headquarters, and working on new communication trench and Front line trenches.	
	16		Company engaged in making Trench Mortar emplacements, Dug-outs, Brigade Bomb Stores, Divisional Bomb Stores, Ration Stores, Brigade Headquarters, and working on new communication trench and Front line trenches.	
	17		Company engaged in making Trench Mortar emplacements, Dug-outs, Brigade Bomb Stores, Divisional Bomb Stores, Ration Stores, Brigade Headquarters, and working on new communication trench and Front line trenches.	
	18		Company engaged in making Trench Mortar emplacements, Dug-outs, Brigade Bomb Stores, Divisional Bomb Stores, Ration Stores, Brigade Headquarters. New communication trench dug ULSTER AVENUE, and working on Front line trenches.	

Army Form C. 2118

WAR DIARY
or
INTELLIGENCE SUMMARY
(Erase heading not required.)

Instructions regarding War Diaries and Intelligence Summaries are contained in F. S. Regs., Part II. and the Staff Manual respectively. Title Pages will be prepared in manuscript.

Place	Date	Hour	Summary of Events and Information	Remarks and references to Appendices
	19		Company engaged in making Trench Mortar emplacements, Dug-outs, Brigade Bomb Store, Divisional Bomb Store, Ration Store, Brigade Headquarters, and working on new Communication Trenches, and Front line Trenches	
	20		Company engaged in making Trench Mortar emplacements, Dug-outs, Brigade Bomb Store, Divisional Bomb Store, Ration Store, Brigade Headquarters, and working on new Communication Trenches, and Front Line Trenches. (No 6464 L/Cpl Johnston J wounded by machine Gun fire)	
	21		Company engaged in making Trench Mortar emplacements, Dug-outs, Brigade Bomb Store, Divisional Bomb Store, Ration Store, Brigade Headquarters, and working on new Communication Trenches, and Front Line Trenches.	
	22		Company engaged in making Trench Mortar emplacements, Dug-outs, Brigade Bomb Store, Divisional Bomb Store, Ration Store, Brigade Headquarters, and working on new Communication Trenches, and Front line Trenches.	

Army Form C. 2118

WAR DIARY
or
INTELLIGENCE SUMMARY
(Erase heading not required.)

Instructions regarding War Diaries and Intelligence Summaries are contained in F. S. Regs., Part II. and the Staff Manual respectively. Title Pages will be prepared in manuscript.

Place	Date	Hour	Summary of Events and Information	Remarks and references to Appendices
	23		Company engaged in making Trench Mortar emplacements, Dug-outs, Brigade Bomb Stores, Divisional Bomb Stores, Ration Stores, Brigade Headquarters, and working on new communication trenches and Front line trenches.	
	24		Company engaged in making Trench Mortar emplacements, Dug-outs, Brigade Bomb Stores, Divisional Bomb Stores, Ration Stores, Brigade Headquarters, and working on new communication trenches and Front line trenches.	
	25		Company engaged in making Trench Mortar emplacements, Dug-outs, Brigade Bomb Stores, Divisional Bomb Stores, Ration Stores, Brigade Headquarters, and working on new communication trenches and Front line trenches.	
	26		Company engaged in making Trench Mortar emplacements, Dug-outs, Brigade Bomb Stores, Divisional Bomb Stores, Ration Stores, Brigade Headquarters, and working on new communication trenches and Front line trenches. (No. 5757 & L.Cpl. Smyth S died of wounds received from rifle fire)	

Army Form C. 2118

WAR DIARY
or
INTELLIGENCE SUMMARY

(Erase heading not required.)

Instructions regarding War Diaries and Intelligence Summaries are contained in F.S. Regs., Part II. and the Staff Manual respectively. Title Pages will be prepared in manuscript.

Place	Date	Hour	Summary of Events and Information	Remarks and references to Appendices
	27		Company engaged in making trench Mortar emplacements, Dug-outs, Brigade Bomb Stores, Divisional Bomb Stores, Ration Stores, Brigade Headquarters, and working on new Communication Trenches and Front line Trenches.	
	28		Company engaged in making trench Mortar emplacements, Dug-outs, Brigade Bomb Stores, Divisional Bomb Stores, Ration Stores, Brigade Headquarters, and working on new Communication Trenches and Front line Trenches.	
	29		Company engaged in making trench Mortar emplacements, Dug-outs, Brigade Bomb Stores, Divisional Bomb Stores, Ration Stores, Brigade Headquarters, and working on new Communication Trenches and Front line Trenches.	
	30		Company engaged in making trench Mortar emplacements, Dug-outs, Brigade Bomb Stores, Divisional Bomb Stores, Ration Stores, Brigade Headquarters, and working on new Communication Trenches and Front line Trenches.	

Army Form C. 2118

WAR DIARY
or
INTELLIGENCE SUMMARY
(Erase heading not required.)

Place	Date	Hour	Summary of Events and Information	Remarks and references to Appendices
	31		Company moved from MARTINSART to FORCEVILLE. Company accommodated in Billets, after being 4 months working in front line trenches, with working parties of 400 to 700 daily. A very large amount of work was done, building dugouts, & improving front & support lines after under very heavy fire & often gets a weeks work there was too work to shew than before we started, owing to the Bombardments.	

L.C. Boyle. Major R.E.
O.C., 150th FIELD COY. R.E.

36th Divisional Engineers

150th FIELD COMPANY R. E.

JUNE 1916

Army Form C. 2118

WAR DIARY
or
INTELLIGENCE SUMMARY
(Erase heading not required.)

Instructions regarding War Diaries and Intelligence Summaries are contained in F.S. Regs., Part II. and the Staff Manual respectively. Title Pages will be prepared in manuscript.

Place	Date 1916	Hour	Summary of Events and Information	Remarks and references to Appendices
FORCEVILLE	June 1		Company engaged in Company Drill, Musketry, Demolitions, setting out work.	
	2		Company engaged in Company Drill, Musketry, Demolitions, setting out work.	
	3		Company engaged in Company Drill, Musketry, Demolitions, setting out work.	
	4		Company engaged in Company Drill, Musketry, Demolitions, setting out work.	
	5		Company engaged in Company Drill, Musketry, Demolitions, setting out work.	
	6		Company engaged in Company Drill, Musketry, Demolitions, setting out work. The Company are resting after 4 months continuous trench work.	
	7		Parties engaged in Workshop. Parties engaged making wire entanglements.	

Army Form C. 2118

WAR DIARY
or
INTELLIGENCE SUMMARY
(Erase heading not required.)

Instructions regarding War Diaries and Intelligence Summaries are contained in F.S. Regs., Part II. and the Staff Manual respectively. Title Pages will be prepared in manuscript.

Place	Date	Hour	Summary of Events and Information	Remarks and references to Appendices
	8		Parties engaged in Workshop. Parties engaged in making wire entanglements	
	9		Parties engaged in Workshop. Parties engaged in making wire entanglements	
	10		Parties engaged in Workshop. Parties engaged in making wire entanglements.	
	11		Parties engaged in Workshop. Parties engaged in making wire entanglements.	
	12		Parties engaged in Workshop. Parties engaged in making wire entanglements. No 2 Section moved to Dugouts behind fuel line trenches.	
	13		Parties engaged in Workshop. Parties engaged in making wire entanglements. No 2 Section engaged in making Carts for gas cylinders & storing same	

1875 Wt. W593/826 1,000,000 4/15 J.B.C. & A. A.D.S.S./Forms/C. 2118.

Army Form C. 2118

WAR DIARY
or
INTELLIGENCE SUMMARY
(Erase heading not required.)

Instructions regarding War Diaries and Intelligence Summaries are contained in F. S. Regs., Part II. and the Staff Manual respectively. Title Pages will be prepared in manuscript.

Place	Date	Hour	Summary of Events and Information	Remarks and references to Appendices
	14		Parties engaged in workshops. Parties engaged in making wire entanglements. No 2 Section engaged in making cases for gas cylinders & storing same.	
	15		Parties engaged in workshops. Parties engaged in making wire entanglements. No 2 Section engaged in making cases for gas cylinders & storing same.	
	16		Parties engaged in workshops. Parties engaged in making wire entanglements. No 2 Section engaged in making cases for gas cylinders & storing same.	
	17		Parties engaged in workshops. Parties engaged in making wire entanglements. No 2 Section engaged in making cases for gas cylinders & storing same.	

WAR DIARY

or

INTELLIGENCE SUMMARY

(Erase heading not required.)

Army Form C. 2118

Instructions regarding War Diaries and Intelligence Summaries are contained in F. S. Regs., Part II. and the Staff Manual respectively. Title Pages will be prepared in manuscript.

Place	Date	Hour	Summary of Events and Information	Remarks and references to Appendices
	18		Parties engaged in Workshops. Parties engaged in making wire entanglements.	
	19		No 2 Section engaged in making cases for gas cylinders and storing same. Parties engaged in Workshops. Parties engaged on making wire entanglements.	
	20		No 2 Section engaged in making cases for gas cylinders and storing same. Parties engaged in Workshops. Parties engaged on making wire entanglements.	
	21		No 2 Section engaged in making cases for gas cylinders and storing same. Parties engaged in Workshops. Parties engaged in making wire entanglements. No 2 Section engaged in making cases for gas cylinders and storing same.	
	22		Parties engaged in Workshops. Parties engaged in making wire entanglements. No 2 Section engaged in making cases for gas cylinders and storing same.	

Army Form C. 2118.

WAR DIARY
or
INTELLIGENCE SUMMARY.
(Erase heading not required.)

Instructions regarding War Diaries and Intelligence Summaries are contained in F. S. Regs., Part II. and the Staff Manual respectively. Title pages will be prepared in manuscript.

Place	Date	Hour	Summary of Events and Information	Remarks and references to Appendices
	23		C company (two strongest) moved into Dugouts. Priestly & Almode Shephard Wood.	
	24		Parties engaged in maintaining communication and other trenches, clearing rides and building bridges over trenches, working on Stokes Mortar emplacements, working on water supply, all under very heavy shell fire.	
	25		A party of 2 N.C.Os and 4 sappers were supplied as working party to 9th Roy. Inniskilling Fusiliers but were put off. Going all the stores moved up from Ros castle to Inverness Strut. Kept 4 main trenches continuously open, under heavy bombardment.	
	26		Maintaining trenches clearing fallen timber etc from rides and trenches. Taking up strips to forward dump in front line, Keeping all communication trenches open which were continually being destroyed by heavy bombardment. Repairing water supply pipe which was damaged by shell fire.	

WAR DIARY
or
INTELLIGENCE SUMMARY.
(Erase heading not required.)

Army Form C. 2118.

Place	Date	Hour	Summary of Events and Information	Remarks and references to Appendices
	27		Maintaining trench retaining water supply, clearing roads through and to enable troops to move into position for advance. Repaired existing water supply pumps which had been destroyed by shell fire. All the work was done under constant enemy counter attack. Casualty 64276 Cpl Bolton W J.R. wounded. 64242 L/Cpl Rolland R shell wound. 64342 Sapr. Metcalf D. shell shock. 62246 Pion Wilson H. shell shock. 64401 Sapr. Stringham J.O. shell shock	
	28		Repaired several places in water pipe which had been damaged by bombardment, the tank having been hit by shell which we were able to repair and restore water supply. Making heavy fenced mortar emplacement. Casualty 64425 Sapr. Hogg J. shell shock	
	29		Keeping communication trenches open and roads through open near clear & moving up R.E. stores to front line. Repairing water supply pipes. Casualty 57512 Sapr. Pulford H. shell shock.	

WAR DIARY
or
INTELLIGENCE SUMMARY.

Army Form C. 2118.

Place	Date	Hour	Summary of Events and Information	Remarks and references to Appendices
	30		Completed Heavy trench mortar emplacement. Opened up all communication and assembly trenches. Put up guide posts through wood and in front line to "take off". Moved all wire, bridged all trenches ready for the movement of troops for the attack. Cavalry 4012 Inf. Common W until dark.	

L C Boder
Major R.E.
O.C 150th Field Coy R.E.

36th Divisional Engineers

150th FIELD COMPANY R. E.

JULY 1916:

Army Form C. 2118.

WAR DIARY
or
INTELLIGENCE SUMMARY.
(Erase heading not required.)

Instructions regarding War Diaries and Intelligence Summaries are contained in F.S. Regs., Part II. and the Staff Manual respectively. Title pages will be prepared in manuscript.

Place	Date 1916	Hour	Summary of Events and Information	Remarks and references to Appendices
THIEPVAL WOOD	July 1.	7.0.a.m.	No.1 Section under Lieut. R.P. Peacock, moved off with 11th Bn. Royal Inniskilling Fus. a company of which was allotted this task with his section of Limberladen Tripods. Lieut Peacock lost his men out and advanced with the Battalion. Lieut. Peacock was killed immediately. All the N.C.Os except one were killed or wounded and only six men of the Section were left and these did not reach the Trenches.	
		11.30.a.m.	Received instructions from 6.A.B. to put in repair the tramline running up Paisley avenue and the valley between Elverlois Post and Thiepval Wood. No.4 Section was put on this work immediately and worked until 8.0.p.m. till driven off by heavy bombardment, which caused damage to the tramway. No.3 Section was sent out to continue the repair of the tramway which they worked at till 11.0.p.m. Keeping it in repair and also gun emmas intermittent fire. No.2 Section did very good work in organising and carrying up R.E. stores from the backward dumps to forward dumps in the front line. Organising infantry parties of men who brought back prisoners there being the only men available they were ultimately taken off to carry up ammunition when No.3 Section carried up so much stores as was possible. No 2 Section who relieved and were detailed to enable wounded to be evacuated, working until late into the night they made stretchers which were on great demand.	

Casualties:
103028 Sapper Montgomery H. wounded. 81A309 Sgt Shrowder J. wounded. 64489 Lt. Jones L wounded.
64424 " Pattison R.T. wounded. 57501 78111 Jr. wounded. 64203 Porter A. wounded.
34400 " Holgson J.A. wounded. 57976 L/pl. Kenny S. wounded. 65506 Hinds J. wounded.
64450 2/pl. Catterall wounded. 57790 L/pl. Cantlon wounded 64497 Keeton E. missing
64461 Sapper McArdle E.M. missing 64332 J.M. Driscoll J.E. missing 14064.L.M. Johnston wounded

Army Form C. 2118

WAR DIARY
or
INTELLIGENCE SUMMARY
(Erase heading not required.)

Instructions regarding War Diaries and Intelligence Summaries are contained in F.S. Regs., Part II. and the Staff Manual respectively. Title Pages will be prepared in manuscript.

Place	Date	Hour	Summary of Events and Information	Remarks and references to Appendices
	July 1		64417 Sapper Andrews & W. missing. 57416 Sapper Burrows R.J., 54562 Sapper Dempster W. missing	
	2		64453 " Fallon J.D. Missing	
			Company worked in evacuation of wounded, making stretchers and organising carrying parties both at THIEPVAL and SWALLOWS nest.	
MARTINSART		1.30 pm	Recived instructions to move back to MARTINSART.	
		6.0 pm	Arrived at MARTINSART and accommodated in billets	
FORCEVILLE	3		Company moved to FORCEVILLE and accommodated in billets	
	4		Cleaning up billets and checking stores	
AVELUY	5		Company moved to bivouac AVELUY to work under 12th Division. Left bivouac at BOUZINCOURT	
	6		Transferred stores from MARTINSART WOOD Dump to OVELIERS Dump. Transferred to N.N.N.N. Recived instructions from 6.R.E. 12th Division that we should be	

1875 Wt. W593/826 1,000,000 4/15 J.B.C. & A. A.D.S.S./Forms/C. 2118.

Army Form C. 2118

WAR DIARY
or
INTELLIGENCE SUMMARY
(Erase heading not required.)

Place	Date	Hour	Summary of Events and Information	Remarks and references to Appendices
	7	8.0 p.m.	Company in reserve for tomorrow's action and would receive orders later in the day. Received orders to rendezvous at Gardners Post.	W. 23. c. 2. 0.
		12.0 Midnt	Stood too under 18th Divisional Engineers Operation Order No 18 of 6 7/16 to be in readiness for the attack which took place this morning at Zero 8 a.m.	
		10 p.m	Received orders to proceed with two Sections, and 30 Pioneers and 85 Infantry who were about to take up necessary materials for consolidation purposes and to consolidate point X 14. c. 9. 7. Sections 1 & 4 under Lieut Jameson set out at 10 p.m. with carrying parties and infantry, which also included sappers carrying tools of consolidation. Materials, in torrents of rain. They moved off to the front and arrived at 5 0. p.m. during to heavy shell and Machine Gun fire work was found to be impossible till after dark. The infantry carrying parties were required for support purposes in the trenches and what little consolidation could be done was done till driven off by heavy fire.	
		3.0 p.m.	Received orders from 74th Brigade to release roads ALBERT – BAPUME for	

WAR DIARY
or
INTELLIGENCE SUMMARY

(Erase heading not required.)

Army Form C. 2118

Place	Date	Hour	Summary of Events and Information	Remarks and references to Appendices
		10.0 p.m.	transport, transport to report to X.th Corps before Ypres to draw what artillery bridges were possible. Transport reported at 10 p.m. that no bridges were available so carried up what materials was available to point W.19.a.9.9. Meanwhile Sections 2 & 4 which left at 9 p.m. with 30 Pioneers were hard at work repairing the road. They worked on this till 2.30 a.m. when they were relieved by another Field Company. A considerable portion of the road was made available for transport. Casualties 57633 Sapper Worthington D. killed. 64326 Dr. Wells J. killed accidentally.	
	8	7.0 a.m	Received instructions to report to 76th Brigade which I did immediately and awaited instructions. Received instructions to take B Company in readiness to proceed to consolidation point X.8.d.2.4. which infantry were about to take. Sections 1 & 4 and transport were employed in carrying up stores. Sections 2 & 3 stood to to proceed on receiving orders.	
		11. a.m	Received instructions to consolidate point X.8.C.8.3. The infantry then	

WAR DIARY
or
INTELLIGENCE SUMMARY.

(Erase heading not required.)

Army Form C. 2118.

Place	Date	Hour	Summary of Events and Information	Remarks and references to Appendices
			being holding the line X8.d.1.8 - X.8.d.7.0. Forty infantry was detailed as a carrying and working party which had long been handed to him at 12.30 pm. and proceeded to forward dump collected materials and proceeded to location Sections 2 & 3 under Lieut. Abis proceeded from Ypres to forward dump to take up tools and materials to the front for consolidation purposes. They collected materials and worked through the trenches under shell and machine gunfire, and arrived at their destination when it was found impossible to consolidate owing to shell and machine gunfire. The infantry having been driven out of the forward line fell back to point X.8.C.8.3. The sections returned at 5.0 a.m.	
		5.0am		
	9	7.0 a.m	Received instructions from C.R.E. 18th Division that I was to receive instructions from C.R.E. 25th Division. I reported to 75th Brigade when I was informed that I was to be relieved by 106th Field Coy R.E. to whom I handed over.	

Company moved to BEAUVAL.

Army Form C. 2118

WAR DIARY
or
INTELLIGENCE SUMMARY
(Erase heading not required.)

Instructions regarding War Diaries and Intelligence Summaries are contained in F.S. Regs., Part II. and the Staff Manual respectively. Title Pages will be prepared in manuscript.

Place	Date	Hour	Summary of Events and Information	Remarks and references to Appendices
BEAUVAL	10		Company arrived at BEAUVAL and accommodated in billets.	
BEAUMETZ	11		Company moved to BEAUMETZ and entrained at	
BERGUETTE	12		Company arrived at BERGUETTE and detrained.	
CAMPAGNE	13		Company arrived at CAMPAGNE and accommodated in billets	
SERQUES	13		Company arrived at SERQUES and accommodated in billets	
~~LEDRINGHAM~~	14		Company ~~arrived~~ in billets	
	15		Company engaged cleaning billets, and checking stores delivery return	
	16		Company engaged in running exercise, route march, Bathing	
	17		Company engaged in running exercise, Route March, Bathing	
	18		Company engaged in Bridging, lecture on Drill, lecture on explosives	
	19		Company engaged in Bridging, lecture Drill, Bathing Shooting.	

WAR DIARY or INTELLIGENCE SUMMARY

Army Form C. 2118

Place	Date	Hour	Summary of Events and Information	Remarks and references to Appendices
	20		Company engaged on running, surveying, surveying, map reading, Bathing, Bridging Shooting	
	21		Company engaged on running, surveying, Map reading, Bathing, Bridging, Shooting	
LEPRINGHYN	22		Company engaged on survey of proposed camp site	
	23		Moved to LEDRINGHEM. E.M. accommodated in billets	Bivouac.
			Company moved to Point L.33.d. and accommodated in bivouac	
CROIX DE POPERINGHE	24		The march to this hill proved trying to the men. Stragglers were numbers of the staff who turned up. Company was moved to Croix de Poperinghe and accommodated in huts	Maj. men sent an "H"
LEDON	25		Company moved to LEDON and accommodated in huts	
	26		Company engaged on cleaning up billets & unpacking transport	
	27		Company engaged in cleaning up billets, unpacking transport and stacking stores, going round huts	
	28		Parties employed in inspecting trenches and ascertaining work to be done	

Army Form C. 2118

WAR DIARY
or
INTELLIGENCE SUMMARY
(Erase heading not required.)

Instructions regarding War Diaries and Intelligence Summaries are contained in F. S. Regs., Part II. and the Staff Manual respectively. Title Pages will be prepared in manuscript.

Place	Date	Hour	Summary of Events and Information	Remarks and references to Appendices
	29		Parties engaged on inspecting trenches, ascertaining work to be done, and arranging for extra Dumps. Shelters west of main trenches of Neuve.	
	30		Parties engaged on construction of advanced report centre, reclamation of line, and digging communication trenches.	
	31		Parties engaged on construction of advanced report centre, reclamation of line, and digging communication trenches.	

J C Boyle, Major R.E.
O.C., 150th FIELD COY. R.E.

Vol II

Confidential

War Diary

of

150th Field Coy. R.E.

August, 1916

WAR DIARY
or
INTELLIGENCE SUMMARY
(Erase heading not required.)

Army Form C. 2118

Instructions regarding War Diaries and Intelligence Summaries are contained in F. S. Regs., Part II. and the Staff Manual respectively. Title Pages will be prepared in manuscript.

Place	Date 1916	Hour	Summary of Events and Information	Remarks and references to Appendices
LE DON	Aug 1.		Parties engaged in construction of advanced report centre, excavating, digging communication trenches and pumping out Dugouts.	
	2		Parties engaged in construction of advanced report centre, excavating, digging communication trenches and pumping out Dugouts	
	3		Parties engaged in construction of advanced report centre, excavating, digging communication trenches and pumping out Dugouts	
	4		Parties engaged in construction of advanced report centre, excavating, digging communication trenches and pumping out Dugouts	

Army Form C. 2118

WAR DIARY
or
INTELLIGENCE SUMMARY

(Erase heading not required.)

Instructions regarding War Diaries and Intelligence Summaries are contained in F. S. Regs., Part II. and the Staff Manual respectively. Title Pages will be prepared in manuscript.

Place	Date	Hour	Summary of Events and Information	Remarks and references to Appendices
	5		Parties engaged in construction of advanced report centre, Brigade H.Qrs. Shelters, Company shelters & digging communication trenches. Party engaged in Workshop	
	6		Parties engaged in construction of advanced report centre, Brigade H.Qrs. Shelters, Company shelters, digging communication trenches. Party engaged in Workshop	
	7		Parties engaged in construction of advanced report centre, Brigade H.Qrs. Shelters, Company shelters & digging communication trenches. Party engaged in Workshop	
	8		Parties engaged in construction of advanced report centre, Brigade H.Qrs. Shelters, Company shelters & digging communication trenches. Party engaged in Workshop.	

WAR DIARY
or
INTELLIGENCE SUMMARY

(Erase heading not required.)

Army Form C. 2118

Place	Date	Hour	Summary of Events and Information	Remarks and references to Appendices
	9		Parties engaged on construction of advanced report centre, Brigade H.Qrs. shelters, Company shelters and digging communication trenches. Parties engaged on workshops. My Captain tells i an expert workshop has been put in to making communication heads. So that 25 skilled helpers & an expert party will be working within m.s the supervision of an expert. I wonder do the Germans utilise their experts in this manner?.	
	10		Parties engaged on construction of advanced report centre, Brigade H.Qrs shelters, Company shelters, working in front line and in communication trenches. Parties engaged in workshops.	

Army Form C. 2118

WAR DIARY
or
INTELLIGENCE SUMMARY

(Erase heading not required.)

Instructions regarding War Diaries and Intelligence Summaries are contained in F.S. Regs., Part II. and the Staff Manual respectively. Title Pages will be prepared in manuscript.

Place	Date	Hour	Summary of Events and Information	Remarks and references to Appendices
	11		Parties engaged in construction of advanced shelters report centre, Brigade H.Qrs. shelters Company shelters, working in Front line and in communication Trenches. Parties engaged in Workshop.	
	12		Parties engaged in construction of advanced report centre, Brigade H.Qrs. shelters Company shelters working in Front line and in communication trenches. Parties engaged in Workshop.	
	13		Parties engaged in construction of advanced report centre, Brigade H.Qrs. shelters Company shelters, working in Front line and in communication trenches. Parties engaged in Workshop.	
	14		Parties engaged in construction of advanced report centre, Brigade H.Qrs. shelters Company shelters, working in Front line and in communication trenches. Parties engaged in Workshop.	

WAR DIARY
or
INTELLIGENCE SUMMARY

(Erase heading not required.)

Army Form C. 2118

Instructions regarding War Diaries and Intelligence Summaries are contained in F.S. Regs., Part II. and the Staff Manual respectively. Title Pages will be prepared in manuscript.

Place	Date	Hour	Summary of Events and Information	Remarks and references to Appendices
	15		Parties engaged on construction of advanced report centre, Brigade H.Qrs. shelters, Company shelters, working on front line and on communication trenches. Parties engaged in Workshops.	
	16		Parties engaged on construction of advanced report centre, Brigade H.Qrs. shelters, Company shelters, working on front line and on communication trenches. Parties engaged in Workshops.	
	17		Parties engaged on construction of advanced report centre, Brigade H.Qrs. shelters, Company shelters, working on front line and on communication trenches. Parties engaged in Workshops.	

Army Form C. 2118

WAR DIARY
or
INTELLIGENCE SUMMARY
(Erase heading not required.)

Place	Date	Hour	Summary of Events and Information	Remarks and references to Appendices
	18		Parties engaged in construction of advanced report centre, Brigade H.Qrs. shelters, Company shelters, working on Front line and in communication trenches. Parties engaged in Workshop.	
	19		Parties engaged in construction of advanced report centre, Brigade H.Qrs. shelters, Company shelters, working on Front line and in communication trenches. Parties engaged in Workshop.	
	20		Parties engaged in construction of advanced report centre, Brigade H.Qrs. shelters, Company shelters, working on Front line and in communication trenches. Parties engaged in Workshop.	

Instructions regarding War Diaries and Intelligence Summaries are contained in F.S. Regs., Part II. and the Staff Manual respectively. Title Pages will be prepared in manuscript.

Army Form C. 2118

WAR DIARY
or
INTELLIGENCE SUMMARY

(Erase heading not required.)

Instructions regarding War Diaries and Intelligence Summaries are contained in F. S. Regs., Part II. and the Staff Manual respectively. Title Pages will be prepared in manuscript.

Place	Date	Hour	Summary of Events and Information	Remarks and references to Appendices
	21		Parties engaged in construction of advanced report centre, Brigade H.Qrs. shelters, Company shelters, working in Front line and in Communication trenches. Parties engaged in Workshops.	
	22		Parties engaged in construction of advanced report centre, Brigade H.Qrs. shelters, Company shelters, working in Front line and in Communication trenches. Parties engaged in Workshops.	
	23		Parties engaged in construction of advanced report centre, Brigade H.Qrs. shelters, Company shelters, working in Front line and in Communication trenches. Parties engaged in Workshops.	

1875 Wt. W593/826 1,000,000 4/15 J.B.C. & A. A.D.S.S./Forms/C. 2118.

Army Form C. 2118

WAR DIARY
or
INTELLIGENCE SUMMARY
(Erase heading not required.)

Instructions regarding War Diaries and Intelligence Summaries are contained in F. S. Regs., Part II. and the Staff Manual respectively. Title Pages will be prepared in manuscript.

Place	Date	Hour	Summary of Events and Information	Remarks and references to Appendices
	24		Parties engaged in construction of advanced report centre, Brigade H. Qrs. Shelters, Company shelters, working on Front line and in communication trenches. Parties engaged in Workshops.	
	25		Parties engaged in construction of advanced report centre, Brigade H. Qrs. Shelters, Company shelters, working in Front line and in communication trenches. Parties engaged in Workshops.	
	26		Parties engaged in construction of advanced report centre, Brigade H. Qrs. Shelters, Company shelters, working on Front line and in communication trenches. Parties engaged in Workshops. No infantry working parties available	

Army Form C. 2118.

WAR DIARY
or
INTELLIGENCE SUMMARY
(Erase heading not required.)

Instructions regarding War Diaries and Intelligence Summaries are contained in F. S. Regs., Part II. and the Staff Manual respectively. Title Pages will be prepared in manuscript.

Place	Date	Hour	Summary of Events and Information	Remarks and references to Appendices
	27		Parties engaged in construction of advanced report centre, Brigade H.Qrs shelters, Company shelters, working on front line and on Communication trenches. To Infantry working parties. Parties engaged in Workshops.	
	28		Parties engaged in construction of advanced report centre, Brigade H.Qrs shelters, Company shelters, working on front line and on Communication trenches. To Infantry working parties. Parties engaged in Workshops.	
	29		Parties engaged in construction of advanced report centre, Brigade H.Qrs shelters, Company shelters, working on front line and on Communication trenches. Parties engaged in Workshops. No day or night Infantry parties owing to 2s going in. Germans a rotten smell from two day.	

2449 Wt. W14957/M90 750,000 1/16 J.B.C. & A. Forms/C.2118/12.

Place	Date	Hour	Summary of Events and Information	Remarks and references to Appendices
	30		Parties engaged on construction of advanced report centre, Brigade H.Qrs shelters, Company shelters, working in front line and on communication trenches. Parties engaged on Workshop. Very wet, no night parties.	
	31		Parties engaged on construction of advanced report centre, Brigade H.Qrs shelters, Company shelters, working in front line and on Communication trenches. Parties engaged on Workshop. Night parties detailed away to some tactical manoeuvre which it is hoped will not occur many Sundays.	

J.W.B. Clyde, Major R.E.
O.C. 150th FIELD COY. R.E.

Vol 12

Confidential

War Diary

of

150th Field Coy R.E.

September 1916

Army Form C. 2118

WAR DIARY
or
INTELLIGENCE SUMMARY
(Erase heading not required.)

Instructions regarding War Diaries and Intelligence Summaries are contained in F. S. Regs., Part II. and the Staff Manual respectively. Title Pages will be prepared in manuscript.

Place	Date 1916	Hour	Summary of Events and Information	Remarks and references to Appendices
LE DON	Sept 1		Parties engaged in construction of advanced report centre, Brigade Hdqrs. Company Dugouts, working on front line and in Communication Trenches. Parties engaged in workshops.	
	2		Parties engaged in construction of advanced report centre, Brigade Hdqrs. Company Dugouts, working on front line and in communication trenches. Parties engaged in Workshops.	
	3		Parties engaged in construction of advanced report centre, Brigade Hdqrs. Company Dugouts, working on front line and in communication trenches. Parties engaged in Workshops. Received orders to move to M. 35. c. 5.1. on 5th Sept. and relieve 82 Field Coy R.E.	

Army Form C. 2118.

WAR DIARY
or
INTELLIGENCE SUMMARY

(Erase heading not required.)

Instructions regarding War Diaries and Intelligence Summaries are contained in F. S. Regs., Part II. and the Staff Manual respectively. Title Pages will be prepared in manuscript.

Place	Date	Hour	Summary of Events and Information	Remarks and references to Appendices
	4		Company engaged in hecking Transport and arranging to hand over to 82nd Field Coy. R.E.	
M.35.b.6.1.	5		Company moved complete to Camp at M.35.b.6.1. (Sheet 28 S.W.) Company accommodated in huts.	
	6		Parties engaged on Perring Brigade Area and arranging what work was to be undertaken	

2449 Wt. W14957/M90 750,000 1/16 J.B.C. & A. Forms/C.2118/12.

WAR DIARY or INTELLIGENCE SUMMARY

Army Form C. 2118.

Place	Date	Hour	Summary of Events and Information	Remarks and references to Appendices
	7		Parties engaged in visiting Brigade area and arranging what work was to be undertaken.	
	8		Section 1. handed to 109 Inf Brigade for work in front line. Sections 2, 3 & 4 engaged in working in support line. Parties engaged in workshop making shelters for store. Engine Drivers employed on Baths.	
	9		Section 1. working on Front line maintenance, improvement and erecting shelters. Sections 2, 3 & 4 redeeming, framing, fronterying support tent and erecting shelters. Parties engaged in workshops & etc.	

Place	Date	Hour	Summary of Events and Information	Remarks and references to Appendices
	10		Front	
			Section 1 working on Left Sub-Sector No1 maintaining, repairing, raising parapet and deepening HAPPY MOMENTS.	
			Sections 2, 3 & 4 reclaiming, framing, revetting, repairing dug-out line and erecting shelters.	
			Parties engaged in Workshops & Baths.	
			Two Companies of Pioneers reclaiming, framing, revetting PICCADILLY and KINGSWAY.	
	11		Two sections engaged to support at BUS FARM for an advance of wire, and was returned on a fatigue by the other Section.	
			No 1. Section working on front. Sub-Sector three maintenance and repairing, raising parapet and deepening HAPPY MOMENTS.	
			No 2. Section digging trench 150 yards joining up Right and Left Sectors of Support Trench.	
			Sections 3 & 4 reclaiming and repairing dug-out line.	
			Two Companies of Pioneers reclaiming, framing, revetting PICCADILLY and KINGSWAY.	
			Parties engaged in Workshops and Baths.	

Army Form C. 2118

WAR DIARY
or
INTELLIGENCE SUMMARY
(Erase heading not required.)

Instructions regarding War Diaries and Intelligence Summaries are contained in F. S. Regs., Part II. and the Staff Manual respectively. Title Pages will be prepared in manuscript.

Place	Date	Hour	Summary of Events and Information	Remarks and references to Appendices
	12		No 1 Section working on Front line maintenance, repairing, raising parapet and deepening HAPPY MOMENTS and exiting shelters.	
			No. 2. 3 & 4 Sections reclaiming, framing, revetting, firestepping support line, and erecting shelters.	
			A Company of 14th Bn V.S.B attached to No 1 Section for Front line maintenance work	
			Two companies of Pioneers reclaiming, framing, revetting PICCADILLY and KINGSWAY.	
			No Infantry working parties for Sections 2.3 & 4. Parties engaged on Workshops etc.	
	13		No 1 Section working on Front line maintenance, repairing, raising parapet and deepening HAPPY MOMENTS and erecting shelters.	
			No 2. 3. & 4 Sections reclaiming, framing, revetting, firestepping support line and erecting shelters.	
			Two Companies of Pioneers reclaiming, framing, revetting PICCADILLY and KINGSWAY. Work considerably interfered with owing to very wet weather. Parties engaged on Workshop etc.	

1875 Wt. W593/826 1,000,000 4/15 J.B.C. & A. A.D.S.S./Forms/C. 2118.

WAR DIARY
or
INTELLIGENCE SUMMARY
(Erase heading not required.)

Army Form C. 2118

Place	Date	Hour	Summary of Events and Information	Remarks and references to Appendices
	14		No 1. Section working on Front Line maintenance, repairing raising parapet and deepening HAPPY MOMENTS Cd. revetting shelters. No 2.3.4 Sections reclaiming, framing, revetting, deepening support line and erecting shelters. Two companies of Pioneers reclaiming, framing, revetting PICCADILLY and KINGSWAY. Parties engaged in Workshops ozo bths. Work considerably interfered with owing to very wet weather	
	15		No 1. Section working on Front Line maintenance, repairing parapet and deepening HAPPY MOMENTS and erecting shelters No 2.3.4 Sections reclaiming, framing, revetting, deepening support line and erecting shelters. Two companies of Pioneers reclaiming, framing, revetting PICCADILLY and KINGSWAY. Parties engaged in Workshops and baths. Supplying fatigues for Loopholes and other explosives for cutting enemy wire, which was a great success	

WAR DIARY
or
INTELLIGENCE SUMMARY
(Erase heading not required.)

Army Form C. 2118

Place	Date	Hour	Summary of Events and Information	Remarks and references to Appendices
	16		No 1 Section working on Front line maintenance, repairing, raising parapet and deepening HAPPY MOMENTS and erecting shelters. No 2, 3 & 4 Sections reclaiming framing, revetting, fortifying support line and erecting Shelters. Two companies of Pioneers reclaiming, framing, revetting PICCADILLY and KINGSWAY. Parties engaged in workshop and baths. No Infantry working parties owing to our bombardment of enemy's front line which damaged our trenches to a considerable extent. One of our Howrs landing in at the end of HAPPY MOMENTS, which had to be demolished causing a large crater which I think did more harm than the enemy bombardment.	
	17		No 1 Section carrying out repairs necessary to front line system after bombardment. No 2, 3 & 4 Sections carrying out repairs necessary to Support line after bombardment. Parties engaged in workshops & Baths.	

WAR DIARY
or
INTELLIGENCE SUMMARY
(Erase heading not required.)

Army Form C. 2118

Place	Date	Hour	Summary of Events and Information	Remarks and references to Appendices
	18		No 1. Section carrying out repairs necessary to front line system after bombardment.	
			No. 2. 3. & 4 Sections carrying out repairs necessary to support line after bombardment.	
			Parties engaged in Workshops and Baths	
			No Infantry working parties owing to reply work greatly interfered with owing to very wet weather	
			Two companies of Pioneers reclaiming, framing, revetting, PICCADILLY and KINGSWAY.	
	19		No 1 Section working on front line maintenance repairing racing parapit and deepening HAPPY MOMENTS	
			No 2. 3. & 4 Sections reclaiming, framing, revetting, juristifying support line and erecting shelters	
			Two companies of Pioneers reclaiming, framing, revetting, PICCADILLY and KINGSWAY.	
			No night parties owing to anticipated gas "attack which had to be put off owing to wind changing.	

Army Form C. 2118

WAR DIARY
or
INTELLIGENCE SUMMARY
(Erase heading not required.)

Instructions regarding War Diaries and Intelligence Summaries are contained in F.S. Regs, Part II. and the Staff Manual respectively. Title Pages will be prepared in manuscript.

Place	Date	Hour	Summary of Events and Information	Remarks and references to Appendices
	20		No 1. Section working on Front line maintenance, repairing, raising parapit and deepening HAPPY MOMENTS & erecting shelters	
			No. 2, 3, & 4 Sections reclaiming, framing, revetting, firestepping, Support line and erecting shelters	
			Two Companies Pioneers reclaiming, framing, revetting PICCADILLY and KINGSWAY.	
			Parties engaged in workshops and Baths	
	21		No 1 Section working on Front line maintenance repairing, raising parapit and deepening HAPPY MOMENTS & erecting shelters	
			No. 2, 3, & 4 Sections reclaiming, framing, revetting, firestepping, Support line and erecting shelters	
			Two Companies Pioneers reclaiming, framing, revetting PICCADILLY and KINGSWAY	
			Parties engaged in Workshops and Baths	

Army Form C. 2118.

WAR DIARY
or
INTELLIGENCE SUMMARY.
(Erase heading not required.)

Place	Date	Hour	Summary of Events and Information	Remarks and references to Appendices
	22		No. 1 Section working on Front Line maintenance, repairing, raising parapet and deepening HAPPY MOMENTS & erecting shelters	
			No. 2, 3 & 4 Sections reclaiming, framing, revetting, revetting, support line and erecting shelters.	
			Two Companies Pioneers reclaiming, framing, revetting PICCADILLY and KING'S WAY.	
			Parties engaged in Workshops and Baths	
	23		No. 1 Section working on Front Line maintenance, repairing, raising parapet and deepening HAPPY MOMENTS & erecting shelters.	
			No. 2, 3 & 4 Sections reclaiming, framing, revetting, revetting, Support line and erecting shelters.	
			Two Companies Pioneers reclaiming, framing, revetting PICCADILLY and KING'S WAY.	
			Parties engaged in Workshops and Baths.	

WAR DIARY
or
INTELLIGENCE SUMMARY.
(Erase heading not required.)

Army Form C. 2118.

Instructions regarding War Diaries and Intelligence Summaries are contained in F. S. Regs., Part II. and the Staff Manual respectively. Title pages will be prepared in manuscript.

Place	Date	Hour	Summary of Events and Information	Remarks and references to Appendices
	24		No 1 Section working on Front line maintenance, repairing parapet and deepening HAPPY MOMENTS and erecting shelters	
			No 2, 3 & 4 Sections reclaiming trench, resetting, revetting, support line and erecting shelters	
			No Infantry working parties sent to us.	
			No 2, 3 & 4 Sections relieved No 1.3 Sections at 3 P.M.	
	25		No 1 Section working on Front line maintenance, repairing parapet and deepening HAPPY MOMENTS and erecting shelters	
			No 2, 3 & 4 Sections reclaiming trench, resetting, revetting, support line and erecting shelters	
			A certain amount of damage has been caused by enemy fire, repair work being carried on with	
			Two companies of Pioneers reclaiming, reveting reeting PICCADILLY and KINGSWAY parties engaged in Workshops and Roads.	

WAR DIARY
or
INTELLIGENCE SUMMARY
(Erase heading not required.)

Army Form C. 2118

Instructions regarding War Diaries and Intelligence Summaries are contained in F.S. Regs., Part II. and the Staff Manual respectively. Title Pages will be prepared in manuscript.

Place	Date	Hour	Summary of Events and Information	Remarks and references to Appendices
	26		No 1 Section working on Front Line maintenance, repairing, raising parapet and deepening HAPPY MOMENTS & erecting shelters	
			No. 2, 3 & 4 Sections reclaiming, framing, revetting, prettifying support line and erecting shelters	
			Two companies of Pioneers reclaiming, framing, revetting PICCADILLY and KINGSWAY	
			Parties engaged in Workshops and Baths.	
	27		No 1. Section working on Front Line maintenance, repairing, raising parapet and deepening HAPPY MOMENTS & erecting shelters.	
			No. 2, 3 & 4 Sections reclaiming, framing, revetting, prettifying support line and erecting shelters.	
			Two companies of Pioneers reclaiming, framing, revetting PICCADILLY and KINGSWAY.	
			Parties engaged in Workshops making Bangalore torpedoes and other devilment.	

Army Form C. 2118.

WAR DIARY
or
INTELLIGENCE SUMMARY.

(Erase heading not required.)

Instructions regarding War Diaries and Intelligence Summaries are contained in F. S. Regs., Part II. and the Staff Manual respectively. Title pages will be prepared in manuscript.

Place	Date	Hour	Summary of Events and Information	Remarks and references to Appendices
	28		No 1. Section working on Front Line maintenance, repairing, raising parapit and deepening HAPPY MOMENTS and erecting shelters.	
			No. 2. 3. & 4. Sections reclaiming, framing, revetting, firestepping support line and erecting shelters.	
			Laying tramway between FORT EDWARD and REGENT STREET.	
			Parties engaged in Workshops preparing charges and frames and repairs to tools.	
			Two companies of Pioneers reclaiming, framing, revetting PICCADILLY & KINGSWAY.	
	29		No 1. Section working on Front line maintenance, repairing, raising parapit and deepening HAPPY MOMENTS and erecting shelters.	
			No. 2. 3. & 4. Sections reclaiming, framing, revetting, firestepping support line and existing shelters.	
			Laying tramway between FORT EDWARD and REGENT STREET.	
			Erecting Dug outs for Machine Gun emplacements.	
			Two companies of Pioneers reclaiming, framing, revetting PICCADILLY & KINGSWAY.	
			Parties engaged in Workshops preparing charges for explosives, making frames	

Place	Date	Hour	Summary of Events and Information	Remarks and references to Appendices
	30		No 1 Section working on front line maintaining, repairing, revising parapet and deepening HAPPY MOMENTS and erecting shelters	
			No 2.3.4 Sections reclaiming framing, revetting, fortifying support line and erecting shelters	
			Laying tramway between FORT EDWARD and REGENT STREET	
			Erecting dugouts M.G. emplacements and T.M. positions	
			Two Companies of Pioneers reclaiming revetting framing PICCADILLY & KINGSWAY.	
			Workshop party making shelters &c for trench works.	
			Party of eight men viz :- First party 64349 Cpl Cush J.H. 64263 Sgt Young Q. Second party 57474 2/Cpl Sibbald. 64315 Sgt McCormick D. Third party 57539 Cpl. Thompson R. 57585 Sgt Hughes W. Fourth party 64395 Cpl Bryan W. 57594 Cpl Johnston J. were attached to raiding party of 10 R.I. Inns. Fusiliers.	
			Parties divided into four groups. 1 N.C.O. and 1 sapper went with each group and each man had with them a 7 lb bag of ammonal and 4 slabs guncotton done up in 2 charges with fuse etc ready for demolition. Each party got into	

WAR DIARY
or
INTELLIGENCE SUMMARY.
(Erase heading not required.)

Army Form C. 2118.

Instructions regarding War Diaries and Intelligence Summaries are contained in F. S. Regs., Part II. and the Staff Manual respectively. Title pages will be prepared in manuscript.

Place	Date	Hour	Summary of Events and Information	Remarks and references to Appendices
			and remained in them for over 30 minutes. The Bosch lines with their portion had taps along the trenches as well as across No Mans Land, and these taps proved very useful in showing the men the way back. Dugouts were bombed and blown up as the party were coming back. A machine gun was captured by Lieut Morris & 2.R. Innis Fus. who informed me L/Cpl Bryans was the greatest help to him in getting it, bombing in front of him, and he blew up emplacement & Dugouts as far as I can ascertain were nine shelters or/& Dugouts on the way back. The Dugouts & emmunition tubes in the Bosch lines and those needed a wide track and clearing for the raiding party. The trenches were in a tattered condition but apparently we kept in repair, but the communication trenches were very bad, and tired and fairly with todo. All Dugouts, Bomb Stores met with were well demolished. Unfortunately L/Cpl Thompson R.J. was killed by I think, a rifle grenade. All the R.E. party and their work well and the O.C. Raiding Party and	

2353 Wt. W2544/1454 700,000 5/15 D. D. & L. A.D.S.S./Forms/C. 2118.

Army Form C. 2118.

WAR DIARY
or
INTELLIGENCE SUMMARY.
(Erase heading not required.)

Instructions regarding War Diaries and Intelligence Summaries are contained in F. S. Regs., Part II. and the Staff Manual respectively. Title pages will be prepared in manuscript.

Place	Date	Hour	Summary of Events and Information	Remarks and references to Appendices
			the Battalion expressed their appreciation of the valuable assistance given the party by these men	

J.C.Stoke
Major R.E.
O.C., 150th FIELD COY. R.E.

vol 13

Confidential

War Diary

of

150th Field Coy R.E.

October 1916

Army Form C. 2118.

WAR DIARY
or
INTELLIGENCE SUMMARY.
(Erase heading not required.)

Instructions regarding War Diaries and Intelligence Summaries are contained in F. S. Regs., Part II. and the Staff Manual respectively. Title pages will be prepared in manuscript.

Place	Date 1916	Hour	Summary of Events and Information	Remarks and references to Appendices
DRANOUTRE	Oct 1.		No 1. section working on front line maintenance, framing, raising parapet and deepening, parapet HAPPY MOMENTS and erecting shelters. No 2.3. + 4 sections revetting framing support line + raising shelters. Workshops parties making shelters for trench work. Tramlines being laid.	
	2.		No 1. section working on front line maintenance, framing, raising parapet and deepening HAPPY MOMENTS and erecting shelters. No 2.3 + 4 sections revetting framing support line and erecting shelters. Workshops parties making shelters for trench work. Tramlines being laid. Wire entanglements revetting framing PICCADILLY + KINGSWAY.	

Army Form C. 2118.

WAR DIARY
or
INTELLIGENCE SUMMARY.
(Erase heading not required.)

Place	Date	Hour	Summary of Events and Information	Remarks and references to Appendices
	3		No 1 Section working on front line maintenance, framing, racing parapet and deepening HAPPYMOMENTS and erecting shelters; repairing damage done by enemy bombardment.	
			No. 2, 3 & 4 Sections revetting framing, support line and erecting shelters, and revetting also tramlines being laid from FORT EDWARD also to REGENT STREET and from R.E. FARM to NORTH SHAFT.	
			Two Companies Pioneers revetting framing PICCADILLY and KINGSWAY. Shelters for M.G. team being erected also O.P. Workshops parties making shelters for trench work.	
	4		No 1 Section working on front line maintenance, framing, racing parapet and deepening HAPPY MOMENTS and erecting shelters; repairing damage done by enemy bombardment.	
			No. 2, 3 & 4 Sections revetting framing, support line and erecting shelters tramlines being laid from FORT EDWARD to REGENT STREET and from R.E. FARM to NORTH SHAFT.	
			Two Companies Pioneers revetting framing PICCADILLY and KINGSWAY. Shelters for M.G. team being erected also O.P. Workshops parties making shelters for trench work.	

WAR DIARY

or

INTELLIGENCE SUMMARY

(Erase heading not required.)

Army Form C. 2118

Place	Date	Hour	Summary of Events and Information	Remarks and references to Appendices
	5		No 1. Section working on front line maintenance, framing, revetting parapet and deepening HAPPY MOMENTS and erecting shelters. No 2. 3. & 4. Sections revetting framing support line and erecting shelters tramlines being laid from FORT EDWARD to REGENT STREET and from R.E. FARM to NORTH SHAFT. Two Companies Pioneers revetting, framing PICCADILLY and KINGSWAY shelters for M.G. team being erected also O.P. Workshop parties making shelters for trench work.	
	6		No 1. Section working on front line maintenance, framing, revetting parapet and deepening HAPPY MOMENTS and revetting shelters. No 2. 3. & 4. Sections revetting framing support line and erecting shelters tramlines being laid from FORT EDWARD & REGENT STREET and from R.E FARM to NORTH SHAFT. Two Companies Pioneers revetting framing PICCADILLY and KINGSWAY shelters for M.G. team being erected also O.P. Workshop parties making shelters for trench work. 64264 Sapper McClure H killed by sniper.	

WAR DIARY
or
INTELLIGENCE SUMMARY
(Erase heading not required.)

Army Form C. 2118

Place	Date	Hour	Summary of Events and Information	Remarks and references to Appendices
	7		No 1 Section working on front line maintenance, framing, racing parapit and deepening HAPPY MOMENTS and erecting shelters. No 2, 3 & 4 Sections revetting framing support line and erecting shelters. Tramlines being laid from FORT EDWARD to REGENT STREET and from R.E. FARM to NORTH SHAFT. Two Companies Pioneers revetting framing PICCADILLY and KINGSWAY. Workshops parties making shelters for trench work. Shelters for M.G. team being erected also O.P.	
	8		No 1 Section working on front line maintenance, framing racing parapit and deepening HAPPY MOMENTS and erecting shelters. No 2, 3 & 4 Sections revetting framing support line and erecting shelters. Tramlines being laid from FORT EDWARD to REGENT STREET and from R.E. FARM to NORTH SHAFT. Shelters for M.G. team being erected also O.P. Workshops parties making shelters for trench work. No. 1 & 3 Sections relieved No 2 & 4 Sections at BUS FARM.	

Army Form C. 2118.

WAR DIARY
or
INTELLIGENCE SUMMARY

(Erase heading not required.)

Instructions regarding War Diaries and Intelligence Summaries are contained in F. S. Regs., Part II. and the Staff Manual respectively. Title Pages will be prepared in manuscript.

Place	Date	Hour	Summary of Events and Information	Remarks and references to Appendices
	9		No 1. Section working on front line maintenance, framing, moving, parapet and deepening HAPPY MOMENTS and erecting shelters. No 2. 3 & 4 Sections revetting, framing support line and erecting shelters. Tramlines being laid from FORT EDWARD to REGENT STREET. Tram from R.E. FARM to NORTH SHAFT. Shelters for M.G. team being erected also O.P. Two Companies Pioneers revetting, framing PICCADILLY & KINGSWAY. Workshops parties making shelters for trench works.	
	10		No 1. Section working on front line maintenance, framing, moving, parapet and deepening HAPPY MOMENTS and erecting shelters. No 2. 3 & 4 Sections revetting, framing support line and erecting shelters. Tramlines being laid from FORT EDWARD to REGENT STREET and from R.E. FARM to NORTH SHAFT. Shelters for M.G. team being erected also O.P. Two Companies Pioneers revetting, framing PICCADILLY & KINGSWAY. Workshops parties making shelters for trench work. Sapper Horton D. No. 57423 & Sapper Crangle D. 84387 wounded in action.	

Army Form C. 2118.

WAR DIARY
or
INTELLIGENCE SUMMARY
(Erase heading not required.)

Instructions regarding War Diaries and Intelligence Summaries are contained in F. S. Regs., Part II. and the Staff Manual respectively. Title Pages will be prepared in manuscript.

Place	Date	Hour	Summary of Events and Information	Remarks and references to Appendices
	11		No 1. Section working on front line maintenance, framing, raising parapet and deepening HAPPY MOMENTS and erecting shelters. No. 2, 3, & 4 Sections erecting framing, support line and erecting shelters. Tramlines being laid from FORT EDWARD to REGENT STREET and from R.E. FARM to NORTH SHAFT. Shelters for M.G. Team being erected also O.P. Two Companies Pioneers erecting framing, PICCADILLY & KINGSWAY. Workshops parties making shelters for French work.	
	12		Company entertained to a day's outing at BAILLEUL	

WAR DIARY
or
INTELLIGENCE SUMMARY

(Erase heading not required.)

Army Form C. 2118.

Place	Date	Hour	Summary of Events and Information	Remarks and references to Appendices
	13		No 1. Section working on Front Line maintenance, framing, raising parapet and deepening HAPPY MOMENTS and sterling shelters. No. 2. 3. 4. Sections revetting, framing, dugout line & erecting shelters. Tramlines being laid from FORT EDWARD to REGENT STREET and from R.E. FARM to NORTH SHAFT. Shelters for M.G. team being erected also O.P. Two Companies Pioneers revetting framing PICCADILLY & KINGSWAY Workshop Parties making shelters for trench work.	
	14		No 1. Section working on Front Line maintenance, framing, raising parapet and deepening HAPPY MOMENTS & erecting shelters. No. 2. 3. 74. Sections revetting, framing, dugout line & erecting shelters. Tramlines being laid from FORT EDWARD to REGENT STREET and from R.E. FARM to NORTH SHAFT. Shelters for M.G. team being erected also O.P. Two Companies Pioneers revetting framing PICCADILLY & KINGSWAY Workshop Parties making shelters for trench work. 64394 Sergt. McCullough W killed in action.	

WAR DIARY
or
INTELLIGENCE SUMMARY

Army Form C. 2118.

Place	Date	Hour	Summary of Events and Information	Remarks and references to Appendices
	15		No 1. Section working on front line maintenance, framing, raising parapet and deepening HAPPY MOMENTS & erecting shelters. No. 2.3 & 4. Sections revetting framing, support line, and erecting shelters. Tramlines being laid from FORT EDWARD & REGENT STREET and from R.E. FARM to NORTH SHAFT. Shelters for M.G. team being erected also O.P. Workshops Parties making shelters for trench work.	
	16		No 1. Section working on front line maintenance, framing, raising parapet and deepening HAPPY MOMENTS & erecting shelters. No. 2.3 & 4. Sections revetting framing, support line, and erecting shelters. Tramlines being laid from FORT EDWARD to REGENT STREET and from R.E. FARM to NORTH SHAFT. Shelters for M.G. team being erected also O.P. Two Companies Pioneers revetting framing PICCADILLY & KINGSWAY. Workshops Parties making shelters for trench work.	

Army Form C. 2118.

WAR DIARY
or
INTELLIGENCE SUMMARY

(Erase heading not required.)

Place	Date	Hour	Summary of Events and Information	Remarks and references to Appendices
	17		No. 1 Section working on front line maintenance, framing, revetting parapet and deepening HAPPY MOMENTS and erecting shelters. No. 2. 3 + 4 Sections revetting, framing, support line, and erecting shelters. Tramlines being laid from FORT EDWARD to REGENT STREET and from R.E. FARM to NORTH SHAFT. Shelters for M.G. Team being erected also O.P. Two Company Pioneers revetting, framing, PICCADILLY + KINGSWAY. Workshop Parties making shelters for trench work.	
	18		No. 1 Section working on front line maintenance, framing, revetting parapet and deepening HAPPY MOMENTS and erecting shelters. No. 2. 3 + 4 Sections revetting, framing, support line, and erecting shelters. Tramlines being laid from FORT EDWARD to REGENT STREET and from R.E. FARM to NORTH SHAFT. Shelters for M.G. Team being erected also O.P. Two Company Pioneers revetting, framing, PICCADILLY + KINGSWAY. Workshop Parties making shelters for trench work.	

WAR DIARY
or
INTELLIGENCE SUMMARY

(Erase heading not required.)

Army Form C. 2118.

Place	Date	Hour	Summary of Events and Information	Remarks and references to Appendices
	19		No 1. Section working on Front line maintenance, framing, revetting parapet, and deepening HAPPY MOMENTS and erecting shelters. No. 2, 3, & 4 Sections revetting, framing dugout lining and erecting shelters Tramlines being laid from FORT EDWARD to REGENT STREET and from R.E. FARM to NORTH SHAFT. Shelters for M.G. team being erected also O.P. Two Companies Pioneers revetting, framing PICCADILLY & KINGSWAY Workshop parties making shelters for French work.	
	20		No 1. Section revetting on Front line maintenance, framing, revetting parapet, and deepening HAPPY MOMENTS & erecting shelters. No. 2. 3. & 4 Sections revetting framing dugout lining & erecting shelters. Tramlines being laid from FORT EDWARD to REGENT STREET and from R.E. FARM to NORTH SHAFT. Shelters for M.G. teams being erected also O.P. Two Companies Pioneers revetting, framing PICCADILLY and KINGSWAY. Workshop parties making shelters for French work.	

Army Form C. 2118.

WAR DIARY
or
INTELLIGENCE SUMMARY

(Erase heading not required.)

Instructions regarding War Diaries and Intelligence Summaries are contained in F. S. Regs., Part II. and the Staff Manual respectively. Title Pages will be prepared in manuscript.

Place	Date	Hour	Summary of Events and Information	Remarks and references to Appendices
	21		No.1. Section working on front line maintenance, framing, revering parapet, and loopholing HAPPY MOMENTS & erecting shelters. No. 2, 3, 7+ Sections revetting, framing support lines & erecting shelters. Tramlines being laid from FORT EDWARD to REGENT STREET and from R.E. FARM to NORTH SHAFT. Shelters for M.G. team being erected, also O.P. Two Companies Pioneers revetting framing PICCADILLY and KINGSWAY. Workshops parties making shelters for trench work.	
	22		No.1. Section working on front line maintenance, framing, revering parapet, and loopholing HAPPY MOMENTS + erecting shelters. No. 2, 3, 74 Sections revetting, framing support lines erecting shelters. Tramlines being laid from FORT EDWARD to REGENT STREET and from R.E. FARM to NORTH SHAFT. Shelters for M.G. team being erected also O.P. Workshops parties making shelters for trench work	

Place	Date	Hour	Summary of Events and Information	Remarks and references to Appendices
	23		No.1. Section working on front line maintenance, framing, revising parapet, and deepening HAPPY MOMENTS and erecting shelters. No. 2. 3. 4. Sections revetting, framing, support line and erecting shelters. Tramlines being laid from FORT EDWARD to REGENT STREET and from R.E. FARM to NORTH SHAFT. Shelters for M.G. team being erected also O.P. Two Companies Pioneers revetting, framing PICCADILLY and KINGSWAY Workshops parties making shelters for french work.	
	24		No.1. Section working on front line maintenance, framing, revising parapet, and deepening HAPPY MOMENTS, and erecting shelters. No. 2. 3. 4. Sections revetting, framing, support line and erecting shelters. Tramlines being laid from FORT EDWARD to REGENT STREET and from R.E.FARM to NORTH SHAFT. Shelters for M.G. team being erected also O.P. Two Companies Pioneers revetting, framing PICCADILLY and KINGSWAY Workshops parties making shelters for french work.	

Army Form C. 2118.

WAR DIARY
or
INTELLIGENCE SUMMARY
(Erase heading not required.)

Place	Date	Hour	Summary of Events and Information	Remarks and references to Appendices
	25		Nos 1 & 3 Sections working on front line maintenance, forming raising parapet and deepening HAPPY MOMENTS and erecting shelters	
			No. 2 & 4 Sections revetting, framing, support line and erecting shelters Tramlines being laid from FORT EDWARD to REGENT STREET and from R.E. FARM to NORTH SHAFT. Shelters for M.G. team being laid also O.P. Two Companies Pioneers revetting framing PICCADILLY & KINGSWAY Workshop parties making shelters for trench work	
	26		Nos 1 & 3 Sections working on Front line maintenance framing raising parapet and deepening HAPPY MOMENTS erecting shelters	
			No 2 & 4 Sections revetting, framing, support line and erecting shelters Tramlines being laid from FORT EDWARD to REGENT STREET and from R.E.FARM to NORTH SHAFT. Shelters for M.G. team being laid also O.P. Two Companies Pioneers revetting framing PICCADILLY & KINGSWAY Workshop parties making shelters for trench work	

Army Form C. 2118.

WAR DIARY
or
INTELLIGENCE SUMMARY
(Erase heading not required.)

Instructions regarding War Diaries and Intelligence Summaries are contained in F. S. Regs., Part II. and the Staff Manual respectively. Title Pages will be prepared in manuscript.

Place	Date	Hour	Summary of Events and Information	Remarks and references to Appendices
	27		No 1 & 3 Sections working on Front line maintenance, framing, revertting parapet and deepening HAPPY MOMENTS and revetting shelters.	
			No. 2 & 4 Sections revetting framing support line and revetting shelters.	
			Tramlines being laid from FORT EDWARD to REGENT STREET and from R.E. FARM to NORTH SHAFT	
			Shelters for M.G. team being erected also O.P.	
			Two Companies Pioneers revetting, framing, PICCADILLY and KINGSWAY.	
			Workshop parties making shelters for trench work.	
	28		No 1 & 3 Sections working on Front line maintenance, framing, revetting parapet and deepening HAPPY MOMENTS & erecting shelters	
			No 2 & 4 Sections revetting framing support line and erecting shelters.	
			Tramlines being laid from FORT EDWARD to REGENT STREET and from R.E. FARM to NORTH SHAFT	
			Shelters for M.G. team being erected also O.P.	
			Two Companies Pioneers revetting, framing PICCADILLY and KINGSWAY	
			Workshop parties making shelters for trench work	

Army Form C. 2118.

WAR DIARY
or
INTELLIGENCE SUMMARY

(Erase heading not required.)

Instructions regarding War Diaries and Intelligence Summaries are contained in F. S. Regs., Part II. and the Staff Manual respectively. Title Pages will be prepared in manuscript.

Place	Date	Hour	Summary of Events and Information	Remarks and references to Appendices
	29.		No 1 & 3 Sections working on Front line maintenance, framing, sawing, parapet and deepening HAPPY MOMENTS and erecting shelters. No 2 & 4 Sections rivetting, framing, support line, and erecting shelters. Tramlines being laid from FORT EDWARD to REGENT STREET and from R.E. FARM to NORTH SHAFT. Shelters for M.G. team being erected also O.P. Workshops parties making shelters for trench work.	
	30		No 1 & 3 Sections working on Front line maintenance, framing, sawing, parapet and deepening HAPPY MOMENTS and erecting shelters. No 2 & 4 Sections rivetting, framing, support line and erecting shelters. Tramlines being laid from FORT EDWARD to REGENT STREET and from R.E. FARM to NORTH SHAFT. Shelters for M.G. team being erected also O.P. Workshops parties making shelters for trench work. Two companies Pioneers rivetting.	

Army Form C. 2118.

WAR DIARY
or
INTELLIGENCE SUMMARY
(Erase heading not required.)

Instructions regarding War Diaries and Intelligence Summaries are contained in F. S. Regs., Part II. and the Staff Manual respectively. Title Pages will be prepared in manuscript.

Place	Date	Hour	Summary of Events and Information	Remarks and references to Appendices
	31		No 1 & 3 sections working on front line maintenance, framing, raising parapet and deepening HAPPY MOMENTS and erecting shelters.	
			No 2 & 4 sections revetting framing support line, and erecting shelters.	
			Tramlines being laid from FORT EDWARD to REGENT STREET and from R.E. FARM to NORTH SHAFT.	
			Shelters for M.G. team being erected also O.P.	
			Two Companies Pioneers revetting, framing PICCADILLY & KINGSWAY. Workshop parties making shelters for trench mortars.	
			4 Sappers went out with a raiding party of the 14 & Bn. R.I.R. They took with them bangalore torpedoes, ammonal tubes to destroy enemy wire, which they successfully did; and other explosives for the	

Army Form C. 2118.

WAR DIARY
or
INTELLIGENCE SUMMARY

(Erase heading not required.)

Instructions regarding War Diaries and Intelligence Summaries are contained in F. S. Regs., Part II. and the Staff Manual respectively. Title Pages will be prepared in manuscript.

Place	Date	Hour	Summary of Events and Information	Remarks and references to Appendices
	31		destruction of Dugouts. The tracing party did not succeed in entering the Boche trenches. 64565 Sapper Stewart J. wounded. Several work during the month consisted of maintenance and reclamation of trenches and repairs done by shell fire. Erecting Dugouts, Trench Mortar emplacements, O.P. Dug Dugouts, Laying Trench tramways. Also increasing water supplies	

J. C. Boyle
Major R.E.
O.C. 150th Field Coy. R.E.

Vol 14

Confidential

War Diary

- of -

150th Field Coy R.E.

November, 1916

Army Form C. 2118.

WAR DIARY
or
INTELLIGENCE SUMMARY
(Erase heading not required.)

Secret

Place	Date	Hour	Summary of Events and Information	Remarks and references to Appendices
DRANOUTRE	1916 Nov. 1.		No 1 & 3 Sections working on Front line maintenance, framing, raising parapet and deepening HAPPY MOMENTS and erecting shelters. Maintenance Support line. Stokes Gun emplacements.	
			No 2 & 4 Sections laying tramways from FORT EDWARD to REGENT STREET and from R.E. FARM to S.P.7. Erecting R.A.M.C. shell proof Dressing Station and First Aid Posts. Water supply.	
			Shelters for M.G. team being erected. Also O.P. and dugout for R.F.A. Two companies Pioneers revetting, framing PICCADILLY and KINGSWAY. Workshop parties making shelters etc, for trenches.	
	2.		No 1 & 3 Sections working on Front-line maintenance, framing, raising parapet and deepening HAPPY MOMENTS and erecting shelters. Maintenance Support line. Stokes Gun emplacements.	
			No 2 & 4 Sections laying tramways from FORT EDWARD to REGENT STREET and from R.E. FARM to S.P.7. Erecting R.A.M.C. shell proof Dressing Station and First Aid Posts. Water supply.	
			Shelters for M.G. team being erected. Also O.P. and Dugout for R.F.A. Two companies Pioneers revetting, framing, PICCADILLY and KINGSWAY. Workshop parties making shelters (letrosets) for trenches.	

Army Form C. 2118.

Secret

WAR DIARY
or
INTELLIGENCE SUMMARY

(Erase heading not required.)

Instructions regarding War Diaries and Intelligence Summaries are contained in F. S. Regs., Part II and the Staff Manual respectively. Title Pages will be prepared in manuscript.

Place	Date	Hour	Summary of Events and Information	Remarks and references to Appendices
	3		No 1 + 3 Sections working on front line maintenance, framing, raising parapet and deepening HAPPY MOMENTS and erecting shelters. Maintenance Support line. Stokes Gun emplacements.	
			No. 2 + 4 Sections laying tramways from FORT EDWARD to REGENT STREET and from R.E. FARM to S.P.7. Erecting R.A.M.C. shell proof Dressing Station and first Aid Posts Water supply. Shelters for M.G. team being erected, also O.P. and Dugout for R.F.A. Two Companies Pioneers revetting, framing, PICCADILLY and KINGSWAY. Workshop parties making shelters etc. for trenches.	
	4		No 1 + 3 Sections working on front line maintenance, framing, raising parapet, and deepening HAPPY MOMENTS and erecting shelters. Maintenance support line. Stokes Gun emplacements.	
			No. 2 + 4 Sections laying tramways from FORT EDWARD to REGENT STREET and from R.E. FARM to S.P.7. Erecting R.A.M.C. shell proof Dressing station and first Aid Posts Water supply. Shelters for M.G. team being erected, also O.P. and Dugout for R.F.A. Two Companies Pioneers revetting, framing, PICCADILLY and KINGSWAY. Workshop parties making shelters etc. for trenches.	

WAR DIARY
or
INTELLIGENCE SUMMARY

(Erase heading not required.)

Army Form C. 2118.

Place	Date	Hour	Summary of Events and Information	Remarks and references to Appendices
	5		No 1 & 3 Sections working on front line maintenance, framing, revering parapet, and deepening HAPPY MOMENTS and erecting shelters. Maintenance support line. Stokes Gun emplacement.	
			No 2 & 4 Sections laying Tramways from FORT EDWARD to REGENT STREET and from R.E. FARM to S.P.7. Erecting R.A.M.C. shell proof dressing Station and First Aid Posts. Water supply.	
			Shelters for M.G. team being erected also O.P. and Dugouts for R.A. Workshop parties making shelters etc. for trenches	
			No 1 & 3 Sections relieved No 2 & 4 Sections at BUS FARM.	
	6		No 1 & 3. Sections working on front line maintenance, framing, revering parapet, and deepening HAPPY MOMENTS and erecting shelters. Maintenance support line. Stokes Gun emplacement.	
			No 2 & 4 Sections laying Tramways from FORT EDWARD to REGENT STREET and from R.E. FARM to S.P.7. Erecting R.A.M.C. shell proof dressing Station and First Aid Posts. Water supply.	
			Shelters for M.G. team being erected also O.P. and Dugouts for R.A. Two companies Pioneers revetting, framing PICCADILLY and KINGSWAY. Enemy shelled KINGSWAY, out about going into the trench close to working parties. Workshop parties making shelters etc. for trenches.	

Army Form C. 2118.

Secret

WAR DIARY
or
INTELLIGENCE SUMMARY
(Erase heading not required.)

Instructions regarding War Diaries and Intelligence Summaries are contained in F. S. Regs., Part II. and the Staff Manual respectively. Title Pages will be prepared in manuscript.

Place	Date	Hour	Summary of Events and Information	Remarks and references to Appendices
	7		Owing to very heavy rains no work was possible in trenches. Workshop parties making shelters etc. for trenches. Party engaged on laying tramway.	
	8		All available labour concentrated on damaged front line work, drains and communication trenches, which had been caused by abnormal floods.	
	9		Repair work on trenches, laying tramway	
	10		Repair work on trenches, laying tramway	
	11		LINDENHOEK - REGENT STREET railway connected up and extension to PICCADILLY commenced. Three platoons of Pioneers taken off PICCADILLY and put on to KINGSWAY, which was badly fallen in. PICCADILLY ULSTER ROAD handed over to 109th Inf. Brigade for maintenance.	

2449 Wt. W14957/M90 750,000 1/16 J.B.C. & A. Forms/C.2118/12.

Army Form C. 2118.

WAR DIARY
or
INTELLIGENCE SUMMARY

(Erase heading not required.)

Stevs

Place	Date	Hour	Summary of Events and Information	Remarks and references to Appendices
	12		No 1 & 3 Sections working on front line maintenance, framing raising parapet & deepening HAPPY MOMENTS & erecting shelters.	
			No 2 & 4 Sections laying tramways. erecting R.A.M.C. shell proof Dressing Station and First Aid Posts. Water supply.	
			Shelters for M.G. Team being erected, also O.P. and Dugout for R.F.A. Workshop parties making shelters etc. for Pioneers	
	13		No 1 & 3 Sections working on front line maintenance, framing raising parapet & deepening HAPPY MOMENTS & erecting shelters.	
			No 2 & 4 Sections laying tramways, erecting R.A.M.C. shell proof Dressing Station and First Aid Posts. Water supply.	
			Shelters for M.G. Team being erected, also O.P. and Dugout for R.F.A. Pioneers clearing KINGSWAY and VIGO STREET.	

Secret   Army Form C. 2118.

WAR DIARY
or
INTELLIGENCE SUMMARY

(Erase heading not required.)

Place	Date	Hour	Summary of Events and Information	Remarks and references to Appendices
	14		No 1 + 3 Sections working on front line maintenance, framing raising parapet & deepening HAPPY MOMENTS & erecting shelters.	
			No 2 + 4 Sections laying tramways, erecting R.A.M.C. shell proof Dressing Station and First Aid Posts. Water supply.	
			Shelters for M.G. Team being erected, also O.P. and Dugouts R.F.A.	
			Workshop parties making shelters etc for trenches.	
			Pioneers clearing KINGSWAY and VIGO STREET.	
	15		No 1 + 3 Sections working on front line maintenance, framing and service trench. Urgency visit for clearing wounded from front line down LONG LANE.	
			No 2 + 4 Sections laying tramways, erecting R.A.M.C. shell proof Dressing Station and First Aid Posts. Water supply.	
			Shelters for M.G. Team being erected. also O.P. and Dp Dugouts on front line.	
			Workshop parties making shelters etc, for trenches, preparing explosives, ammonal tubes, and dummy figures to for the Bosch.	
			Pioneers getting face away thro' KINGSWAY where it had fallen in and so that relief may take place through the whole length of it.	

Army Form C. 2118.

Secret

WAR DIARY
or
INTELLIGENCE SUMMARY
(Erase heading not required.)

Place	Date	Hour	Summary of Events and Information	Remarks and references to Appendices
	16		No 1 & 3 Sections repairing front line work, erecting shelters etc.	
			No 2 & 4 Section laying tramways, erecting shelters for R.A.M.C. and water supply	
			Workshops completed septiewers aminonal tubes dummy figures etc for N.Z Royal Enniskilling fusiliers. resetting party	
			Pioneers getting pair way through KINGSWAY.	
	17		No 1 & 3 Sections repairing front line work, erecting shelters etc	
			No 2 & 4 Sections laying tramways, erecting shelters for R.A.M.C. water supply	
			Pioneers getting pair way through KINGSWAY.	
			Very hard frost, work being concentrated on clearing drains preparing to thaw.	
			Workshop parties making shelters etc. for trenches.	

Secret

Army Form C. 2118.

WAR DIARY
or
INTELLIGENCE SUMMARY

(Erase heading not required.)

Instructions regarding War Diaries and Intelligence Summaries are contained in F. S. Regs., Part II. and the Staff Manual respectively. Title Pages will be prepared in manuscript.

Place	Date	Hour	Summary of Events and Information	Remarks and references to Appendices
	18		No 1 & 3 Sections repairing front line work, erecting shelters etc.	
			No 2 & 4 Sections laying tramways, erecting shelters for R.A.M.C. water supply.	
			Pioneers getting fair way through KINGSWAY. Workshop parties making shelters etc. for trenches.	
			No 2 Section relieved No 1 & 3 Sections at BUS FARM.	
	19		No 1 & 3 Sections repairing front line work, erecting shelters etc.	
			No 2 & 4 Sections laying tramways, erecting shelters for R.A.M.C. water supply.	
			~~Pioneers getting fair way through Kingsway~~ Workshop parties making shelters etc. for trenches	

WAR DIARY or **INTELLIGENCE SUMMARY**

Army Form C. 2118.

Secret

Place	Date	Hour	Summary of Events and Information	Remarks and references to Appendices
	20		No 1 + 3 Sections repairing front line and support line work, erecting shelters etc. Portion of CLOGHER VALLEY badly blown in and new trench had to be dug. No. 2 + 4 Sections laying tramways, making M.T.M. positions, shell proof shelters for R.A.M.C. Water supply. Pioneers clearing KINGSWAY + PICCADILLY. Workshop parties making frames etc. for trenches.	
	21		No 1 + 3 Sections repairing front line and support line work, erecting shelters etc. No. 2 + 4 Sections laying tramways, making M.T.M. positions, shell proof shelters for R.A.M.C. Water supply. Pioneers clearing KINGSWAY + PICCADILLY. Workshop parties making frames etc. for trenches.	

Army Form C. 2118.

~~Secret~~

WAR DIARY
or
INTELLIGENCE SUMMARY
(Erase heading not required.)

Instructions regarding War Diaries and Intelligence Summaries are contained in F. S. Regs., Part II. and the Staff Manual respectively. Title Pages will be prepared in manuscript.

Place	Date	Hour	Summary of Events and Information	Remarks and references to Appendices
	22		No 1 & 3 Sections repairing front line & support line, erecting shelters etc. No 2 & 4 Sections laying tramway making M.T.M. positions, shell proof shelters for R.A.M.C. Water supply. Pioneers clearing KINGSWAY and PICCADILLY. Workshop parties making frames etc. for trenches	
	23		No 1 & 3 Sections repairing front line & support line, erecting shelters, etc. No 2 & 4 Sections laying tramway making M.T.M. positions, shell proof shelters for R.A.M.C. Water supply. Pioneers clearing KINGSWAY and PICCADILLY. Workshop parties making frames etc. for trenches. Collecting stores from various dumps, removing same preparatory to move.	
	24		No 1 & 3 Sections repairing front line & support line, erecting shelters etc. No 2 & 4 Sections extending tramway, making M.T.M. positions, shell proof shelters for R.A.M.C. Water supply. Pioneers clearing KINGSWAY and PICCADILLY. Workshop parties making frames etc. for trenches. Collecting stores from various dumps & removing same preparatory to move	

WAR DIARY
or
INTELLIGENCE SUMMARY

Army Form C. 2118.

Secret

Place	Date	Hour	Summary of Events and Information	Remarks and references to Appendices
	25		No 1 & 3 Sections repairing front line & support line, erecting shelters etc. No 2 & 4 Sections laying tramways, making M.T.M. positions, erecting shell proof shelters for R.A.M.C. Water supply. Pioneers clearing KINGSWAY and PICCADILLY. The very wet day and work considerably interfered with. Workshop parties making shelters etc. for trenches.	
	26		No 1 & 3 Sections repairing front line & support line, erecting shelters etc. No 2 & 4 Sections laying tramways, making M.T.M. positions, shell proof shelters for R.A.M.C. Water supply. Workshop parties making shelters etc. for trenches.	
	27		No 1 & 3 Sections repairing front line & support line, erecting shelters, etc. No 2 & 4 Sections ballasting tramways, making M.T.M. positions, shell proof shelters for R.A.M.C. Water supply. Pioneers clearing KINGSWAY and PICCADILLY. Workshop parties making shelters etc. for trenches.	

Army Form C. 2118.

Secret

WAR DIARY
or
INTELLIGENCE SUMMARY

(Erase heading not required.)

Instructions regarding War Diaries and Intelligence Summaries are contained in F. S. Regs., Part II. and the Staff Manual respectively. Title Pages will be prepared in manuscript.

Place	Date	Hour	Summary of Events and Information	Remarks and references to Appendices
	28		No 1 & 3 Sections repairing front line and support line, erecting shelters, etc.	
			No 2 & 4 Sections ballasting tramways, making M.T.M. positions, shell proof shelters for R.A.M.C. Water supply.	
			Pioneers clearing KINGSWAY and PICCADILLY	
			Workshop parties making shelters etc. for trenches	
	29		No 1 & 3 Sections repairing front line and support line, erecting shelters etc.	
			No 2 & 4 Sections ballasting tramways making M.T.M. positions, shell proof shelters for R.A.M.C. Water supply.	
			Pioneers clearing KINGSWAY and PICCADILLY	
			Workshop parties making shelters etc. for trenches	

WAR DIARY
or
INTELLIGENCE SUMMARY

Army Form C. 2118.

Secret

Date	Hour	Summary of Events and Information	Remarks and references to Appendices
30		No. 1 & 3 Sections repairing front line and support line, erecting shelters etc.	
		No. 2 & 4 Sections ballasting tramways, making M.T.M. positions, shell proof shelters for R.A.M.C. Water supply	
		Pioneers clearing KINGSWAY and PICCADILLY. Workshop parties making shelters etc for trenches	
		Weather very boisterous & frost line much both. No interference largely with work. Space tools in circulating link has been one this month owing to thinktops.	

J. [signature]
Major R.E.
O.C. 150th FIELD COY. R.E.

Confidential

Vol 15

War Diary

of

150th Field Coy. R.E.

December, 1916

Army Form C. 2118.

WAR DIARY
or
INTELLIGENCE SUMMARY

(Erase heading not required.)

Instructions regarding War Diaries and Intelligence Summaries are contained in F. S. Regs., Part II. and the Staff Manual respectively. Title Pages will be prepared in manuscript.

Place	Date 1916	Hour	Summary of Events and Information	Remarks and references to Appendices
DRANOUTRE M 35 f.4.4	Dec. 1		No 1 & 3 Sections working on Front line & Support line maintenance, erecting shelters etc	
			No 2 & 4 Sections ballasting tramway, erecting R.A.M.C. shelters, water supply Pioneers clearing KINGSWAY & PICCADILLY Workshop parties making shelters etc for trenches	
	2		No 1 & 3 Sections working on Front line & Support line maintenance, erecting shelters etc.	
			No 2 & 4 Sections ballasting tramway, erecting R.A.M.C. shelters. Water supply Pioneers clearing KINGSWAY & PICCADILLY Workshop parties making shelters etc. for trenches.	
	3		No 1 & 3 Sections working on Front line & Support line maintenance erecting shelters etc.	
			No 2 & 4 Sections ballasting tramway erecting R.A.M.C. shelters, water supply. Workshop parties making shelters etc for trenches.	

Army Form C. 2118.

WAR DIARY
or
INTELLIGENCE SUMMARY

(Erase heading not required.)

Instructions regarding War Diaries and Intelligence Summaries are contained in F. S. Regs., Part II. and the Staff Manual respectively. Title Pages will be prepared in manuscript.

Place	Date	Hour	Summary of Events and Information	Remarks and references to Appendices
	4		No. 1. 2. 3 & 4 Sections moved to V. 13 d 3.3. and accommodated in Dugouts. Headquarters and Transport moved to Aldershot Camp T.19 6.5.5. and accommodated in huts	
	5		Parties engaged going over line and arranging for work	
	6		No. 2 & 4 Sections working on Front and Support line. No. 3. Section reclaiming and strengthening locality 3. No. 1. Section on defence of Hill 63. No Infantry parties owing to Brigade relief.	
	7		No. 2 & 4 Sections working in Front and Support line. No. 3 Section reclaiming and strengthening locality No. 3 No. 1. Section on defence of Hill 63.	
	8		No. 2 & 4 Sections working on Front and Support line No. 3 Section reclaiming and strengthening locality No. 3 No. 1. Section on defence of Hill 63. Major Potter R.O. killed in Action.	

Army Form C. 2118.

WAR DIARY
or
INTELLIGENCE SUMMARY

(Erase heading not required.)

Place	Date	Hour	Summary of Events and Information	Remarks and references to Appendices
	9		No. 2 & 4 Sections working on Front and Support Line.	
			No. 3. Section reclaiming and strengthening locality No. 3.	
			No. 1. Section on defence of Hill 63.	
	10		No. 2 & 4 Sections working on Front and Support Line.	
			No. 3. Section reclaiming and strengthening locality No. 3.	
			No. 1. Section on defence of Hill 63.	
	11		No. 2 & 4 Sections working on Front and Support Line	
			No. 3. Section reclaiming and strengthening locality No. 3.	
			No. 1. Section on defence of Hill 63.	
	12		No. 2 & 4 Sections working on Front and Support Line	
			No. 3. Section reclaiming and strengthening locality No. 3.	
			No. 1. Section on defence of Hill 63.	

Instructions regarding War Diaries and Intelligence Summaries are contained in F. S. Regs., Part II. and the Staff Manual respectively. Title Pages will be prepared in manuscript.

Army Form C. 2118.

WAR DIARY
or
INTELLIGENCE SUMMARY
(Erase heading not required.)

Instructions regarding War Diaries and Intelligence Summaries are contained in F. S. Regs., Part II and the Staff Manual respectively. Title Pages will be prepared in manuscript.

Place	Date	Hour	Summary of Events and Information	Remarks and references to Appendices
	13		No. 2 & 4 Sections working in front and support line	
			No. 3 Section reclaiming and strengthening locality No. 3	
			No. 1 Section on defence of Hill 63.	
	14		No. 2 & 4 Sections working in front and support line	
			No. 3 Section reclaiming and strengthening locality No. 3	
			No. 1 Section on defence of Hill 63	
	15		No. 2 & 4 Sections working in front and support line	
			No. 3 Section reclaiming and strengthening locality No. 3	
			No. 1 Section on defence of Hill 63	
	16		No. 2 & 4 Sections working in front and support line	
			No. 3 Section reclaiming and strengthening locality No. 3	
			No. 1 Section on defence of Hill 63.	

Army Form C. 2118.

WAR DIARY
or
INTELLIGENCE SUMMARY

(Erase heading not required.)

Place	Date	Hour	Summary of Events and Information	Remarks and references to Appendices
	17		No 2 & 4 sections working in front & support line	
			No. 3 section reclaiming and strengthening locally No 3	
			No 1. section on defence of Hill 63	
	18		No 2 & 4 sections working on front & support line	
			No. 3 section reclaiming and strengthening locally No 3.	
			No 1. section on defence of Hill 63.	
	19		No 2 & 4 sections working on front & support line	
			No 3. Section reclaiming and strengthening locally No 3.	
			No 1. section on defence of Hill 63.	

Instructions regarding War Diaries and Intelligence Summaries are contained in F. S. Regs., Part II. and the Staff Manual respectively. Title Pages will be prepared in manuscript.

Army Form C. 2118.

WAR DIARY
or
INTELLIGENCE SUMMARY

(Erase heading not required.)

Instructions regarding War Diaries and Intelligence Summaries are contained in F. S. Regs., Part II. and the Staff Manual respectively. Title Pages will be prepared in manuscript.

Place	Date	Hour	Summary of Events and Information	Remarks and references to Appendices
T.23.d.7.9	20		No 2 & 4 Sections working on front & support line	
			No 3. Section reclaiming and strengthening locality No 63	
			No 1. Section on defence of Hill 63.	
	21		No 2 & 4 Sections working on front & support line	
			No 3. Section reclaiming and strengthening locality No 63	
			No 1. Section on defence of Hill 63	
	22		No 2 & 4 Sections working on front & support line	
			No 3. Section reclaiming and strengthening locality No 63	
			No 1. Section on defence of Hill 63	
	23		No 2 & 4 Sections working on front & support line	
			No 3. Section reclaiming and strengthening locality No 3	
			No 1. Section on defence of Hill 63	
			Sections moved from dugouts to billets at T.23.d.7.9.	
			Headquarters moved from Camp T.19.b.5.5. to billets at T.23.d.7.9.	

Army Form C. 2118.

WAR DIARY
or
INTELLIGENCE SUMMARY

(Erase heading not required.)

Instructions regarding War Diaries and Intelligence Summaries are contained in F. S. Regs., Part II. and the Staff Manual respectively. Title Pages will be prepared in manuscript.

Place	Date	Hour	Summary of Events and Information	Remarks and references to Appendices
	24		No 2 & 4 Sections working on Front & Support line. No 3. Section reclaiming and strengthening locality No 3. No 1. Section on defence of Hill 63.	
	25		Christmas Day. No working parties	
	26		No 2 & 4 Sections working on Front & Support line. No 3. Section reclaiming and strengthening locality No 3. No 1. Section on defence of Hill 63.	
	27		No 2 & 4 Sections working on Front & Support line. No 3. Section reclaiming and strengthening locality No 3. No 1. Section on defence of Hill 63.	
	28		No 2 & 4 Sections working on Front & Support line. No 3. Section reclaiming and strengthening locality No 3. No 1. Section on defence of Hill 63.	

Army Form C. 2118.

WAR DIARY
or
INTELLIGENCE SUMMARY
(Erase heading not required.)

Place	Date	Hour	Summary of Events and Information	Remarks and references to Appendices
	29		No working parties on account of relief	
	30		No 1 Section repairing and framing front line, screening and erecting dugouts and support line. Making bridge for tramway to support line.	
			No 2 Section working on S.2 line, Support line framing. Repairing dugouts on front line.	
			No 3. Section reclaiming and draining dugouts and trenches Locality 3. Repairing shelters on Lebidovsky line	
			No. 4. Section working on front line, service trench, and S.2 Line. Advanced Brigade Headquarters. Overhead traverses. Machine Gun dugouts on Front line. Relaying railway line from Hyde Park Corner to front line.	

Army Form C. 2118.

WAR DIARY
or
INTELLIGENCE SUMMARY

(Erase heading not required.)

Place	Date	Hour	Summary of Events and Information	Remarks and references to Appendices
	31		No. 1 Section. Repairing and reaming Front line. Reserving. Erecting Dugouts up support line. Making fridge for Trench Tramway to Support line.	
			No. 2 Section. Working on S.2 and Support line. Tramway. Repairing dugouts on Front line	
			No. 3 Section. Reclaiming and drainage dugouts and trenches Locality 3. Repairing shelters in subsidiary line.	
			No. 4 Section. Working on Front line. Arrie trench and S.2 line. Advanced Traverses. Machine Gun dugouts on Front line. Relaying railway line from Hyde Park Corner to Front line.	

W. Wright
Capt R.E.

Vol 16

(36)

Confidential

War Diary
of
150th Field Coy R.E.

January 1917.

WAR DIARY or INTELLIGENCE SUMMARY

Army Form C. 2118.

Place	Date 1917	Hour	Summary of Events and Information	Remarks and references to Appendices
	Jan. 1.		No. 1. Section repairing and framing Front Line, lowering. Erecting Dugouts in Support Line. Making trench bridge for French tramway to Support Line.	
			No. 2. Section working on S.2. Support Line. Framing & placing Dugouts in Front Line.	
			No. 3. Section reclaiming and drainage dugouts and trenches locality 3. Repairing shelters on Rukloing Line.	
			No. 4. Section working in Front Line, Diverse trench & S.2. Line. Advanced Brigade Headquarters overhead traverses. Machine Gun Dugouts in Front line. Relaying railway line from H.P. Corner to Front Line.	
	2.		No.1. Section repairing and framing Front Line, lowering. Erecting dugouts in support line. Making trench bridge for French tramway.	
			No. 2. Section working on S.2. Support Line. Framing & placing dugouts in trenches locality 3.	
			No. 3. Section reclaiming and drainage dugouts and trenches locality 3. Repairing shelters on Rukloing Line.	
			No. 4. Section working on Front Line, Diverse trench & S.2. Line. Advanced Brigade Headquarters overhead traverses. Machine Gun Dugouts in Front Line. Relaying tramway line from H.P. Corner to Front Line.	

WAR DIARY
or
INTELLIGENCE SUMMARY

(Erase heading not required.)

Army Form C. 2118.

Place	Date	Hour	Summary of Events and Information	Remarks and references to Appendices
	3		No 1. Section repairing and framing Front Line. Screening. Erecting dugouts on support line. Making bridge for french tramway to support line.	
			No. 2. Section working on S.2, support line. Framing. Repairing Dugouts in front line.	
			No. 3. Section reclaiming and drainage dugouts and trenches Locality 3. Repairing shelters on subsidiary line.	
			No 4. Section working on Front Line, service trench and S.2. Line. Advanced Brigade Headquarters. Overhead traverses. Machine Gun dugout on Front Line. Relaying Railway line from Hyde Park corner to Front Line.	
	4		No 1. Section repairing and framing Front Line. Screening. Erecting dugouts on support line. Making bridge for french tramway to support Line.	
			No 2. Section working on S.2, support Line. Framing. Repairing Dugouts in front line.	
			No. 3. Section reclaiming and drainage dugouts and trenches. Locality 3. Repairing shelters on subsidiary line.	
			No.4. Section working on Front Line, service trench, and S.2. Line. Advanced Brigade Headquarters. Overhead traverses. Machine Gun dugout on Front Line. Relaying Railway line from Hyde Park corner to Front Line.	

Army Form C. 2118.

WAR DIARY
or
INTELLIGENCE SUMMARY
(Erase heading not required.)

Place	Date	Hour	Summary of Events and Information	Remarks and references to Appendices
	5		No 1. Section repairing and framing Front Line, loosening erecting dugouts on Support Line. Making bridge for trench tramway to Support Line.	
			No 2. Section working on S.2. Line Support Line. Framing Repairing dugouts in Front Line.	
			No. 3. Section reclaiming and drainage dugouts and trenches Locality 3. Repairing Shelters in Shrobbury Line.	
			No. 4. Section working on Front Line. Rebel Trench, and S.2. Line Advanced Brigade Headquarters. Overhead Traverses. Machine Gun dugout on Front Line. Relaying Railway Line from Hyde Park Corner to Front Line.	
	6		No working Parties owing to Infantry Relief.	
	7		No 1. Section repairing and framing Front Line. Working, erecting dugouts on Support Line. Making bridge for trench tramway to Support Line.	
			No. 2. Section working on S.2. line. Support Line.	
			No. 3. Section reclaiming and drainage dugouts and trenches Locality 3. Repairing shelters in Shrobbury line	
			No. 4. Section working on Front line Front trench, and S.2. line Advanced Repairing Headquarters. Overhead Traverses. Machine Gun Dugout on Front Line. Relaying Railway line from Hyde Park Corner to Front Line.	

Army Form C. 2118.

WAR DIARY
or
INTELLIGENCE SUMMARY
(Erase heading not required.)

Instructions regarding War Diaries and Intelligence Summaries are contained in F.S. Regs., Part II. and the Staff Manual respectively. Title Pages will be prepared in manuscript.

Place	Date	Hour	Summary of Events and Information	Remarks and references to Appendices
	8		No 1. Section repairing and cleaning front line. Screening, erecting dugouts in support line. Making bridge for french tramway to support line.	
			No 2. Section working on S.2. Line support line. Framing. Repairing dugouts on front line.	
			No 3. Section reclaiming and drainage dugouts and trenches locality 3. Repairing shelters in subsidiary line.	
			No 4. Section working on front line, large trench and S.2. line. Advanced Brigade Headquarters. Overhead travers. Machine Gun support on front line. Relaying Railway line from Hyde Park corner to front line.	
	9		No 1. Section reclaiming and drainage dugouts and trenches locality 3. Repairing shelters in subsidiary line.	
			No 2. Section working on S.2. Line support line. Framing. Repairing dugouts on front line.	
			No 3. Section reclaiming and drainage dugouts and trenches locality 3. Repairing shelters in subsidiary line.	
			No 4. Section working on front line, 2nd line trench and S.2. line. Advanced Brigade Headquarters. Overhead travers. Machine Gun dugout in front line. Relaying Railway line from Hyde Park corner to front line.	

WAR DIARY or INTELLIGENCE SUMMARY

Army Form C. 2118.

(Erase heading not required.)

Place	Date	Hour	Summary of Events and Information	Remarks and references to Appendices
	10		No.1. Section repairing and framing Front line. Screening. Erecting dugouts in Support line. Making bridge for French tramway to Support line.	
			No.2. Section working in S.2. Line Support line. Framing. Repairing dugouts on front line.	
			No.3. Section reclaiming and drainage dugouts and trenches locally S.1. Repairing shelters in Subsidiary line.	
			No.4. Section working on Front line. Service Trench, and S.2. line. Advanced Brigade Headquarters. Overhead traverses. Machine Gun dugouts on Front line. Relaying Railway line from Hyde Park corner to Front line.	
	11		No.1. Section repairing and framing Front line. Screening. Erecting dugouts in Support line. Making bridge for French tramway to Support line.	
			No.2. Section working in S.2. line Support line. Framing. Repairing dugouts in Front line.	
			No.3. Section reclaiming and drainage dugouts and trenches locally S.1. Repairing shelters in Subsidiary line.	
			No.4. Section working on Front line. Service Trench and S.2. Line. Advanced Brigade Headquarters. Overhead traverses. Machine Gun Dugouts on Front line. Relaying Railway line from Hyde Park corner to Front line.	
	12		No.1. Section repairing and framing Front line. Screening. Erecting dugouts in Support line. Making bridge for French tramway to Support line.	
			No.2. Section working in S.2. line Support line. Framing. Repairing dugouts in Front line.	
			No.3. Section reclaiming and drainage dugouts and trenches locally S.1. Repairing shelters in Subsidiary line.	
			No.4. Section working on Front line. Service Trench and S.2. line. Advanced Brigade Headquarters. Overhead traverses. Machine Gun Dugouts on Front line. Relaying Railway line from Hyde Park corner to Front line.	

WAR DIARY
or
INTELLIGENCE SUMMARY

(Erase heading not required.)

Army Form C. 2118.

Instructions regarding War Diaries and Intelligence Summaries are contained in F. S. Regs., Part II. and the Staff Manual respectively. Title Pages will be prepared in manuscript.

Place	Date	Hour	Summary of Events and Information	Remarks and references to Appendices
	13		No.1. Section repairing and framing Front line. Screening & erecting dugouts in support line. Making of bridge for trench tramway to Support line.	
			No.2. Section working in S.2. Line Support line. Framing & placing dugouts in Front line.	
			No.3. Section reclaiming and drawing dugouts and shelter locally. 3. Placing shelters in Tuxedo[?] Rd.	
			No.4. Section working on Front line. Front trench, and S.2. line. Advanced Brigade Headquarters. Overhead Traverses. Machine Gun dugouts on Front line. Relaying Railway line from Hyde Park Corner to Front line.	
	14		No working Parties owing to Infantry Relief.	
	15		No.1. Section repairing and framing Front line. Screening & erecting dugouts in support line. Making Relief of Trench Tramway to Support line.	
			No.2. Section working on S.2. line Support line. Framing & placing dugouts in Front line.	
			No.3. Section reclaiming and drawing dugouts and shelter locally 3. Placing shelters in Tuxedo[?] Road.	
			No.4. Section working on Front line. Front trench and S.2.line. Advanced Brigade Headquarters. Overhead Traverses. Machine Gun dugouts on Front line. Relaying Railway line from Hyde Park Corner to Front line.	

Army Form C. 2118.

WAR DIARY
or
INTELLIGENCE SUMMARY

(Erase heading not required.)

Instructions regarding War Diaries and Intelligence Summaries are contained in F. S. Regs., Part II. and the Staff Manual respectively. Title Pages will be prepared in manuscript.

Place	Date	Hour	Summary of Events and Information	Remarks and references to Appendices
	16		No. 1. Section repairing and decauvilling front line, covering & erecting dugouts in support line. Making bridge for trench tramway to support line.	
			No. 2. Section working in S.2. line by foot line tramway. Making dugouts in front line.	
			No. 3. Section reclaiming and drainage dugouts and shelters locally 3. Repairing. Shelters in subsidiary line.	
			No. 4. Section working on front line, revise trench and S.2. line. Advanced Brigade Headquarters. Overhead traverses. Machine Gun dugouts on front line. Relaying Railway line from Hyde Park Corner to front line.	
	17		No. 1. Section repairing and tramming front line, covering & erecting dugouts in support line. Making bridge for trench tramway to support line.	
			No. 2. Section working in S.2. line, support line tramway. Repairing dugouts in trenches.	
			No. 3. Section reclaiming and drainage dugouts and shelters locally 3. Repairing. Shelters in subsidiary line.	
			No. 4. Section working on front line, revise trench and S.2. line. Advanced Brigade Headquarters. Overhead traverses. Machine Gun dugouts on front line. Relaying Railway line from Hyde Park Corner to front line.	
	18		No. 1. Section repairing and tramming front line, covering & erecting dugouts in support line. Making bridge for trench tramway to support line.	
			No. 2. Section working in S.2. line by foot line.	
			No. 3. Section reclaiming and drainage dugouts in front line. Repairing dugouts and shelters locally 3. Repairing. Shelters in subsidiary line.	
			No. 4. Section working on front line, revise trench and S.2. line. Advanced Brigade Headquarters. Overhead traverses. Machine Gun dugouts on front line. Relaying Railway line from Hyde Park Corner to front line.	

WAR DIARY
or
INTELLIGENCE SUMMARY

(Erase heading not required.)

Army Form C. 2118.

Instructions regarding War Diaries and Intelligence Summaries are contained in F. S. Regs., Part II. and the Staff Manual respectively. Title Pages will be prepared in manuscript.

Place	Date	Hour	Summary of Events and Information	Remarks and references to Appendices
	19		No 1. Section repairing and framing front line, loosening, erecting dugouts in support line, making bridge for trench tramway to support line.	
			No. 2. Section working in S.2. Line. Support line. Framing Repairing dugouts in front line.	
			No. 3. Section reclaiming and drainage dugouts and shelters thoroughly & Repairing shelters in Subsidiary line	
			No.4. Section working on front line, Revert trench, and S.2. Line	
	20		No.1. Section repairing and framing front line, loosening, erecting dugouts on support line. Making bridge for trench tramway to Support line.	
			No. 2. Section working on S.2. Line, support line framing Repairing dugouts in Front line.	
			No. 3. Section reclaiming and drainage dugouts and shelters, locally & Repairing shelters in Subsidiary line.	
			No. 4. Section working on front line, Revert trench, and S.2. line. Advanced Brigade Headquarters. Overhead traverse. Machine Gun dugouts on front line. Relaying Railway line from Hyde Park Corner to front line.	
	21		No.1. Section repairing and framing Front line, loosening, erecting dugouts on support line. Making bridge for trench tramway to support line.	
			No. 2. Section working on S.2. Line, Support line. Framing. Repairing dugouts on Front line.	
			No. 3. Section reclaiming and drainage dugouts and shelters, loosely & Repairing shelters in Subsidiary line.	
			No.4. Section working on front line, Revert trench, and S.2. line. Advancing Brigade Headquarters. Overhead traverse. Machine Gun dugouts on front line. Relaying Railway line from Hyde Park Corner to front line.	

2449 Wt. W14957/Mg0 750,000 1/16 J.B.C. & A. Forms/C.2118/12.

Army Form C. 2118.

WAR DIARY
or
INTELLIGENCE SUMMARY
(Erase heading not required.)

Instructions regarding War Diaries and Intelligence Summaries are contained in F. S. Regs., Part II. and the Staff Manual respectively. Title Pages will be prepared in manuscript.

Place	Date	Hour	Summary of Events and Information	Remarks and references to Appendices
	22		No Working Parties owing to Infantry Killed during 16 day engaged in bombardment which considerably damaged front line, two sections were sent out at night to repair damage.	
	23		No 1 Section repairing and framing Front Line, lowering tracing dugouts on support line. Making Bridge for 1 trench tramway to Support line.	
			No. 2 Section working on S.2 line, Support line. Framing repairing dugouts on front line.	
			No. 3. Section reclaiming and drawing dugouts and shelter, locality B. Repairing Shelters in Elbsidery line.	
			No. 4. Section working on Front line, lewis Trench and S.2 line. Advanced Brigade Headquarters. Overhead travels. Machine Gun dugouts in Front line. Relaying Railway line from Hyde Park Corner to Front line.	
	24		No 1 Section repairing and framing Front line, lowering tracing dugouts on support line. Making Bridge for 1 trench tramway to Support line.	
			No. 2. Section working on S.2. line, Support line. Framing repairing dugouts in front line.	
			No. 3. Section reclaiming and drawing dugouts and shelter, locality B. Repairing Shelters in Elbsidery line.	
			No. 4. Section working on Front line, lewis Trench and S.2 line. Advanced Brigade Headquarters. Overhead travels. Machine Gun dugouts in Front line. Relaying Railway line from Hyde Park Corner to Front line.	

WAR DIARY
or
INTELLIGENCE SUMMARY

(Erase heading not required.)

Army Form C. 2118.

Instructions regarding War Diaries and Intelligence Summaries are contained in F. S. Regs., Part II. and the Staff Manual respectively. Title Pages will be prepared in manuscript.

Place	Date	Hour	Summary of Events and Information	Remarks and references to Appendices
	25		No. 1. Section repairing and framing Front line, boreening, erecting dugouts in support line. Making bridge for Search Tramway to Support line.	
			No. 2. Sections working in S.2. line Support line. Greaming. Repairing dugouts in front line.	
			No. 3. Section reclaiming and drainage dugouts and shelters, really 3. Repairing shelters in subsidiary line.	
			No. 4. Section working on Front line, wire trench and S.2. line. Advanced Brigade Headquarters. Overhead traverses. Machine Gun dugouts in Front line. Relaying Railway line from Hyde Park Corner to Front line.	
	26		No. 1. Section repairing and framing Front line, boreening, erecting dugouts in Support line, making bridge for trench Tramway to Support line.	
			No. 2. Section working in S.2. line Support line. Greaming. Repairing dugouts in front line.	
			No. 3. Section reclaiming and drainage dugouts and shelters. Really 3. Repairing shelters in subsidiary line.	
			No. 4. Section working on Front line, wire trench, and S.2. line. Advanced Brigade Headquarters. Overhead traverses. Machine Gun dugouts in Front line. Relaying Railway line from Hyde Park Corner to Front line.	
	27-1-17		No. 1.2.3.4. Sections wiring C.T.s + Subs line - Returned bill.	
	28-1-17		Nos. 1.2.3.4. Sections wiring C.T.s. Work line + wire stopping	

C.T.S.

2449 Wt. W14957/M90 750,000 1/16 J.B.C. & A. Forms/C.2118/12.

Army Form C. 2118.

WAR DIARY
or
INTELLIGENCE SUMMARY

(Erase heading not required.)

Instructions regarding War Diaries and Intelligence Summaries are contained in F. S. Regs., Part II. and the Staff Manual respectively. Title Pages will be prepared in manuscript.

Place	Date	Hour	Summary of Events and Information	Remarks and references to Appendices
	29		No. 1. 2. 3. 4. Sections wiring C.Ts. and Subsidiary Line. No. 57513 Corpl. Florence W. wounded in action by Machine Gun.	
	30		No. 1. 2. 3. 4. Sections wiring C.Ts. and Subsidiary Line. Trestletopping ditto	
	31.		No. 1. 2. 3. 4. Sections wiring C.Ts. and Subsidiary Line. Trestletopping ditto	

J. Boyle
Major R.E.
O.C. 150th FIELD COY. R.E.

[Stamp: 150th COY. ROYAL ENGINEERS * ULSTER DIVISION * No. Date 31/1/17]

Vol 17

Confidential

War Diary

of

150th Field Coy R.E.

February 1917.

Army Form C. 2118.

WAR DIARY
or
INTELLIGENCE SUMMARY

(Erase heading not required.)

Instructions regarding War Diaries and Intelligence Summaries are contained in F. S. Regs., Part II. and the Staff Manual respectively. Title Pages will be prepared in manuscript.

Place	Date	Hour	Summary of Events and Information	Remarks and references to Appendices
	1917 Feb. 1		All sections wiring Sub line etc. + finishing CTR	
	2.		Sections wiring defences + finishing C.T.R	
	3.		Section wiring defences. + finishing CT3	
	4.		Section wiring defences, finishing C.T.O.	Laying trackway to gun position & laying harness to gun position
	5.		Section wiring defences + finishing CT0	
	6.		Section wiring defence + finishing CTS &c.	
	7.		Section wiring defences + finishing CT &c	
	8.		Section wiring defences + finishing &c.	
	9.		Section wiring defences, finishing &c.	
	10.		Sections wiring & defences. finishing &c.	
	11.		Section wiring defence.	
	12.		Section wiring defence	
	13.		Section revetting front line + overseeing	
	14.		Section revetting front line & revetting	Laying tramways to gun position

2449 Wt. W14957/M90 750,000 1/16 J.B.C. & A. Forms/C.2118/12.

Army Form C. 2118.

WAR DIARY
or
INTELLIGENCE SUMMARY
(Erase heading not required.)

Instructions regarding War Diaries and Intelligence Summaries are contained in F. S. Regs., Part II. and the Staff Manual respectively. Title Pages will be prepared in manuscript.

Place	Date	Hour	Summary of Events and Information	Remarks and references to Appendices
	15		Relief	
	16		Sections following. Dug out strutted work hampered by hard frost.	
	17		Snowing & windy	
	18		Sections. Dugouts, repairs to trenches etc.	
	19		Sections. Dugouts, repairs to trenches etc.	
	20		Sections. Dugouts, repairs to trenches etc.	
	21		Sections. Dugouts, repairs to trenches etc.	
	22		Sections. Dugouts & repairs to trenches	
	23		Relief	
	24		No Brigade working parties. Dugout & repairs to trenches. Instrn of artillerymen	
	25		" " " "	
	26		3 Sections mining	
	27		2 Secs. hutting, 1 Sec. concrete Batt. Hqrs. 1 Sec dugouts. Tramways, gun emplacements "	

2449 Wt. W14957/M90 750,000 1/16 J.B.C. & A. Forms/C.2118/12.

Army Form C. 2118.

WAR DIARY
or
INTELLIGENCE SUMMARY

(Erase heading not required.)

Instructions regarding War Diaries and Intelligence Summaries are contained in F. S. Regs., Part II. and the Staff Manual respectively. Title Pages will be prepared in manuscript.

Place	Date	Hour	Summary of Events and Information	Remarks and references to Appendices
	28		2 Sections Battery; 1 Section towards Butte Wapres; 1 Sec dugouts, remainder 4 gun emp [illegible]	
			28/2/17	
			C. E. Elmer R.M.R.E.	

Confidential   Vol 18

War Diary
of
150th Field Coy R.E.

March 1917

WAR DIARY
or
INTELLIGENCE SUMMARY

(Erase heading not required.)

Army Form C. 2118.

Instructions regarding War Diaries and Intelligence Summaries are contained in F. S. Regs., Part II. and the Staff Manual respectively. Title Pages will be prepared in manuscript.

Place	Date	Hour	Summary of Events and Information	Remarks and references to Appendices
Aldershot Camp	1/3/17		2 Sections Putting. 1 Sect. Concrete Batto Hqrs. 1 Sect. Framing Dugouts. Gun emplacements etc	
	2/3/17		"	
Kortepyp	3/3/17		"	
	4/3/17		½ Sec. repairing Chambridge Range remainder setting	
	5/3/17		2 Sections putting. 1 Sect. Concrete Batt. Hqs. 1 Sect. Framing Dugouts, Gun emplacements etc	
	6/3/17		"	
	7/3/17		1 Sect. Ruts, 1 Sect moving. 1 Sect. Concrete Batt. Hqs. 1 Sect. Framing dugouts Gun emplacements	
	8/3/17		1 Sect. Ruts, 1 Sect improving huts, 1 Sect. Concrete Batt Hqs, 1 Sect Framing dugouts	
	9/3/17		1 Sect. Ruts, 2 Sect. Concrete Batt Hqrs 1 Sect Framing dugouts, gun pits etc	
	10/3/17		do	do
Mammoth Camp Armentieres	11/3/17		2 Sect moving. 2 Sect. G.H.Q line repairs.	
	12/3/17		2 Sect G.H.Q line. 1 Sect inducting & organizing Camp. 1 Sect build public hut.	
	13/3/17		2 Sect G.H.Q line. 1 Sect Concrete Brigade Hqrs. 1 Sect build officers Mess.	
	14/3/17		2 Sect G.H.Q line. 1 Sect Concrete Brigade Hqs. 1 Sect. building Mess & officers Hospital	
	15/3/17		2 Sect G.H.Q line. 1 Sect Concrete Brigade Hqrs. 1 Sect Hutting	
	16/3/17		2 Sect G. H.Q line. 1 Sect. A Dressing Station & Dugouts. 1 Sect. messing hut work	

Army Form C. 2118.

WAR DIARY
or
INTELLIGENCE SUMMARY
(Erase heading not required.)

Instructions regarding War Diaries and Intelligence Summaries are contained in F. S. Regs., Part II. and the Staff Manual respectively. Title Pages will be prepared in manuscript.

Place	Date	Hour	Summary of Events and Information	Remarks and references to Appendices
Mammoth Camp Pretoria	17/3/17		2 Secs G.H.Q. pkt., 1 Sect Advanced Dressing Station 9 dugouts 1 Sect THQ's took inventory	
	18/3/17		Men had day off. O.C. 150 Relieved from leave.	
	19/3/17		2 Sects G.H.Q. line - 1 Sect Adv. Dressing Station & 1 Sect. buildings hand & left afternoon. C.R.E. called.	
	20.3.17.		2 Sec. G.H.Q line reclamation. 1 Sec. Adv. Dress St. 1 Sec. Hutting. 1 sec. Hutting latrines.	
	21.3.17		2 Sec. G.H.Q. line reclamation 1 Sec. Adv. Dress St. 1 Sec. Hutting hutting, last to took trees showing death.	
	22.3.17		2 sec. G.H.Q. line reclamation. 1 sec. Adv. Dress St. 1 sec. Hutting hutting had intentions with took trees speech.	
	23.3.17		2 sec.'s G.H.Q line reclamation. 1 Sec Adv. Dress St. 1 Sec. Hutting.	
	25.3.17		Divl. semi festival MONSTER PRESBYTERIAN SERVICE by "EX MODERATOR" GENERAL ASSEMBLY	
	26.3.17		1 Sec. G.H.Q. 1 Sec. F.t Victoria Road. H.Q. 1 Sec. M.G. dugouts 1 Sec. Hutting. very wet day.	

2449 Wt. W14957/M90 750,000 1/16 J.B.C. & A. Forms/C.2118/12.

Army Form C. 2118.

WAR DIARY
or
INTELLIGENCE SUMMARY

(Erase heading not required.)

Instructions regarding War Diaries and Intelligence Summaries are contained in F. S. Regs., Part II. and the Staff Manual respectively. Title Pages will be prepared in manuscript.

Place	Date	Hour	Summary of Events and Information	Remarks and references to Appendices
Mermand Camp	28/7/17		1 Sect Re.Lown G.H.Q. 1 Malin Sulp as 1 M.G. Corps cont 1 Station	
	29/7/17		do	
	30.		do	
	31.		help teather is no to a certain ammount interfered with work.	S.P. Pennell Kill do

J G Boyle
Lt Col
O.C. 1.0. M.G. Cop. 29

Vol 19

Confidential

War Diary

of

150th Field Coy. R.E.

April 1917

Confidential

Army Form C. 2118.

WAR DIARY
or
INTELLIGENCE SUMMARY

(Erase heading not required.)

Instructions regarding War Diaries and Intelligence Summaries are contained in F. S. Regs., Part II. and the Staff Manual respectively. Title Pages will be prepared in manuscript.

Place	Date	Hour	Summary of Events and Information	Remarks and references to Appendices
Army Rest Camp	1.4.17		1st Bn. 9. Brigade — PBK Ralli H.Q, O.P etc. Auf. Bn. 1 Sect Hd Zns	
	2.4.17		do above. — wire & Stations. Heavy Snow Storm in aft.	
	3.4.17		Heavy Snow Storm in morning	
	4.4.17			
	5.4.17		Sec. M.G. Coy M. Langlemark 1st Butts. 1st O.P. 1 Sec. Hd Zns	
	6.4.17		do	
	7.4.17		do	
	8.4.17		do	
	9.4.17		do	
	10.4.17		do	
	11.4.17		do	
	12.4.17		do	
	13.4.17		do	Orders rec'd to hand over to new
	14.4.17		do	
	15.4.17		do	
	16.4.17		do	Ord'rs hand'd over to new
	17.4.17			
	18.4.17			
	19.4.17			
	20.4.17			Q.O.C. Visits B.H. Expressed Satisfaction otherwise
	21.4.17			
	22.4.17			

Army Form C. 2118.

WAR DIARY
or
INTELLIGENCE SUMMARY
(Erase heading not required.)

Instructions regarding War Diaries and Intelligence Summaries are contained in F. S. Regs., Part II. and the Staff Manual respectively. Title Pages will be prepared in manuscript.

Place	Date	Hour	Summary of Events and Information	Remarks and references to Appendices
Granville	23.4.19		Sect 1 & 3 moved to Boulogne to erect battalion Rest Camp for 2nd Army. Lt C.A.M. in charge. No 2 Sec erecting O.Ps on Kemmel Hill & No 4 erecting Divl Rest Camp for accommodation of 33 Officers & 260 O.R.	
	24.4.19		Sec 1 & 3 at Boulogne. moved out 15th to camp 3 miles N. of Wimereaux & erecting O.Ps. Kemmel - Completed potential m? in G. of K. line which G.O.C. division remarked on against a whiskey soda & for cigarettes Effect? Ambrigade Hq at the action 3 Car elephants being widely remarked. No 4 Secti still showing wilt. Divl Hq camp B shells of prairie now around H.Q. O.C. hut.	
	25.4.19		Visited Boulogne. Free my 1½ Comp Run - Erecting posts Camp in Sawdhills alone the Sea - Sec No 2 Erecting Concrete O.Ps on Kemmel Hill No 4. erecting Camp & keeping at preparing ground for state Planting potatoes in Camp - Stone Glen - Lt Thorne returns fr 10 days leave.	

2449 Wt. W14957/M90 750,000 1/16 J.B.C. & A. Forms/C.2118/12.

WAR DIARY
or
INTELLIGENCE SUMMARY

(Erase heading not required.)

Army Form C. 2118.

Place	Date	Hour	Summary of Events and Information	Remarks and references to Appendices
Drouvin	26/4/17		2 Sects Boulogne erecting Rest Camp for 2nd Army. 1 Sects had day off. 1st Canterbury S.P. in Kemmel Hill & Batts. H.Q. men Zythostein. Wt Thorne allowed 5 POR Bde 17.9 Surface Fougade bomb in advance dep.	
	27/4/17		do	
	28/4/17		do	
	29/4/17		do. A Pipe pushing demonstration where to a Pipe be pushed to its send hole 6.0 aw crater created 20.0 with 4 9.0 deep. Apparatus seemed simple & efficient to accept for certain C.T.S. demos. however lent Pim & Launchbe attack in 2 day trial trial enough hope shown for Corps up h an army selected. C.T. Sentinel Drouse Test	
	30		2 Sections Boulogne marching Rest Camp of 2nd Army	

Army Form C. 2118.

WAR DIARY
or
INTELLIGENCE SUMMARY

(Erase heading not required.)

Place	Date	Hour	Summary of Events and Information	Remarks and references to Appendices
Bruaulk	30/4/17		Recco everting. HQ 6th Caruh. 1st Australn reoccupied concert b/pa on increment title harled by C.S. & 2nd Army PLS. 1st Corps who expressed their approval. The work being done. This represents approval has been a fine effect on Irish Troops who look twice above to a level Moravian. Lattich menn showing labour employed during month. About 300 has previously put in during the month.	

J C Boyles
Major
O.C. 150th FIELD COY. R.E.

1-5-17

Army Form C. 2118.

WAR DIARY
or
INTELLIGENCE SUMMARY
(Erase heading not required.)

Instructions regarding War Diaries and Intelligence Summaries are contained in F.S. Regs., Part II. and the Staff Manual respectively. Title Pages will be prepared in manuscript.

Appendix A.

Place	Date	Hour	Summary of Events and Information	Remarks and references to Appendices
			Working Parties During April	
				Infantry	Sappers	
Locaton + work						
Kemmel Small Shelters			320	02	
-do- Calais Shelters			110	131	
-do- O.P.			1198	347	Put men under O.P. hut on hill. Dugouts 2. look Legs. trench. revetting. Trench covers. Park [?] group power lies back
-do- Brickfield wiring			30	23	
Fort Victoria Bde H.Q.			533	153	Reinforced concrete shelters built after concrete is
G.H.Q. 2 Line			180	50	
Lindenhoek Dressing Station			595	114	A S.A.A. Amm. reinforced shelter built. All cut offs of trenches and [?] in present [?].
Hammer Farm Dugout			105	45	
Crown [?]			98	22	
-do- 1 Spy Farm wiring			435	63	
Spy Farm M.G. Shelter Dugout			263	159	
			3864	1264	

WAR DIARY
or
INTELLIGENCE SUMMARY

(Erase heading not required.)

Army Form C. 2118.

Place	Date	Hour	Summary of Events and Information			Remarks and references to Appendices
			Location of Work	Working Parties	Materials	
				Infantry / Sappers / (during day) Sappers		
Appendix "A" Continued			Frenchmans Farm Dugout	65 / 8 /		
			Fort Regina Dugout	87 / 22 /		
			Regent Street O.P.	- / 4 /		
			-do- Printing	- / 17 /		
			Newport dugouts water supply	- / 4 /		
			Vine Street -do-	- / 2 /		
			Stores loading and Carrying parties in all works	931 / 50 /		
			Total for 31st.	4950 / 1371 /		

Vol 20

Confidential
—————
War Diary
—————
of
—
150th Field Ock E
—————
May 1945

Army Form C. 2118.

WAR DIARY
or
INTELLIGENCE SUMMARY
(Erase heading not required.)

Instructions regarding War Diaries and Intelligence Summaries are contained in F. S. Regs., Part II. and the Staff Manual respectively. Title Pages will be prepared in manuscript.

Place	Date	Hour	Summary of Events and Information	Remarks and references to Appendices
Steenwerck	1.5.17		2 Sections tidying Rest Camp for 36th Div & Army at Boulogne. Improving life by the Indian in perfect weather	
	2.5.17		1 Sect. Building H.Q. Div Camp — do —	
	3.5.17		1 Sect. Constructing new intersect O.P.'s at known site. do	
	4.5.17		Scott Jones went to Paris. That he will see the Grand Battlefield. do Lt BARNES proceeded on leave	
	5.5.17		to England do	
	6.5.17		do do went round with CRE staging selecting sites for concentration Camps re Bailed screen Blinds Show hours from MESSINES RIDGE.	
	7.5.17		ULSTER DIVISIONAL HORSE SHOW	

WAR DIARY
or
INTELLIGENCE SUMMARY

(Erase heading not required.)

Army Form C.-2118.

Instructions regarding War Diaries and Intelligence Summaries are contained in F. S. Regs., Part II. and the Staff Manual respectively. Title Pages will be prepared in manuscript.

Place	Date	Hour	Summary of Events and Information	Remarks and references to Appendices
Brandhoek	9.5.17		2 sectis Intern: Portsmouth for 2nd Army near Belgian sea men. 1 sect. being re-equipped. enemy C.B. on Kinnoul Hill. 1 sect. ranging huts.	
	9.5.17		do.	
	10.5.17		do.	
	11.5.17		do. 1 sect ranging mins extension to S.team Farm for hot soup bacon. Very hot day.	
	12.17		2 sectis hutting at Pontoques for men. another battery advanced. 1 sect. hidden O.P. in Kinnoul Hill.	
	13.17		Reported further at Pontoque - no men. enemy erecting but H.Q. Rither Camp brannels. Seen our new Drive in a minutes 1 place to enemy huts - andecks. Completion O.P. Kinnoul Hill, making 2 hides to Artillery on all OPs shell emplacements to render to a standlight Gunner further in bath Supply to prevent enemy	

Army Form C. 2118.

WAR DIARY
or
INTELLIGENCE SUMMARY.
(Erase heading not required.)

Instructions regarding War Diaries and Intelligence Summaries are contained in F. S. Regs., Part II. and the Staff Manual respectively. Title pages will be prepared in manuscript.

Place	Date	Hour	Summary of Events and Information	Remarks and references to Appendices
	14.5.17		2 sects huttng at Boulogne sur mer - 1 sect hutting at Brimeux. HQ aid camp + their camps in neighbourhood. 1 sect OP's shelter hut supply horse vans -	
	15.5.17		do. On HQ. Completed - HQ. moved to to their new Quarantine camp -	
	16.5.17		2 sect Hutting Boulogne. 1 sec hutting standing at Brimeux. 1 sec hutting repair cement OP's shut outs + laying hut supply. Request St Oby ut + at Berio returned for here.	
	17.5.17		2 sect hutting Boulogne. 1 sect huts Brimeux area - 1 sec OP shelter hut supply etc. Hutletting Co. few horse at returning trestles huts Remainder trench latrines for Stock -	
	18/3/17		2 sect Boulogne - 1 sect Brimeux, now Dorre - 1 sect completing OP's + huts out -	

2353 Wt. W2544/1454 700,000 5/15 D. D. & L. A.D.S.S./Forms/C. 2118.

WAR DIARY or INTELLIGENCE SUMMARY

Army Form C. 2118.

Place	Date	Hour	Summary of Events and Information	Remarks and references to Appendices
	18.5.17		Q.O.E. Motor Ambulance [?] for Sec[?] section 9 at the G[?] Unit due at Mobile Camp.	
	19.5.17		2 Sec. Boulogne for Troops. 1 Rec. Ordes and Mortar Supply [?] Run.	
	20.5.17		Section Postern No 1 moved from Boulogne to Dunnes. No 3 351st Sn Co R.E. at ARQUES. No 2 Sec intn Slings Arq. and lower light supply funeral run. No 4 intn. Supply to int area.	
	21.5.17		No 1 Sec[?] arrived from Boulogne. No 3. at ARQUES 20 laundry [?] 2nd A.F.A.K. No 2. Duties thing [?] Newport funeral int. supply. No 4 intn supply had Arn.	
	22.5.17		No 1 Sec. working day at Newport. No 2. Supply Col. Ambulance Water Supply. No 3. at A.R.Q.W.E.S. No 4. Pack [?] Supply Supply. Ang. and M. Regine Shell.	

Army Form C. 2118.

WAR DIARY
or
INTELLIGENCE SUMMARY.
(Erase heading not required.)

Instructions regarding War Diaries and Intelligence Summaries are contained in F. S. Regs., Part II. and the Staff Manual respectively. Title pages will be prepared in manuscript.

Place	Date	Hour	Summary of Events and Information	Remarks and references to Appendices
	23.5.17		No 1 Sect Smythe - Nieuport Aug 016 - No 2 to + from out. WG Suffs at working & relieving of hogts. No 3 at ARGEUS. No 4 Bath area take Supp -	
	24.5.17		No 1 Sect Smythe do do	
	25.5.17		do do do	
	26.5.17		do do do	
	27.5.17		" " " Low's camp. CRE killed - Boche shells -	
	28.5.17		No 1 Sect Popham but f Su 14g which rained out of h - Shelling - No 2. A various trails - Linderhook Bazaam + No 3. M. Watchment - M.A. meeting day in 5 Reinhilt -	

Army Form C. 2118.

WAR DIARY
or
INTELLIGENCE SUMMARY.
(Erase heading not required.)

Instructions regarding War Diaries and Intelligence
Summaries are contained in F. S. Regs., Part II.
and the Staff Manual respectively. Title pages
will be prepared in manuscript.

Place	Date	Hour	Summary of Events and Information	Remarks and references to Appendices
Dunkirk	29/5/17		No 1 Sec. Strengthening Newport bridges. No 2. Working on new bridge in Kentwerck. Cutting tracks for advance — 77 held safely. No 3. On detachment No 4. Sectar, Baix Shelter & back water supply. Camp Shelter driven in till	
	30/5/17		do. do. do.	
	31/5/17		do. do. do. The weather during the whole month has been perfect for working. Preparations for our great naval + military scheme have done — Materials have rather a difficulty in coming along.	

L.C.Boyle.
Major

Vol 21

Confidential

War Diary

of

150th Field Coy. R.E.

June 1917.

Army Form C. 2118.

WAR DIARY
or
INTELLIGENCE SUMMARY.
(Erase heading not required.)

Instructions regarding War Diaries and Intelligence Summaries are contained in F. S. Regs., Part II. and the Staff Manual respectively. Title pages will be prepared in manuscript.

Place	Date	Hour	Summary of Events and Information	Remarks and references to Appendices
Dbunk	1.6.17		No 1 Sect. Completing strengthening of New Post bay & etc. No 2 Making one luce Track for approach of infantry & Cav in manner from Brewing Station. No 3 acc'n in Relatonment. No 4 Constructing shelling dugout	
	2/6/17		do. do. Lt Thorne returns from 108 Brigade who has been running tr guns in ind. Secrets having all work completed — making sketches & —	
	3/6/17		do for offensive. all sections having & officers retained.	
	4/6/17		No 3 Sect. returned. 3 officers practically destroyed Camp shelled & two officers (not included have a narrow escape) war diary) have been scattered & wind's. No casualties. Our 3 shells pitched within 20 yards to both Issued rifles for offensive. by the camp —	

WAR DIARY or INTELLIGENCE SUMMARY

Army Form C. 2118.

Place	Date	Hour	Summary of Events and Information	Remarks and references to Appendices
	5/9/17		All sectors kept quiet & instructed in work of offensive patrol of Brigade	
	6/9/17		All seems quiet. Relieving of Lt. BARNES honoured and also Lt CAM THORNE & Lt PULFORD the latter 3 slightly wounded at duty. Lt Ferries replaced Barnes & Lt Dean 16 R.I.R.(P) sent to assist in Coy. Lt CAM & THORNE unable to go —	
	7/9/17 10.		Known Parry 3 Shells arrived Close French at Dug out 3. 5 A.M. From reply to grnph the setting Lt of mining trail artillery Hun Coy. turned it at 6 a.m. to binocular on Kon [?] turned it [?] to answer 7 am	

WAR DIARY or INTELLIGENCE SUMMARY

Army Form C. 2118.

Place	Date	Hour	Summary of Events and Information	Remarks and references to Appendices
[illegible]	7.6.17		At 8. Ismain received orders to CRS & billet Shing Point No. 7. 8. 9. together No 2 under Lt Jones moved off with No 25. Staff & supplies to Kendidate. No 7 Pt. 9/10 R Ln. 7 consolidated stays at 6.30 am No 3 Sect under Lt Carr moves off at 6.35 am forward with No 9 Pt. No 4 Sect under 2/Lt P. BRUNKATE moved off at 8.20 a.m to consolidate S.P. No 8 their so they returned to camp about 9 am Lancy ambulance rendered assistance to parties at 8.30 am rendezvous in this formation Section 1 & Pt. 20 infantry, 9 R.W.F. S.P. 1a. at 9 am Lt Thorne in charge of with Section 1 & Pt. 20 infantry 9 R.W.F. & [illegible]	

WAR DIARY or INTELLIGENCE SUMMARY

Army Form C. 2118.

Place	Date	Hour	Summary of Events and Information	Remarks and references to Appendices

16th Bde for information re situation
asked us the when Lt Thorne received
orders from B.O.C. 16? to proceed to Consolidate
No. 2, 3, 4 sections reported having arrived at their
posts. I proceeded out to inspect their
posts. I found them a strong post with a
rock point from which to look. No 1 Section
2 M.G emplacements in each. Start work early
from I had just been able to
form till Sunday morning. Lt Thorne was put
starting them in conjunction with 16 Bde by
R.M. Fraser So Welsh & the South of
Ireland Australia a pontoon the Orange
together influence a little

Place	Date	Hour	Summary of Events and Information	Remarks and references to Appendices
	3/6/17		Recc't orders from CRE. yesterday at 10 a.m. to Construct a new MURELINE - the original guides who assured us 3ft with 10ft Boyaus & leaved in dug that for Sects 1 & 4 and 2 & 3 known it at 6 ft 6 in turn made his between the pts D 27 b 50 & 31182 Sects 1 & 4 trace Sullivans & 2 & 3 trace R. Way Capt Oliver. Speed by many materials to mule spare transport as far as possible. Put to shell most. Section tracing. Got up materials etc. hive within 500 yards of the work & gallery has could have given me to the site hole. This has been inspected with to-opper before first — [signed] We do we memorial	

WAR DIARY or INTELLIGENCE SUMMARY

Army Form C. 2118.

Place	Date	Hour	Summary of Events and Information	Remarks and references to Appendices
	5/9		Off at 1.15 p.m. as above. I attached myself to Reserve dump at BULL BEEF FARM left with Erich with Capt Murray & went in (own car) between Sches & the Materials transport which he did with much success & returned to rest Kitchens at the 56th at dusk — when they had to wait till Shelling by Bocke was over. Boche kept heavy shrapnel up to between the main line opposite our own held at Aftillus O21b75 - G27b68 - O27b15 - 6 - the aft. Northern trench the 16th Div East & & & s/r line Hanch the 25th Div the	

reported to O.C. 14 Batt. R.I.R who was holding
the line + actually handing over to 9 R.I.F.
He showed me where he felt he had to keep had
out. Since then there could I decided to take
in - + on arrival of our 2+3 two Lewis
out had to be used — resistant
Then 2 cc etc but meanwhile there
there shells a could keep
my Lewis got shells a could keep
from the Boche hosts help up a
ferrage in front for a rescue force to be
had sent as Stock Lewis been taken
the new enemy before up they [illegible]

WAR DIARY
or
INTELLIGENCE SUMMARY

Army Form C. 2118.

Place	Date	Hour	Summary of Events and Information	Remarks and references to Appendices
	26/7		Continued line started before 10 2 x 3 trains from at 2 am from a line almost complete & all materials pushed & restocked from F before daylight So G r not begun our parties first. RES arrived each in camp 5 a.m. & each 1 x A arrived to returned late. Tepebir & CRE line of hurdles & high trestles was most difficult. These our party helped 8th guides supplied. Road to be finished. Our men laterally tired out. Whole experience by up. Left in up on the day —	

Especially when the numbers of shrapnel in
the Turkish a soda bath & a shell &
shrapnel of both Mortars + 75 m [?] get
about me [all?] with little ground- Why Turks
was like a charnel house strewn with [?]
dead men horses [?] though [?] never get
this the "Stinking [?]" [?] [?] & [?]
with [?] had [?] had [?] there sleep at the
days— a 15" [?] dud lay at the
X roads— [?] a 5 one thing I find not
[?] on [?] must have [?] the
[?] [?] Got back [?] 10 p.m
[?] [?] G.O.C. [?] [?] wound
had seen— [?] a heavy [?]
[?] [?] all the [?]—

Place	Date	Hour	Summary of Events and Information	Remarks and references to Appendices
	9/6/17		Rec'd orders 12 Noon to move back into MONMOUTH CAMP which we did shortly afterwards. Got them to a early tea — the Coues have served out.	
	10/6/17		Men all resting — after a few hrs in hot Screens pits & dugs — Relieved 100 infantry & their unit	
	11/6/17		Sect'n drilling & cleaning up —	
	12/6/17		Football match v 122 w >) Co. be won. Very heavy thunderstorm in the afternoon.	
	13/6/17		Co: moved & camp at N 25 d A. - hutted Block line in huts with tickets which we are to occupy. Met General Plumer C.i.g. 2nd Army —	

WAR DIARY
or
INTELLIGENCE SUMMARY.

Army Form C. 2118.

Place	Date	Hour	Summary of Events and Information	Remarks and references to Appendices
	14/6/17		In Camp M 28 d 11 "Beaumetz" hut to mule at Orac	
	15/6/17		All Ranks Paraded and Kippers here & all sects kent at service. Inspects line — Rec'd instruct for up of fresh line further forward. No to div to hrs of fence line. Supply tank put up	
	16/6/17		Put up 12 lins of wire entanglement —	
	17/6/17		Heading up troopers Instruct C.R.S. in morning. For own tent inspected wire & relief french —	
	18/6/17		Rec'd new staff nco from 6t & 14 Res Bgl & 82 Bn. 1/Lieut Thorne went to hospital. Thunderstorm	
	19/6/17		Notice O.C. 81 & 82 Btns to went this : look with them turning & take mer up flares. Evening blew thro levels secure art	

Army Form C. 2118.

WAR DIARY
or
INTELLIGENCE SUMMARY.
(Erase heading not required.)

Place	Date	Hour	Summary of Events and Information	Remarks and references to Appendices
B	20.6.17		Moved to N.6.6.2.2. Threw lines to 7.10.a.8.4. Cited line to line on main line - Sec. B.	
	21.6.17		1 & 2 tried by night. Sent returned up - wet night.	
	22.6.17		C.R.E. ceased - Sec. B. 3rd put up 2000 yds wire	
	23.6.17		Remoulins with C.R.E. - Recon. in afternoon Sec 1 & 2 put up 700 yds wire at Northern end of Sector	
	24.6.17		Notice to Royaux working parties for digging to commence	
	25.6.17		B. Section wiring main line + 500 infantry digging trenches. 2/Lt Cam returned from leave	
	26.6.17		2 Sec. wiring - reserve line + 500 infantry digging - temporarily. All night work	

Army Form C. 2118.

WAR DIARY
or
INTELLIGENCE SUMMARY.
(Erase heading not required.)

Instructions regarding War Diaries and Intelligence Summaries are contained in F.S. Regs., Part II. and the Staff Manual respectively. Title pages will be prepared in manuscript.

Place	Date	Hour	Summary of Events and Information	Remarks and references to Appendices
	27/6		2 sections working on Maedelstede line & 30' infantry and 1 section Bunny on improving I Camp shelters & Dugouts. Shrapnel to mined trench to Rene dues	
	28/6		Resting. Handed over work to 182nd Co. R.E.	
	29/6		Resting. Camp shelled 4 Ormes of mine erected	
	30/6		Marched when to to POPPERINGHE - Hittin Pin for the night - Came out after being since June 28th 1916 in Front line trenches	

J.C. Boyle
Major
O.C. 150th FIELD COY. R.E.

Vol 22

Confidential

War Diary

of

150th Field Coy R.E.

July, 1917

WAR DIARY
or
INTELLIGENCE SUMMARY.
(Erase heading not required.)

Army Form C. 2118.

Place	Date	Hour	Summary of Events and Information	Remarks and references to Appendices
	1.9.17		Snow left POPERINGHE marched to WORMHOUDT. Billeted in 2 comfortable farms. A bad march but no men fell out.	
	2.9.17		Marched from WORMHOUDT to MERKEGHEM. Settled down in Billets.	
	3.9.17		C.R.E. called - informed us we are lent for be till further [?] to XIX Corps.	
	4.9.17		Wells started. SUS - just outside Village of Merckeghem on the Bollezeele Road. Major Boyle leaves to report to [?] Rouen	
	5.9.17		4 wells underway & about 12' deep.	
	6.9.17		4 wells now about 15' Struck water at this depth in [?] of them.	

Army Form C. 2118.

WAR DIARY
or
INTELLIGENCE SUMMARY.
(Erase heading not required.)

Place	Date	Hour	Summary of Events and Information	Remarks and references to Appendices
MEREKEGEM	7/7/17		Started four new Wells – in field next to that with our original four wells. The wells totally supply water to proposed XIV Corps reinforcement Camp in these fields. Four 200 gallon tanks to the otherwise supplied on for each pair of wells for storage. Effective strength of Coy 5 Officers 206 other ranks	
	8/7/17		C.R.E. 36th Division approves of huth Well being sunk in same field as the four new ones - Approx yield of these new wells when finished estimated at 4000 gallons a day. Capt H.M. FORDHAM R.E. joined Coy as O.C. from 290th A.T. Coy R.E. Effective Strength 6 Officers + 205 O.R.	
	9/7/17		huth Well started - C.R.E visited wells water in all 1st 9 wells. 3 O.R. returned from leave. Effect. Strength 6.0 209 O.R.	
	10/7/17		Nos 3,2,+8 Wells Sunk Stand day ready for finishing off rest in progress Officer Capt OTWAY R.E rejoined unit from leave Two O.R. on leave	Effective strength 7 Officers + 204 O.R.

Army Form C. 2118.

WAR DIARY
or
INTELLIGENCE SUMMARY.
(Erase heading not required.)

Place	Date	Hour	Summary of Events and Information	Remarks and references to Appendices
MERCKEGHEM	11/7/17		Nos 3 + 7 Wells finished C.R.E. Visited works - Nos 1-5 Wells & 7 ogo dugout remainder the finished off. One Sapper casualty on works due to accident. 2. O.R. Sent on leave. 3 shift 2 off 204 O.R.	
	12/7/17		Nos 4 and 8 Wells finished - two 400 gallon tanks arrived stages for tanks commenced. All Wells nearing completion	
	13/7/17		Shift as previous day. C.R.E. Visited works, staging for tanks finished, two tanks erected - All wells finished and pumped day to test 24 hour test for capacity. Captain H.M. Fordham + 1 O.R. Went on leave. Strength 6. Off 203 O.R. Captain H. Otway takes over command of Company.	STO
	14/7/17		Clearing up site round wells. Received orders to move on 15/7/17. Strength. 6 Off 203 O.R.	STO

2353 Wt. W2544/1454 700,000 5/15 D. D. & L. A.D.S.S. Forms/C. 2118.

Army Form C. 2118.

WAR DIARY
or
INTELLIGENCE SUMMARY.
(Erase heading not required.)

Instructions regarding War Diaries and Intelligence Summaries are contained in F. S. Regs., Part II. and the Staff Manual respectively. Title pages will be prepared in manuscript.

Place	Date	Hour	Summary of Events and Information	Remarks and references to Appendices
Rest 27. C.30.G.2.5.	15/7/17		Company left MERCKEGHEM at 5 A.M. — Advance Guard left Rest Party of 1 Officer + 8 cyclists to complete firing of fumpto to. Company arrived New Camp at Sheet 27 at 9 P.M. Erected two line. Petrol Huts, and made usual Camp arrangements. Strength 6 Offs. 203 O.R.	Nil
	16.7.17		Received positions of shallow wells to be sunk in the Area — Continued sinking of 3 wells and sent out Recce Party to locate further test bore. C.R.E. trailer works. 2. O.R. Wound to leave 2 O.R. Returned from Base Camp. 2. O.R. sent to hospital. Strength 6 Offs. 205 O.R.	Nil
	17.7.17.		3 wells progressing favourably — shortage of timber for casing and framing, causing considerable delay. One Section busy erection of 3 Nissen Huts. 2 O.R. sent to Hospital. Sick Strength 6 Offs. 203. O.R.	Nil
	18.7.17		One Section erecting Nissen Huts. No timber available for wells. Unarmed	

Army Form C. 2118.

WAR DIARY
or
INTELLIGENCE SUMMARY.
(Erase heading not required.)

Place	Date	Hour	Summary of Events and Information	Remarks and references to Appendices
Sheet 27. C.30.6.2.5.			of Company employed in training, weather showery. O.Rs. involved works. Strength 6 Offs. 203 O.R.	/43
	19.7.17.		Small quantity of timber arrived. Started work on wells again. 3 test bores found satisfactory given water at 8 to 10 feet depth. 3 O.R. went on leave. Strength 6 Off. 299 O.R.	/43
	20.7.17.		Still short of timber — all wells down — all wells completed except 2 wooden sections being under Section officers. Receive notification that 2nd Lt C.E. THORNE of this Company has been awarded the MILITARY CROSS. 3 O.R. returned from leave. Strength 6 Offs. 203 O.R.	/43
	21/7.		One section on wells, timber shortage for other wells. Remainder of Company training. Strength 6 Offs. 203 O.R.	/43

WAR DIARY
or
INTELLIGENCE SUMMARY.

Army Form C. 2118.

Place	Date	Hour	Summary of Events and Information	Remarks and references to Appendices
Shad 27. C.30.b.2.5.	22/7/17	—	Sunday – Day devoted to Rest and Company Sports. 2 O.R. went on leave. Strength 6 Offs. 201 O.R.	A.P.O
"	23/7/17		Tenders arrived to enable us will be continued. Remainder of Co. training. 3 O.R. Reinforcement arrived. 2 O.R. came back off leave. 1 O.R. proceeded on leave 1 O.R. transferred to C.R.E. 38th Div. Haddelburn to 123 Coy. Strength 6 Offs. 204 O.R.	A.P.O
"	24/7/17		Captain Otway, 4 Officers & 120 O.R. moved to YPRES to be attached for work to C.R.E. 55th Divsn. in accordance with orders by C.R.E. 38th Divsn. H.Q. Mounted Section Neuran at C.30.b.2.5. Whilst on above Report to C.C.E. 55th Divsn. take over all work from the 3 Field Companies of 55th Division, and Pioneer Battalion. Work consists of maintenance of all roads & Bridges across Canal Road YPRES, mark roads to front line, maintenance of front line tracks, construction of assembly trenches etc. 300 Infantry attached	A.P.O

WAR DIARY or INTELLIGENCE SUMMARY

Army Form C. 2118.

Place	Date	Hour	Summary of Events and Information	Remarks and references to Appendices
	24/7/17		Bn. 13 Officers + 3 Sections moved into Elythed Huts in CANAL BANK area. One Officer + 1 Section remain in billets at VLAMERTINGHE to conduct all further work etc. from there etc. Spasmodically shelled on CANAL BANK by all calibres all night. Heavy gas shelling from 12.30 A.M. to 3.30 A.M. again from 5 A.M. to 5.30 A.M. Strength 8 Off. 202 O.R.	
	25/7/17		Very heavy shelling in all areas, particularly CANAL BANK + approaches all morning up to 1 P.M. One 17" dropping on CANAL BANK approach dug out. Worker Parties out by day + night – At night all Bridges approaches heavily shelled – Lt. S.P. WHELON R.E. killed, wounded on CANAL BANK in trenches. 1 N.C.O. (Sergt.) shell shocked, 1 N.C.O. (Corpl.) + 1 Sapper wounded all by same shell. Officer brought up from back billets to replace casualty + took section left in charge of C.S.M. Capt. A.M. FORDHAM returned from leave. Strength 8 Off. 199 O.R.	

2353 Wt. W2544/1454 700,000 5/15 D. D. & L. A.D.S.S. Forms/C 2118.

WAR DIARY
or
INTELLIGENCE SUMMARY

Army Form C. 2118.

Place	Date	Hour	Summary of Events and Information	Remarks and references to Appendices
	26/8/17		Co. Still located as before. Forward Sections carrying out the same work. Night parties constantly shelled o/c to work by H.E. & gas. CANAL BANK roadways very heavily shelled all night by all calibres. Several shell hits on dugouts. Men strained. Cook house and ward kennie demolished. Tank causeway across Canal Charles Henry Causeway blown in. Map ref. Belgium 6&14 I47 20R.	
	27/8/17		Co. Still located as before. Forward sections carrying out same work. Work at night very difficult owing to shelling & gas. Canal Bank & dugouts heavily shelled during shortly & evening. 166 A Brigade got 1 NCO & 4 men to accompany ration party. O.C. arranges ration with Brigade H.Q. Later Rain's part ponied. 1 N.C.O. (Sergt.) slightly wounded & Pappr. badly wounded on canal. 1 N.C.O. 2/Corpl. collapsed in trench. (Shock) & taken to hospital. Very heavy shelling all night. All calibres up to 9.2".	

Army Form C. 2118.

WAR DIARY
or
INTELLIGENCE SUMMARY.
(Erase heading not required.)

Instructions regarding War Diaries and Intelligence Summaries are contained in F. S. Regs., Part II. and the Staff Manual respectively. Title pages will be prepared in manuscript.

Place	Date	Hour	Summary of Events and Information	Remarks and references to Appendices
	17"		Two of Wheel dropped within 50 yds of dug out. 2 Special parties of 1 NCO + 5 Sappers each arranged for parties on raids, with the intention of looking for Bosche traps &c, but did not get beyond German lines. By strength 3 off 103 O.R.	
	28/7		Co. Located as before. Forward Echelons work as before. 166 I.B. say raid is on for the afternoon — set up 1 NCO + 4 Sappers carrying 8 made up charges of gun-cotton of 8 lbs each. Raid most successful to my far took done by Sappers — 2 large dug outs in 2nd German line + the communication trench being blown in. One Sapper wounded bombing on raid. Very heavy shelling all night especially on Cross Bank. Heavy gas shells from 12.30 P.M. to 5.30 P.M. Remainder wore all the time. Casualties. 1 Sapper shell shocked 2 Sappers wounded. By strength 6 off 128 O.R.	

Army Form C. 2118.

WAR DIARY
or
INTELLIGENCE SUMMARY.
(Erase heading not required.)

Place	Date	Hour	Summary of Events and Information	Remarks and references to Appendices
	29/7/17		Co. located as before. Forward sections work as before. Hostile shelling machine gun all around — Quiet in afternoon. Very active shelling all night on front support lines, working parties etc. very little work done. Fair to heavier at & time at very intense. Quiet night on CARR BANK after 9 P.m. Between 8 & 9 P.m. 6.17" shells dropped at vicinity of Dug outs. Gas-shelled shrapnel were from 1.30 A.M. to 3 A.M. Casualties: 1 Sapper wounded — 2 Sapper shell shock.	Coy strength 6 off. 185. O.R.
Hut 27 2. 16 Central	30/7/17		Received orders to hand over work to 419 Field Co. All work continued till 1 P.M. Forward Section left CARRA Dugouts at 2 P.M. & Shell shelter. Jerry back Section at Mill NAMERTINGE. Lower provision at 6.05 + all four Sections proceed to rest at L.16 Central where they are joined by Horses & Horse lines. Rest of Personnel in the early hours of the morning who proceeded to WINEZEELE arriving at 4 P.m. Duffel 10 P.m. with 122 & Coy to proceed to Camp.	Coy strength 5 off. 185 O.R.

Army Form C. 2118.

WAR DIARY
or
INTELLIGENCE SUMMARY.
(Erase heading not required.)

Instructions regarding War Diaries and Intelligence Summaries are contained in F. S. Regs., Part II. and the Staff Manual respectively. Title pages will be prepared in manuscript.

Place	Date	Hour	Summary of Events and Information	Remarks and references to Appendices
Shorncliffe L.16 a Central	31/7		Company under Canvas. Day spent in returning Camp and making necessary arrangements, wet in afternoon though 2nd Divisional Camp.	
			O-Staff. 5 O/R. 184 O.R.	Ors
			2. O.R. proceeded on Leave.	

J.H. Thomson Capt M.A S.
for O.C. 13th
C.A.S.C.
31/7/17

Vol 23

Confidential

War Diary

- of -

150th Field Coy. R.E.

August, 1917.

WAR DIARY
or
INTELLIGENCE SUMMARY.

Army Form C. 2118.

Place	Date	Hour	Summary of Events and Information	Remarks and references to Appendices
BELGIUM FRANCE. Sheet 27. L.16.a.2.4	1/8/17	—	Company under canvas — Rainy heavily — impossible to carry out any training. 6. O.R. proceeded to WINNEZEELE to each baths houses. 2nd Lt. JAMES DAINTITH R.E. joined for duty. 2nd Lt. BENNETT 10th R. Innis Fus + 101 O.R. from 100th Coy joined for duty + remainder attached. Co Strength 7 Offs. 202 O.R. Att'd Strength 1 Off. 191 O.R.	S.A.O
"	2/8/17		Company under CANVAS. Morning wet & showery — Afternoon very wet. Carried some drill + physical training. Co Strength 7 Off. 201 O.R. Attached Strength 1 Off. 100 O.R.	S.A.O
"	3/8/17		Day very wet — Received orders to be ready to move tomorrow. Coy practised in occupying trenches. Co Strength 7 Off. 201 O.R. Att'd Strength 1 Off. 95 O.R.	S.A.O

WAR DIARY
or
INTELLIGENCE SUMMARY

Army Form C. 2118.

Place	Date	Hour	Summary of Events and Information	Remarks and references to Appendices
Sheet 27			Day fine with light showers	
L.16.a.24	4/6/17		Received orders for Company and attached Infantry to move at 1 P.M. today. Co follows H.Q. Staff however.	
			Portion Those Cimes to H.8 a 5.9 Sheet 28. Remainder of Company and	
			attached Infantry & Engineers on CANAL at I.1.b.6.00. Sheet 28.	
			Move completed successfully	Appx
			Company Strength 7 Off. 200 O.R.	
			MT. Infantry 1 Off. 94 O.R.	
Sheet 28	5/6/17		Major A.M. FORBIRAM R.E. + 4 Others and attached Infantry carted	
H.8.a 5.9 &			at CANAL Dugouts I.1.B.6.00 - Work carrying Decauville Track forward.	
I.1.B.6.00.			Company Cross Country North thereto. Co working in 3 Shews Reliefs	Appx
			H.Q. Section & R.E. transport located at H.8.a 5.9 Lieut CAPTAIN OTWAY R.E.	
			Bomb dropped by E.A. in horse lines at 2 P.M. Casualties among horses	
			Sapt + R.C. Corporal + 1 driver also killed 1 mule wounded 1 horse	
			1 Sapper killed forward	
			Co Strength 7 Off. 196 O.R. Attached Infantry 1 Off. 95. O.R.	

WAR DIARY
or
INTELLIGENCE SUMMARY.
(Erase heading not required.)

Army Form C. 2118.

Place	Date	Hour	Summary of Events and Information	Remarks and references to Appendices
	6/8/17		Co General as before. Work carried on as before. Work started on a coys track. Arrived at St Jean.	Neuve- St Jean
			Putney Road where it disappears in German front line system, and on track to Boss ART FARM	
			All Co TRANSPORT engaged in bringing up material to forward	
			dumps. NEUTJE ST JULIEN ROAD Co Strength. 7 Off. 203 O.R.	Offrs
			Saved oxens ho have loads Allied Infantry 1 Off. 96 O.R.	
	7/8/17		Co located as before. Day work on forward tracks stopped & to dangerous	
			2 Sections on night work on tracks. One section alleying alignment of No 6	
			Track / day. One section Uproing Bridge over CANAL which was damaged by	
			Shell fire. Co Transport engaged all day in bringing up supplies	
			highly by Brigades to help to follow up the work (material to St Jean Dump)	
			1 Sapper raped by Shell. Co Strength. 7 Off. 201 O.R.	Offrs
			WELT JE ST JEAN ROAD shewed Allied Infantry 1 off. 94 O.R.	
			between German 2nd + 3rd Line	

Army Form C. 2118.

WAR DIARY
or
INTELLIGENCE SUMMARY.
(Erase heading not required.)

Place	Date	Hour	Summary of Events and Information	Remarks and references to Appendices
	8/8/17		Co. worked as before. Forward sections employed as on previous day. Repairs to Bridge strenuous. Very heavy shower about noon making transport very difficult. No 6 Track Blue head good from Rail Transport from T.I. 6.75 Thro LaBRIQUE to Bilge Track. Co. strength 7 offs. 194 OR. and from there to front line a back attached Infantry. 1 off. 93 OR. Attached Infantry Track	SKO
	9.8.17		Co. worked as before. Forward sections employed as before. Works for neighbourhoods on no 6 Track. Party of 100 Infantry promoted by Brigade in two forward Centres. Worked where BILGE TR. crosses St JEAN - WEALTJE R-. Co strength 7 offs. 194 OR. Attached Infantry. 1 off. 91. OR	SKO
	10.8.17		Co. worked as before. One section taken across to trunk line. Work started on Duckwalk Gangway Bomb Store. Remainder of sections on trunk & duck board tracks. Co. strength 7 offs. 194 OR. Attd Infantry 1 off. 92 OR	

Army Form C. 2118.

WAR DIARY
or
INTELLIGENCE SUMMARY.
(Erase heading not required.)

Instructions regarding War Diaries and Intelligence Summaries are contained in F. S. Regs., Part II. and the Staff Manual respectively. Title pages will be prepared in manuscript.

Place	Date	Hour	Summary of Events and Information	Remarks and references to Appendices
	11.8.17		Co located as before. 3 Sections working on No 6 Track - also BOSSAERT FARM - Work on Bomb Store continued instruction.	
			H forward Dumps by day & night. Coy Strength 7 off. 193 O.R. Attached Infantry 1 off. 89 O.R.	J/40
	12.8.17		Co located as before. Work as before. P of W Coy 2 of our 5 while SJ ST JEAN. 1 Sapper killed 2 others wounded. Co Strength 7 off. 190 O.R.	J/40
			A.I.P. Infantry	
	13.8.17		3 Sections working on No 6 track. 2 by night forward of Bilge Trench one by day Back. — Work continued on Bomb Store. Before Coy. 2 Lt DAINTITH killed on No 6 Track. Transport advanced to Bilge Trench Dugout — ST JEAN. one Sapper killed in action three others wounded in action. Coy Strength 6 off / 186 O.R.	##
	14.8.17		Back Track of No 6 completed from Bd. Trench across ADMIRAL'S ROAD to WELTJE — ST JULIEN Rd. Linking up No 6 wheel transport track to forward portion of track. Commencing at old German front line as attached map. Coy Strength 6 off. 184 O.R.	##

A 6945   Wt. W14422/M1160 350,000   12/16   D.D.& L.   Forms/C./2118/14.

WAR DIARY or INTELLIGENCE SUMMARY

Army Form C. 2118.

Place	Date	Hour	Summary of Events and Information	Remarks and references to Appendices
Inward Billet D.1 B.6-Q	15/9/17		No 6 Track completed - Bomb store and P. of W. Cage completed. Battalion under Lt Arneyate left at 9.30pm to get into position with 11th R.I.R. on Black Line CAPRICORN TREINCH S.34. The Battalion had two men hit going Northly across the duckboards at approx C.19. C.13. SPREE FARM. Coy strength 6 Off. 186 O.R.	
	16/9/17	12.30am	No 3 & 4 Coys under H St Cur went forward to 11th Inniskilling HQs at WIELTJE Dugouts at 12.30am and there waited to go forward. Coy strength 3 Off. 176 O.R.	
CAPRICORN TRENCH C.18 D.21		2.15am	Shell hit No 4 Section in Capricorn Trench wounding officer Lieut. Sergeant Heverwher. Only 2 are left effective. The four after getting away wounded, returned to WIELTJE to R.E. work of consolidation then possible. Then attached Infantry (who 14 R.I.R.) were absorbed by this Battalion and held the line returned to Billets heartbreaking on relief.	

Place	Date	Hour	Summary of Events and Information	Remarks and references to Appendices
	16/9/17	6.30am	No 3 Section left WIELTJE and went forward with Major NOTT C.O. of 11th In-Frs to advanced Bn H.Qrs at WINE HOUSE. Then Steam went forward with C.O. and it was decided to consolidate Fort Hill behind just S. of BORDER HOUSE. Lt CAM came back to get the section attacked heavily out of a shell a trench near WINE H.Q. however had the forward line BORDER H.Q. Heyron in No 8 trench line St Andres killed at about 9 a.m. Lt Petersen tried to get forward but the fire was too heavy and after several casualties the attempt was abandoned at 11 a.m. and section returned to Aggye dugout WIELTJE. TRANSPORT 9 mules from the Coy went up from 16 R.I.R. Pioneer horses coy Park transport under "Lt BENNETT 10th In-Frs. The attack was under Officer. It was intended that they should bring it water trees &c. after zero and possible and dump from the free divisional Mgt. Wing work which was then done by No 102 section on the left of the Divisional front working on the left of the 121 trench &	

WAR DIARY
or
INTELLIGENCE SUMMARY.
(Erase heading not required.)

Army Form C. 2118.

Place	Date	Hour	Summary of Events and Information	Remarks and references to Appendices
	16/8/17		The mules left Dev Pack Camp fully loaded & reported at WIELTJE Dugouts at 5.15am. The Hy rain which came on the station did lett most of them going forward	
			At 10.30pm they were ordered to Pack Camp & as the 109th Bgd did not consider that there was any forward of their getting forward to St. THORNE by change of Nos 1-2 & strong detachmt at SWEITSE at 9 am. It was in charge of the highest among at SCHULER FARM and it was hoped to chance structuring them going fastly daylight. The tactical situation however rendered this impossible and at 11.30am Lt Thorne returned to his destination at the CANAL Bank Billets & took NO with his orders going back	
				Coy strength 3 off/ 176 O.R.

WAR DIARY
or
INTELLIGENCE SUMMARY.
(Erase heading not required.)

Army Form C. 2118.

Place	Date	Hour	Summary of Events and Information	Remarks and references to Appendices
Hq a 59	17/8/17		Hand over all Work & Dumps to 279 to Coy 2nd also all wagon lines at H2 a 5.9. Lt A Ferrier & Lt Blanden Tents transfer from 121 Brigade to duty	
I.B.6.0				
			Coy strength 3 off 176 O.R.	
Hut 27	18/8/17		Move tho I Area Winne Zeele (J.6.a.1.7) Dismounted par Ln Hut 27 2nd 3 Infantry of 109 Bgde taken over Lorries from VLAMERTINGHE	
J.6.a.1.7			"C" Bennett & attached infantry to their Battalions	
			Coy strength 3 off 174 O.B.	#
	19/8/17		Camp fatigues — Kit Inspection — Goodshed Inspection	
			Coy strength 3 off 176 O.R.	#
	20/8/17		Coy fatigues Transport Inspection open order drill — Box movement exercise — 2 3rds	
			Coy strength 3 off 176 O.R.	#
	21/8/17		Ditto Lt Ferrier and Sgt Crisp sent on to Bapaume as advance party to take over Billets.	
			Coy strength 3 off 176 O.R.	#

Army Form C. 2118.

WAR DIARY
or
INTELLIGENCE SUMMARY.
(Erase heading not required.)

Instructions regarding War Diaries and Intelligence Summaries are contained in F.S. Regs., Part II. and the Staff Manual respectively. Title pages will be prepared in manuscript.

Place	Date	Hour	Summary of Events and Information	Remarks and references to Appendices
Nieppe J.6.a.1.7	22/8/17		Some work done for farmers. Coy in keep of 3 inches wagon. Still needing orders for Transport packs for horses.	
			Coy strength 3 off, 176 O.R.	
	23/8/17		Paraded in full marching order as usual. Transferred at 11.30am. Left Cainfort 11.45am. G.S. Limbahead in Train. Arrived CAESTRE 3pm. Transport horses entrained by 4.10pm. Train started at 6.20pm. Sgt Thompson 2 O.R. rejoined Coy at CAESTRE.	
			Coy strength 3 off, 176 O.R.	
France Sheet 57.C	24/8/17		Arrived at BAPAUME. N.15 a.m. D.Krames – Guides in camp by Lt FERRIER. Proc'd Camp at 0.10.C.1.6 8.30am. Camp Ligny.	
			Coy strength 3 off, 176 O.R.	

WAR DIARY
or
INTELLIGENCE SUMMARY.
(Erase heading not required.)

Army Form C. 2118.

Place	Date	Hour	Summary of Events and Information	Remarks and references to Appendices
O.10 e.1.6	25/9/17		Held kit + Rifle Inspection - in morning	
			Coy employed in cleaning trench & generally during afternoon.	
			LT A FERRIER RE. thus N.C.Os proceeded to BERTINCOURT to take	
			over work from 90th Field Coy R.E. Coy strength 3 Off. 176 O.R.	
	SUNDAY 26/9/17		Church parades for C of E + C of I 11.15 am	
			other Denominations 10.30 am	
			☩ Lt. H.C ELLIOT + Lt. C.L. KNOX joined for duty posted to Nos 2 & 3 sections respectively.	
			Coy strength 5 Off. 178 O.R.	
	27/9/17		Drill Parades &c. Transport work on wagons harness generally	
			Attended Conference with S.O.E. 109th Bgde. re work in line	
			Weather wet moderate gale.	
			Coy strength 5 Off. 178 O.R.	

WAR DIARY
or
INTELLIGENCE SUMMARY

Army Form C. 2118.

Place	Date	Hour	Summary of Events and Information	Remarks and references to Appendices
O.10.c.1.6	28/9/17		Coy Employed on Transport Work generally - Conference with all Battalion Comdrs of 109 B'gde. Arranged for Lt FERRIER + Lt ELLIOT to Undertake work in line	
			"Lt BLAGDEN returned to B'gd own Coy 109 Inf's Coys.	
			Coy strength 5 Off/ 178 O.R	
O.10.c.16	29/9/17	8am	Left Camp at 8am with whole Coy transport proceeded to BERTINCOURT	
BERTIN COURT 57.c P7.b.64			Arrived at Back Billet with whole Company. HQ's transport and also 1 + 3 Section Billetted here. Inspected site for NISSEN HUTS in N. 3 Area.	
HERMIES J23.d.5.0			Section 2 + 4 Sent forward to Billets in HERMIES 5pm transport for these two sections following later whole arrived at forward Billet J 23 d.5.0 correct	
			Coy strength 5 Off/178 O.R	
57.c P7.b.64 + J.23.d.5.0	30/9/17		Started Work on NISSEN HUTS with part of No 1 + 3 Sections + on Road sweeping HERMIES ROAD. Working party from 9th + 10th INNISKILLINGS & Mr Atchinson Hut bus. R.E. No 2 + 4 Section at work improving trenches from DEMICOURT Junction of	

WAR DIARY
or
INTELLIGENCE SUMMARY.
(Erase heading not required.)

Army Form C. 2118.

Place	Date	Hour	Summary of Events and Information	Remarks and references to Appendices
57e Q.7.8.64.30/9/17 Jas d. 3ff			Railway removal East of HERMIES.	
			Coy strength 5 off 179 O.R.	
	31/8/17		Work as before. Messen hut removed at BUS for D.A.D.O.S 35th DIV. men sent to Div Dump	
			Coy strength 5 off 172 O.R.	

J. H. Fordham
O.C. 150th FIELD COY R.E.

h o 6 Track (Wheeled)   Red

do   Pack   Green

Trench board Tracks   Brown

Where recovered road has been used as part of Pack Track it is shown Green

Vol 24

Confidential

War Diary

of

150th Field Coy. R.E.

September 1917

Army Form C. 2118.

WAR DIARY
or
INTELLIGENCE SUMMARY.
(Erase heading not required.)

Instructions regarding War Diaries and Intelligence Summaries are contained in F. S. Regs., Part II. and the Staff Manual respectively. Title pages will be prepared in manuscript.

Place	Date	Hour	Summary of Events and Information	Remarks and references to Appendices
Sheet 57.c				
Book@W.R 27.b.64	1/9/17		Work on Nissen huts from standings for truck Batolbury continued	
			Advance huts for 110 F.Ambulance continued	#
HERNESS 57.c.23.d.50 Forward Bill.R			Mess Hut for D.A.D.O.S Practically complete	
	2/9/17		Work continued on shelters, drainage of S.T. abutment on Deep Dugout for 199 to 2W by Inf Bn Mining	
			Communication Trench from Post R12 to D.a.5.95 to K1.D.12 to Long 579. 1790.R	
57.c @7.b.64 3.23.d.50	2/9/17		Other Work as before. Hut for D.A.D.O.S completed	#
			Way Tunnel 584. 1940.R	
	3/9/17		Work commenced re-metalling service rm RUYAULT COURT — BERTIN COURT ROAD	
			Other Work as before.	
			Day strength 5th 1250.R	#
	4/9/17		Work as previous days. 10 Pioneers 16 (R.I.F) attached as working party for Rec Screening	
			Day strength 5th 1820.R	#

WAR DIARY
or
INTELLIGENCE SUMMARY.
(Erase heading not required.)

Army Form C. 2118.

Place	Date	Hour	Summary of Events and Information	Remarks and references to Appendices
57.C P7 b.6.4 J.23 d.50	5/9/17		Progress made with hessian Hut screening. One Adrian Hut screened. Hessian to be used for a Bogie Cinema Theatre	
			Work on line as before – Owing to readjustment of fronts 109 Bgde trench slightly reduced and new reciefs of line from Puisieux Rd at K.7.C.7.5 to the HERMIES - HAVRINCOURT ROAD at K.26.a.0.4. Coy strength 5 Off 132 O.R.	
	6/9/17		Huts for D.A.D.O.S. erected at Divisional Baths completed. Other work as progress as before. New C.T. from Post R.13 to Post R.12 is from K.27.d.a.2 to K.27.d.50.05 completed except for Trench Boards etc. Coy Strength 5 Off 202 O.R.	
	7/9/17		Work on before. Huts at BERTINCOURT & work in sub-way. Tramway & widening Fire Trenches between Posts R.12 R.13 & putting in Cavalry & Rifle Shelters. Coy Strength 5 Off. 202.O.R.	
	8/9/17		Work as before. Lt. A. FERRIER has proceeded to the H.Q. 7y.C.R.E. 25th Division. Coy strength 6 Off. 202.O.R.	

WAR DIARY
INTELLIGENCE SUMMARY

Army Form C. 2118.

Place	Date	Hour	Summary of Events and Information	Remarks and references to Appendices
57.c P1.7 6.d J33.a.5.0	9/9/17		Work as before. Revetting of fire bays & fosts in line commenced. Work commenced refacing Road near 109 Bgde H.Qrs. Bgy strength 6 off. 202 O.R.	
	10/9/17		Afflayheap from approx P4 a.68 to J34 d.9.0 Work as before. ADRIAN hut for Bgde H.Q. the huns completed. In BERTINCOURT — Repairs to screening on BERTINCOURT—RUYAULCOURT ROAD huns completed & Road safe from View. Bgy strength 6 off. 202 O.R.	
	11/9/17		Work as before. In to-some to Back Crown "A" Relieved from 121 field Coy Tents attached to duty. New work commenced on screening HERMIES BERTINCOURT ROAD	
	12/9/17		This road was screened from P8 a.18 to P2 — c.25. Bgy strength 6 off. 202.O.R. Work as before. Nissen Huts in Back area also commenced for 164 M.G. Coy. Bgy strength 6 off. 202 O.R.	
	13/9/17		Work as before. Road from HERMIES to Boylnf. at J34 d.1.9 hour. Site from View — Yehicles can now pass safely from BERTINCOURT to HERMIES via RUYAULCOURT. Screens from Boylhcp to P2 c.25 still the Ruylht Bgy strength 6 off. 202 O.R.	

WAR DIARY or INTELLIGENCE SUMMARY

Army Form C. 2118.

Place	Date	Hour	Summary of Events and Information	Remarks and references to Appendices
as before	12/9/17		Work as before - MISSEN HUTTING of BERTINCOURT - Leave nominal following a few. Work for 109 T.M. Battery. Coy Strength 6 Off. 202 O.R.	
	15/9/17		Work commenced on Sifle Range O.9.2.66 erecting safety bar to the first on Rifle Range. Work for 109 T.M. Battery. Work as before when aid at BERTINCOURT + BUS + ROAD Screening on BERTINCOURT - ROYAL COURT ROAD. Coy Strength 6 Off. 201 O.R.	
	Sunday 16/9/17		Line work as before comp work in Back Billet from 8 to 9:30 am - Work on hutting - Road Screening Suspended - Church Parade at 11am - Instruction in Back Billet resting during afternoon - Work on Rifle Range Completed - PEERIEF Practice Carried out by Coy Strength 6 Off. 201 O.R.	
	17/9/17		Work on hutting site at BERTINCOURT - Road Screening & Line work as before. Coy Strength 6 Off. 201 O.R.	

Place	Date	Hour	Summary of Events and Information	Remarks and references to Appendices
	18/9/17		Work as before. 2/Lt BRUNYATE rejoins Coy from Sick leave. Coy strength 7 off. 200 O.R.	
	19/9/17		Line Work as before. No horse bussed. Hut's available for storing off some unnecessary traps to help up transport. Coy strength 7 off. 200 O.R.	
BERTINCOURT				
	20/9/17		Line work as before. Bankers started in BERTINCOURT. Road repairing. A hutting at BUS for F.A. W. etcetera. Coy strength 7 off. 201 O.R.	
	21/9/17		Line work as before. Road from K.25.a.6.3 to K.25.b.08 handed over. Passage of finishing to 699 projective work at BERTINCOURT & BUS. kept. Coy strength 7 off. 201 O.R.	

WAR DIARY
or
INTELLIGENCE SUMMARY.
(Erase heading not required.)

Army Form C. 2118.

Place	Date	Hour	Summary of Events and Information	Remarks and references to Appendices
Sheet 57E T.23.d.50 HERMIES Back Billet	22/9/17		Work in front & Back areas as before at BERTINCOURT. New tents sent up to H&M troops. Huge floor strutting = ammunition — enough for....	
P7.b.6.4 BERTINCOURT	23/9/17		Coy Strength 7 Off. 202. O.R. Network Back areas as up on Coy Bn. 1 proof + Bullet proof shelters in place. Ready for zero 1110am Church parade for all denominations at 1110am Work in line — Revetting, Elephant shelters, and overlay of line as before. New line of strong points from K19.C12 round that R.5+R, lted dated. Coy Strength 7 Off. 202. O.R.	#
	24/9/17		Work in line as before — Work continues at BERTINCOURT on Bon. Strongs generally etc + shelters for artillery Bgde. H.Q.s Coy Strength 7 Off. 202. O.R.	#

WAR DIARY
INTELLIGENCE SUMMARY

Army Form C. 2118.

Place	Date	Hour	Summary of Events and Information	Remarks and references to Appendices
As before	25/9/17		Work on line as before. New Regt Aid Post 50% Completed - Work on new Rifle Range in hand. Work commenced on clearing site for Mens Gat. Way Bayes H.Qrs. - U St Regaives return to this from company. Coy Strength 7 Off. 201 O.R.	
	26/9/17		Work Line and Back area as before. Material put up at night trine new Switch line from O.R.1, across to R.1.6 in front line officer Via R.1 a 17.R.3. Coy Strength 7 Off. 204 O.R.	
	27/9/17		Work as before. Wiring party had usual setting up. Coy Strength 7 Off. 204 O.R.	
	28/9/17		Work as before. Switch line wired with double belt of double apron fence from R.R.1 to R.1.6 in front line during night by 16.RIR(P). Coy Strength 7 Off. 204 O.R.	
	29/9/17		Work generally on before. Hutting for 110 F.A. at Bus Row completed. Second double belt of wire completed on Switch line. Coy Strength 7 Off. 204 O.R.	

Army Form C. 2118.

WAR DIARY
or
INTELLIGENCE SUMMARY.

(Erase heading not required.)

Place	Date	Hour	Summary of Events and Information	Remarks and references to Appendices
In Camp	30/9/17		Work in line as before has ceased. Sans restel there to about 10 white crosses	
			averaging per day.	
			Work down in BERTINCOURT bright way through dense standing	
			Coy resting total obey	///
			Coy strength 7 offs 294 O.R.	
			J. Fortescue Hayes	
			Major	
			O.C. 150th FIELD COY. R.E.	

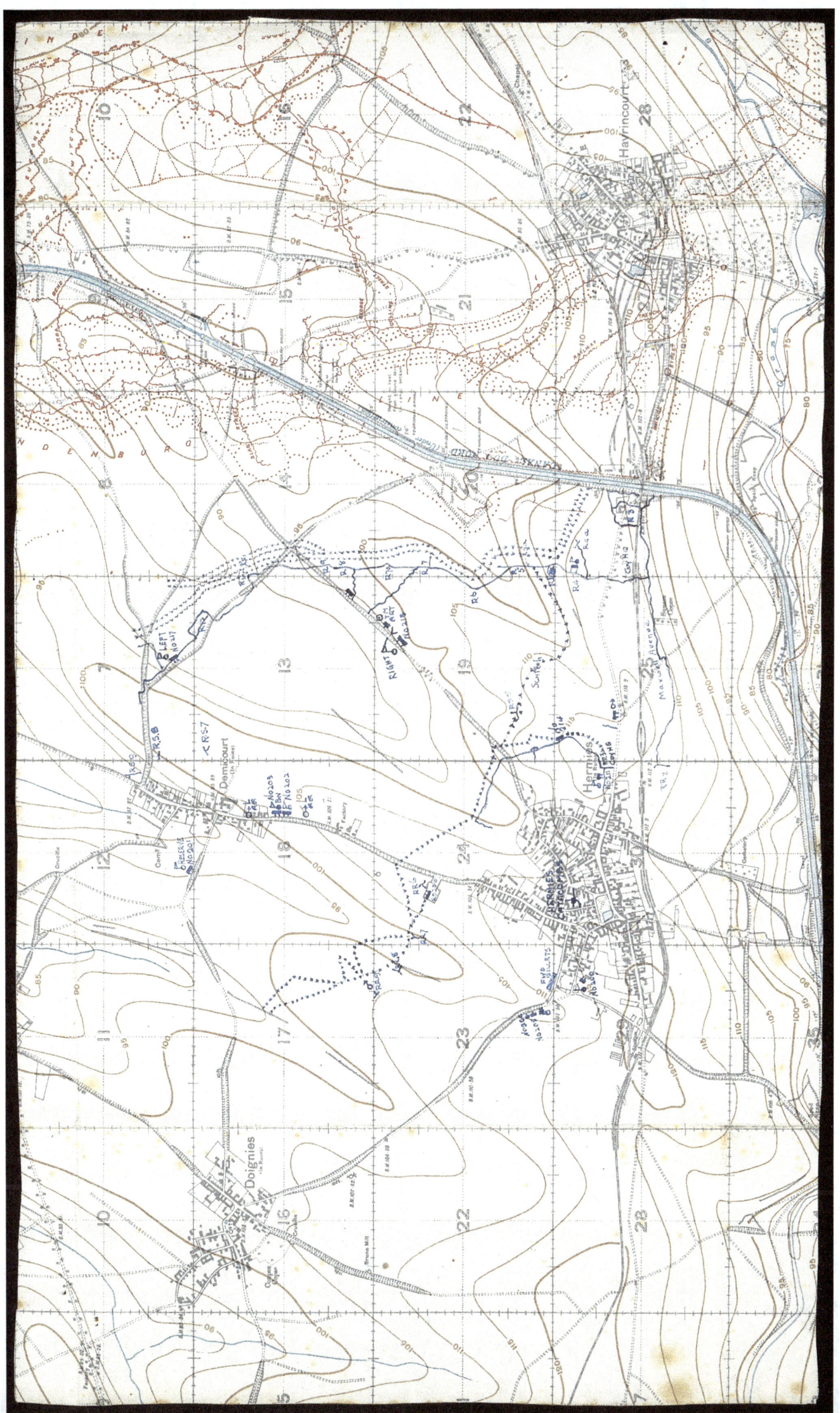

Confidential

War Diary

of

150th Field Coy. R.E.

October 1917

WAR DIARY
or
INTELLIGENCE SUMMARY.
(Erase heading not required.)

Army Form C. 2118.

Place	Date	Hour	Summary of Events and Information	Remarks and references to Appendices
BERTINCOURT & HERMIES P.7.6.7. K.23.D.50	1/7/10		Work at BERTINCOURT carried on as before. I.E. section at Large Elephant Shelters in Village. Improvements to Bgde Cinema Hall - Screening at BERTINCOURT. HERMES ROAD - Hutting 109th Inf. Bgde Headquarters at P.8.a.3.9. Work in line as before. — 16 RIR (P) commenced 250 x hand-switch line from Post RTR to Post in front line R.L.b. Coy Strength 7 Off. 203 O.R.	
	2/7/10		Work in BERTINCOURT & line as before. — New but L line now also covered left of 2.9. Coy Strength 7 Off. 203 O.R.	
	3/7/10		Work on line as before. New switch line continued. — Work at BERTINCOURT as before, and about 200 yards of new Artillery cable (173) 15 pair at P.7 by O. Coy Strength 7 Off. 203 O.R.	
	4/7/10		Work in Line & Back area as before. Coy Strength 7 Off. 203 O.R.	

WAR DIARY
or
INTELLIGENCE SUMMARY.
(Erase heading not required.)

Army Form C. 2118.

Place	Date	Hour	Summary of Events and Information	Remarks and references to Appendices
	5/10/17		Enterd line dug to 4ft of 5ft throughout & to large extent. Wiring & Tactical Rays commenced. Other work as before in trens + Back Areas. Coy Strength 7 Off. 208 O.R.	#
	6/10/17		Flying Traverses erected in Switch line & the steps revetted - Drains started. Other work as before. Y. Beat Over Certify hut allottion at Egl.Erma Theatre commenced. Coy Strength 7 Off. 208 O.R.	
	Sunday 7/10/17		No Work in Back Areas — other work as before Coy Strength 7 Off 208 O.R.	
	8/10/17		Work in line and Back areas as before - new portion of Switch line from R.1.2. Through R.1.0 to R.3 taped. Coy Strength 7 Off. 208 O.R.	

Army Form C. 2118.

WAR DIARY
or
INTELLIGENCE SUMMARY.
(Erase heading not required.)

Instructions regarding War Diaries and Intelligence Summaries are contained in F. S. Regs., Part II. and the Staff Manual respectively. Title pages will be prepared in manuscript.

Place	Date	Hour	Summary of Events and Information	Remarks and references to Appendices
	9/10/17		Work in line as before. Work continued at night on new Switch line drainage. Weather very wet. Div: Siev: cc Switch from R4b-R4a-R3 battle dug until weather clears. Work in Back Areas as before. Coy Strength 7 Off. 208. O.R. *On attached G.S. 36th Division.	#/10
	10/10/17		Work as previous day. Coy Strength 7 Off. 208. O.R.	#/10
	11/10/17		Work as previous day - Switch line drainage continued. Work hampered by very wet weather. Coy Strength 7 Officers 208.O.R.	#
	12/10/17		Weather very wet. Work as before. Coy Strength 7 Off. 208. O.R.	#
	13/10/17		Work as before. Coy Strength 7 Off. 208. O.R.	#
	14/10/17 Sunday		Line Work as usual - No work in Back Billets were left in Back Areas during - . Urgent repairs begining on Regt ROYAL COURT ROAD. Coy Strength 7 off 208 O.R.	#

Army Form C. 2118.

WAR DIARY
or
INTELLIGENCE SUMMARY.
(Erase heading not required.)

Instructions regarding War Diaries and Intelligence Summaries are contained in F. S. Regs., Part II. and the Staff Manual respectively. Title pages will be prepared in manuscript.

Place	Date	Hour	Summary of Events and Information	Remarks and references to Appendices
	15/10/17		Work as before in various trades areas. Coy Strength 7 Off 208 O.R.	
	16/10/17		Work as before - Additional Tile drains being laid in Pltt road at REFCLEN court bath completed. Renewing on ROULERS ROAD repairs on existing completed roads how closed from view - Capt J. H. OTWAY proceed on ten days leave to U.K. Coy Strength 7 Off 208 O.R.	
	17/10/17		Work as before - Drainage of new Dutch line now half completed front line drainage scheme now in hand. Coy Strength 7 Off 208 O.R.	
	18/10/17		Work as before. Coy Strength 7 Off 208 O.R.	
	19/10/17		Work as before. 3 recruits came to join 2 Lt A TERRIER went to Divn H.Q. YPRES to be attached to C.R.E. E Section. Coy Strength 7 Off 212 O.R.	

Place	Date	Hour	Summary of Events and Information	Remarks and references to Appendices
	20/10/17		Work on defences. A line & back areas, her switch line to be known as "LURGAN SWITCH". Coy Strength 7 Off. 212 O.R.	
	Sunday 21/10/17		Work on line & defences. Leitons at Back Billet employed in front - no work outside except at Art. O.P.s & guns. by 1 Off. 40 O.R's. Arty O.S.	
	22/10/17		Work in Back area as before. 16 R.I.R.(?) cut the day working at LURGAN SWITCH from R.1.6. through R.4 to R.5. Bulk of work about 80% of entire excavating required — trench section tube or shown in hereshear. Fire step to be cut as required — Parting to the same as the rest of the line. Coy Strength 7 Off. 9 2 238.	2/0 7 20 - 5
	23/10/17		Work in back areas & front line as before — 2 Coy Canow wents for 16 RIR Fort of LURGAN SWITCH & fright advanced line by 1 Off 34 O.R.	

WAR DIARY
or
INTELLIGENCE SUMMARY.
(Erase heading not required.)

Army Form C. 2118.

Place	Date	Hour	Summary of Events and Information	Remarks and references to Appendices
	24/10/17		Work in forward track areas as before. Coy Strength 7 Off 212 O.R	#34/10
	25/10/17		Work as before. Digging forward part of LURGAN SWITCH to R4 & R2.3 completed. Coy Strength 7 Off 212 O.R	#25/10
	26/10/17		Work as before in line + Back areas. Coy Strength 7 Off 211 O.R	#26/10
	27/10/17		Work as before. Duck boards laid in new front line LURGAN SWITCH R4L & R3. Trench ladders fixed F.J. Coy Strength 7 Off 211 O.R wall E.T.S	#27/10
	28/10/17 Sunday		Only work in Back area on 173. Out 03 y/e A.D.Goes front line. Work as before. One officer was made on revetting R.D posts. Coy Strength 7 Off & 212 O.R	#28/10

1/2 R.D. I - 2 - 3 + 4 Capt J.H. OTWAY R.E. returned from leave.

WAR DIARY
INTELLIGENCE SUMMARY

Army Form C. 2118.

Place	Date	Hour	Summary of Events and Information	Remarks and references to Appendices
	29/7		Work as before in line + BERTINCOURT - all down in BERTINCOURT + BUS	
			habitats for safety precautions - all Coy strengths 7 off. & 11.O.R.	
			deep dugouts in front line as before	
	30/7		Work as before in line to back areas	
	31/7		Work in 6th area in like Boards tabs out B of BERTINCOURT	
			Coy" B gtn. H.Q " Cut B g E reopen practically 7 off 100 O.R	

O.C. 156th FIELD Coy. R.E.

War Diary
of
OC 150' Field Coy RE
For November 1917

M 26

WAR DIARY
or
INTELLIGENCE SUMMARY.
(Erase heading not required.)

Army Form C. 2118.

Place	Date	Hour	Summary of Events and Information	Remarks and references to Appendices
BERTINCOURT HERMIES	1/1/17		Work generally as before	
			Road continued - 173 OR to Bgde + 109th Bgde HQ. Two continued of one elephant shelter in BERTINCOURT. No 1 & 2 sections of No.4 Coy strength 7 off. 211 O.R.	
	2/1/17		In BERTINCOURT as before. No.3 & 4 Sections in forward billet HERMIES	
			Work as before. 16th R.I.R. (?) commenced to take up tramway road from Slagheap to HERMIES. 1st company to lay to crater at P.3.a.7.3	
			Coy strength 7 off. 210 O.R.	
	3/1/17		Demolition of two arch of broken bridge over canal at J.34.D.1.7 commenced. The end of bridge abutment towards neither bank strong enough to work as before.	
			Coy strength 7 off. 208 O.R.	

WAR DIARY
or
INTELLIGENCE SUMMARY.
(Erase heading not required.)

Army Form C. 2118.

Place	Date	Hour	Summary of Events and Information	Remarks and references to Appendices
	4/1/17 Friday		Demolition of bridge continued other work as before	
			Coy Strength 7 Off. 208 O.R.	
	5/1/17		News of our own troops in D.O.R. APs at J.29.a.50 & J.18.a.40. Clearing of Bridge debris commenced. Clearing dug-outs at HERMIES – HAVRINCOURT ROAD commenced with working parties of 100 Infantry other work as before.	
			Coy Strength 7 Off. 208 O.R.	
	6/1/17		Work as before. Debris of bridge cleared & tow-path on both sides of canal cleared.	
			Coy Strength 7 Off. 208 O.R.	
	7/1/17		All work as before	
			Coy Strength 7 Off. 207 O.R.	
	8/1/17		All work as before	
			Coy Strength 7 Off. 207 O.R.	

Army Form C. 2118.

WAR DIARY
or
INTELLIGENCE SUMMARY.
(Erase heading not required.)

Instructions regarding War Diaries and Intelligence Summaries are contained in F. S. Regs., Part II. and the Staff Manual respectively. Title pages will be prepared in manuscript.

Place	Date	Hour	Summary of Events and Information	Remarks and references to Appendices
	9/17		Work as before on HERMIES ROAD Road to HERMIES & whole Bn guts.	#9/11
			Coy Strength 7 Off. 207 O.R.	
	10/17		Work as before - also new work started today. A Elephant shelter at Bt BN Hrs HERMIES and screening of road from J.20 central southwards to the CEMETRY J.36.a	#10/11
			Coy strength 7 Off. 207 O.R.	
			Work was also started in BERLIN COURT to erect as possible hasty Elephant shelters the Bn Hqs weather proof but splinter proof. That the work in rendering other elephants Bomb proof was STOPPED	
			Coy strength 7 Off. 207 O.R.	#10/11
	11/17	Away	All work as previous days. one freed at afternoon J.29 O.4.1 for Pct W Cage	#11/11
	12/17		Officious day also work on Divis: Bomb Store at Stanleal J.34.d.9.4. reg the arrival of 1 Off 207 O.R.	#12/11
			Coy Strength 7 Off. 207 O.R.	

Army Form C. 2118.

WAR DIARY
or
INTELLIGENCE SUMMARY.
(Erase heading not required.)

Place	Date	Hour	Summary of Events and Information	Remarks and references to Appendices
	13/7		All work as before. Screening of Road from BERTINCOURT to HERMIES Complete. This road is practically above forms. Coy strength 7 Off. 207 O.R.	A/11 A/18
	14/7		Work as before. Diversion at entries on HERMIES Road at B3a been passable. Coy Strength 7 Off 207 O.R.	A/16 A/17
	15/7		Work as before. Also a start made on repairing HERMIES - GRAINCOURT Road Coy Strength 7 Off 207 O.R.	A/15 A/17
	16/7		Work as before in Forward area. Hd Qrs & here 1st & 3rd Sections ordered to METZ and arrived 6pm. Transport with Capt Otway RE went to BARASTRE O.10.c.2.5 & arrived 5pm. 50 bayards & Officers reported at HERMIES & BRONFAY for attachment to 30 Inf. & down lines. the other Sections to METZ with hd to 3 Sections Coy Strength 2 Officers 206 O.R.	A/19

WAR DIARY
or
INTELLIGENCE SUMMARY.
(Erase heading not required.)

Army Form C. 2118.

Place	Date	Hour	Summary of Events and Information	Remarks and references to Appendices
	17/11/17		and 50 O.R	
			249 O.R. and 1 & 3 Sections proceeded Preston in HAVRINCOURT WOOD	
			Q.15. C.6.f. & proceeded to erect shelters for 150 hfs of 1st & 2nd Bn Rf	
			Nos 2 + 4 Sections located as before. Transport located at BARASTILE	2/40
			as before. 2 Pontoon Wagons and 1 Trestle Wagon with Coal & the Lephistone	
			1 Cucumber, also 6 Drivers and 12 horses lent on attachment to 122 Field Co.	
			Coy Strength 4 Officers & O.R. 296	
	18/11/17		Nos 1 + 3 Sect - attached HQ work as before & unloading trains & road material	
			Nos 2 +4 Sections + attached R.E. Coys less as before. 1 Sis. Batln 40 Yorkshire	
			carried on the days work. Roads etc all should smooth for Sudden burst in HERMIES	
			Shelters for R.P.M. + Bn. H.Q. + Store practically completed. 80 As. and 5 Sappers	Nil
			Let C. No 2 ry Sections by 122 Fld Co for work	
			Transport as before	
			Coy Strength Officers 4 O.R. 206	
	19/11/17		Company Strenth as on 18th. Nos 1 + 3 Sections did some work in unloading	
			trains at METZ B.W. 54 - 12. TRESCAULT RAILHEAD Q. 10. a. 25. 25.	

WAR DIARY
or
INTELLIGENCE SUMMARY.
(Erase heading not required.)

Army Form C. 2118.

Place	Date	Hour	Summary of Events and Information	Remarks and references to Appendices
			Sections 2 & 4 - All work completed except Dub Field H.2.	Sp.3.
			Coy. Strength Officers 4, OR. 204	
	20/11		Company located as before. British forces attacked in force a two front lines Zero hour 6.20 A.M. At 8 A.M. party of 12 O.R. with Lt. Knox R.E. followed wire Cavalry tanks to clear path for Cavalry from Q.5.6.8.8. to RIBECOURT. This party cut & cleared all pieces of wire Ex/H. At 10 A.M. N° 1 & 3 Sections & aff. Infantry went forward to RIBECOURT, filled in head crossing STATION AVENUE at L.25.6.2.3. then cleared & made good whole road through village to L.25.a.95.95. Completed at 1 p.m. N° 2 Section & aff. Infy. captured an Indigny old front line at K.14.C.6.1 also in Cherry road from K.13.d.8.3. to 6, K.15.a.5.3. N° 4 Section taped out track from K.25.a.7.3. to K.20.d.2.7. & filled in Shell holes, also improved ramp up Canal bank & also carried a tape track to K.16.C.9.8.	two

WAR DIARY
or
INTELLIGENCE SUMMARY.
(Erase heading not required.)

Army Form C. 2118.

Place	Date	Hour	Summary of Events and Information	Remarks and references to Appendices
			4 Pack Animals with an N.C.O. were sent forward to HERMIES at 4 hours after ZERO to await instructions. These were not employed.	
	21/11/17		Org. Strength Officers 7, O.R. 206	
			Nos 1 & 3 Sections & AHQ.Hqrs. & Nos 2 & 4 Sections & AHQ Hqrs by locations as before. Transport & Horse Lines under Capt OTWAY R.E. moved from BARASTRE O.I.O.C.2.5 to VELU WOOD at J.31.C.50.50 when personnel were accommodated in tents. Move completed 9.30 P.M. Nos 1 & 3 Sections & attached Infantry continued Crater diversion at K.36.c.7.7 working in 3 Reliefs, commencing at 4 P.M. By 10 P.M. a 9 ft. Unit was open. No.4 Ration noted. No.2 Section worked except for 1 Officer & one B.R. who with some Infantry were employed on light transport.	
			Org. Strength Officers 7, O.R. 206	

WAR DIARY or INTELLIGENCE SUMMARY

Army Form C. 2118.

Place	Date	Hour	Summary of Events and Information	Remarks and references to Appendices
	22/1/17		Co. located as at Army of 21/1/=. N°s 1 & 3 Section rand Bf. Completed Corbie Diversion at K.36.c.7.7. N°2 Section Repair road to DEMICOURT. N°4 Section Rel'd in reserve all day & improve & turning on returning Tracks. Cpy. Strength Officers 7. OR 336.	J/no
	23/1/17		N°s 2 & 4 Section rand Bf. party located as on 22nd Transport Lines as before. H.Q.C. & N°s 1 & 3 Section rand party moved to J.30.d. near HERMIES & were Accomod. in Huts. All Sections working on repairs &c to HERMIES road. Cpy. Strength Officers 7. OR 206	J/no

WAR DIARY or INTELLIGENCE SUMMARY

Army Form C. 2118.

Place	Date	Hour	Summary of Events and Information	Remarks and references to Appendices
	24/7/17		Co located as before. — The 4 Sections + all Infantry with 200 of Labour Co. Employed on Clearing, cleaning & making good all roads in HERMIES, also HERMIES-DEMICOURT ROAD to Far forward as SUGAR FACTORY. Coy. Strength Officers 4/ O.R. 236.	yes
	25/7/17		The Whole to be employed as on 24 on Co located as before — Repairs to roads in HERMIES. Coy Strength Officers 4/ O.R. 228	yes
	26/7		Co located as before — 2 Sections on roads in HERMIES - also 1 Section from WINDY CORNER J.29.c.40.95. Working N. side of track continued from J.34.c.95 practically completed BERTINCOURT Road to J.34.c.95. Support Line from K.1.6.8.7 on 2 Sections Commenced to Rivet and Support Line from K.26.a.9.6 BAPAUME – CAMBRAI - road to CAMm. at K.26.a.9.6 Coy. Strength, Officers 4/ O.R 218	

WAR DIARY
or
INTELLIGENCE SUMMARY.

Army Form C. 2118.

Place	Date	Hour	Summary of Events and Information	Remarks and references to Appendices
	24/11		Co located as before. Work on trench Coy strengths. Coy Strength Officers 7. O.R. 208	
	25/11		Co located as before. Took the North Co Trench that had the General HQ Tea Room. Hornies + trenches of Shelters commenced to house all the Co in. Coy Strength Officers 7. O.R. 209	
	29/11		Work as previous day. Coy Strength Officers 7. O.R. 209	
	30/11		Co located as before. 3 Sections arrived to commence line W of FLESQUIERES, one section behind Reserve line for Co in TRENCHES. In rear of Shelter of Co in TRENCHES. Coy Strength Officers. O.R. 209	

J Horsey
Capt O.C.

WAR DIARY
150th Field Co. R.E.
November 1917

Confidential   Vol 27

War Diary

of

150ᵗʰ Field Coy R.E.

December, 1917

Army Form C. 2118.

WAR DIARY
or
INTELLIGENCE SUMMARY.
(Erase heading not required.)

Instructions regarding War Diaries and Intelligence Summaries are contained in F. S. Regs., Part II. and the Staff Manual respectively. Title pages will be prepared in manuscript.

Place	Date	Hour	Summary of Events and Information	Remarks and references to Appendices
Field	1/10/17		Co located as follows. H.Q. and 4 Sections with 100 Attached Infantry in Dugouts and billets at HERMIES J.29.b.6.9. Sheet 57.c. 1/40,000 France. Horse Lines and transport under Captain Otway R.E. in VELU WOOD. J.31.c.50.50. 3 Sections working on wiring of Noreuil Line from K.17.a.1.0 to K.17.d.5.9 and taking two M.G. emplacements at K.17.c.8.5 and K.17.d.5.5. One Section working on Company billets + dug outs rooms. HERMIES. Company Strength 7 Off. 208 O.R.	Nil.
	2/10/17		Co located as before. Work as on previous day. Company Strength 7 Off. 208 O.R.	Nil.
	3/10/17		Co located as before. Wiring completed. Work on billets completed. Company Strength 7 Off. 208 O.R.	Nil.
	4/10/17		Horse lines located as before. H.Q. 4 Sections with Infantry moved to Camp in DESART WOOD, + accommodated in tents about P.1.b. Company Strength 7 Off. 208 O.R.	App 2

WAR DIARY
or
INTELLIGENCE SUMMARY.

Army Form C. 2118.

Place	Date	Hour	Summary of Events and Information	Remarks and references to Appendices
	5/12/17		H.Q. 4 Sections & added Infantry located as on previous day. Transport Horselines moved to SOREL LE GRAND W.13.a.1.0. r were accommodated in shelters open standings. Sections employed on wiring the line from R.3.a.4.5 to R.3.c.7.5. and R.3.c.5.2. Wounded in Action $\begin{cases} 2 \text{ N.C.O.s} \\ 1 \text{ Sapper} \\ 3 \text{ A/H Infantry} \\ 2 \text{ A/H Infantry} \end{cases}$ Killed in Action. Company Strength 7 Off. 205. O.R.	JKO
	6/12/17		Horse Lines and Transport as previous day. H.Q. 4 Sections and all Infantry moved to Camp at Q.16.a.1.8. Accommodated in tents. Co employed wiring as on 5th. Company Strength 7 Off. 205. O.R.	JKO

WAR DIARY
or
INTELLIGENCE SUMMARY
(Erase heading not required.)

Army Form C. 2118.

Place	Date	Hour	Summary of Events and Information	Remarks and references to Appendices
	7/4/17		Co located as before. Co Employed burying front line from R.4. c. 35.50 to Stokes Road - Pl. C. 6.7 to Pl. d. 35. 95. Company Strength 7 Off. 205. O.R.	Aro
	8/4/17		Co located as before. burying front line as before 2/Lieut ELLIOTT A.C. wounded in action. Company Strength 6 Officers 205. O.R.	Aro
	9/4/17		Co located as before. work on covering front line traced out by 121 Field Co. Co Commenced trenches on forward slope of HIGHLAND RIDGE. - Reserve Front Line. Company Strength 6 Officers 200.O.R.	Aro
	10/4/17		Co located as before. burying work as before. Jim Stopped work Started on R.2.6.47 to R.8.c.2.6. work Started on Jim Stopper Reserve Fire line trench. Company Strength 6 Officers 197. O.R.	Aro

Army Form C. 2118.

WAR DIARY
or
INTELLIGENCE SUMMARY.
(Erase heading not required.)

Place	Date	Hour	Summary of Events and Information	Remarks and references to Appendices
	11.iv.17		From L.32.c.75.40. to R.1.d.23.45. And on digging a new trench also Reserve Line from R.1.d.25.45. to old front line at R.R.S.O.	AAO
	12.iv.17		C. employed as before. C. employed in digging of Reserve Support line and wiring of Reserve Front line as before. Digging of Assistant Reserve Support line. Company Strength 6 Off. 196 O.R. Co. trained as before. Digging of new Reserve Support line — wiring of Reserve Front line completed. Company Strength 6 Off. 196 O.R.	AAO

Army Form C. 2118.

WAR DIARY
or
INTELLIGENCE SUMMARY.
(Erase heading not required.)

Instructions regarding War Diaries and Intelligence Summaries are contained in F. S. Regs., Part II. and the Staff Manual respectively. Title pages will be prepared in manuscript.

Place	Date	Hour	Summary of Events and Information	Remarks and references to Appendices
	13.12.17		HQ and detrained portion of Co. left Camp near TRESCAULT at 2 P.M. and arrived at SOREL-LE-GRAND at 4 P.M. and were accomodated in Shelters near their own Wagon Lines. Company Strength 6 off. 194 O.R.	Nil.
	14.12.17		Co. located in Shelters at SOREL-LE-GRAND. Co. employed in Heavy transport. Company Strength 6 off. 194 O.R.	Nil.
	15.12.17		Co. to a complete unit. Arrived from SOREL-LE-GRAND at 12 noon. Marching to ROCQUIGNY arriving 3.30 P.M. & were accomodated in tents & open Horse Standings. Co under Command of Capt. J. HOTWAY, Major Fordham having gone on leave. Company Strength 6 off 195 O.R.	Nil.

Army Form C. 2118.

WAR DIARY
or
INTELLIGENCE SUMMARY.
(Erase heading not required.)

Instructions regarding War Diaries and Intelligence Summaries are contained in F. S. Regs., Part II. and the Staff Manual respectively. Title pages will be prepared in manuscript.

Place	Date	Hour	Summary of Events and Information	Remarks and references to Appendices
	16/7/.		Distributed portion of Co marched from ROCQUIGNY to ETRICOURT & entrained there, moving in conjunction with 109th I. Bde. at 4 P.M. Arrived MONDICOURT 10.30 P.M. & marched to village of BOUT des PRES. 1½ miles from DOULLENS on DOULLENS - LUCHEUX - DOULLENS Road. Accommodated in billets. Mounted portion & transport moved by road under Lt FERRIER arriving at COURCELLES COMTE at ROCQUIGNY at 11.30 A.M. arriving at 4 p.m. & were accommodated in tents. Strong hard & roads very difficult. Company Strength 6 Off. 195 O.R.	Pro
	17/7/.		Distributed portion at BOUT des PRES:- Resting and settling into billets. Mounted portion left COURCELLES COMTE at 8 A.M. & reached BOUT des PRES at 7.30 P.M. handled by bad roads. deep sand & roads unfit for badly. Country Covered in deep sand. Company Strength 6 Off. 195 O.R.	Pro

Army Form C. 2118.

WAR DIARY
or
INTELLIGENCE SUMMARY.
(Erase heading not required.)

Place	Date	Hour	Summary of Events and Information	Remarks and references to Appendices
	18/1/17		Co located at BOOT des PRES. Employed in Notby and Refitting Small parties sent out to repair various battalion baths. Snow stopped - freezing hard & roads almost impassable. Company Strength 6 Off. 195. O.R.	JHO
	19/1/17		Co located & employed as before. Weather still hard & freezing. Company Strength 6 Off. 195. O.R.	JHO
	20/1/17		Co treket to Reference to be lent to Canadian Forestry Co to build horse standings in LIC H EOR Wood. Roads very slippery. Still freezing. Company Strength 6 Off. 195. O.R.	JHO
	21/1/17		Co located & employed as before. 2/Lieut STAPYLTON-SMITH J.B. joined for duty. Company Strength 7 Off. 195. O.R.	JHO

Army Form C. 2118.

WAR DIARY
or
INTELLIGENCE SUMMARY.

(Erase heading not required.)

Instructions regarding War Diaries and Intelligence Summaries are contained in F. S. Regs., Part II. and the Staff Manual respectively. Title pages will be prepared in manuscript.

Place	Date	Hour	Summary of Events and Information	Remarks and references to Appendices
	22/12/17		Co Located & Employed as before. Company Strength 7 Off. 194. O.R.	Nil
	23/12/17		Co Located & Employed as before. Company Strength 7 Off. 195. O.R.	Nil
	24/12/17		Co Located & Employed as before and thus getting in weather breaks. Company Strength 7 Off. 196. O.R.	Nil
	25/12/17		Coy Located as before Employed breaking wagons Company Strength 7 Off. 196 O.R.	a.t.
	26/12/17		Coy Located as before Employed as before with addition of washing wagon and cleaning wards. One Officer on'd forward to new area for billeting. 8" snow. Company Strength 7 Off. 196 O.R.	a.t.

A.5834 Wt. W4973/M687 750,000 8/16 D. D. & L. Ltd. Forms/C.2118/13.

Army Form C. 2118.

WAR DIARY
or
INTELLIGENCE SUMMARY.
(Erase heading not required.)

Instructions regarding War Diaries and Intelligence Summaries are contained in F. S. Regs., Part II. and the Staff Manual respectively. Title pages will be prepared in manuscript.

Place	Date	Hour	Summary of Events and Information	Remarks and references to Appendices
27/12/17 Field	27/12/17		Company employed and treated as before along fosters and chaney wagons. Company Strength 7 off. 196.O.R.	At.
	28/12/17		Company treated as before, employed clearing chaney filato. Transport moved off (less tanks) via DOULLENS. They could not get further than PUCHEVILLERS on account of snow drift. Do. Company Strength 7 off. 196.O.R.	At.
	29/12/17		Dismounted portion of company 11 Limbers and 8 carts entrained MONDICOURT station & proceeded via MOREUIL and transported at BOVES. Racked & Domart in V Corps area. Main body of Transport completely held up at PUCHEVILLERS. Company Strength 7 off. 192.O.R.	At.
	30/12/17		Dismounted portion employed empanier filato. Transport left PUCHEVILLERS at 7.30 p.m. Arrived DOMART 10.30 p.m. Company Strength 7 off. 191.O.R.	At.
	31/12/17		Company employed at wild and h.1 and posting. Company Strength 7 off. 191.O.R.	At.

A Ferrio 2/Lt
for O.C. 150th Field Coy R.E.

36D1

Vol 28

Confidential

War Diary

150th Field Coy. R.E.

January 1918.

WAR DIARY
or
INTELLIGENCE SUMMARY.

(*Erase heading not required.*)

Army Form C. 2118.

Instructions regarding War Diaries and Intelligence Summaries are contained in F. S. Regs., Part II. and the Staff Manual respectively. Title pages will be prepared in manuscript.

Place	Date	Hour	Summary of Events and Information	Remarks and references to Appendices

A5834 Wt. W4973 M687 750,000 8/16 D. D. & L., Ltd. Forms/C.2118/13.

Army Form C. 2118.

WAR DIARY
or
INTELLIGENCE SUMMARY.
(Erase heading not required.)

Instructions regarding War Diaries and Intelligence Summaries are contained in F. S. Regs., Part II. and the Staff Manual respectively. Title pages will be prepared in manuscript.

Place	Date	Hour	Summary of Events and Information	Remarks and references to Appendices
DOMART	1/1/18		Coy. in Billets. Drill & training carried on	Coy. Strength 8 O.R. 193
	2/1/18		as before. Major H. M. FORDHAM returned from 14 days leave to U.K. and resumed command of Coy.	Coy. Strength 8 O.R. 193
	3/1/18		Training as before	— do —
	4/1/18		do	— do —
	5/1/18		do	— do —
	6/1/18		do	— do — 8 O.R. 189

Army Form C. 2118.

WAR DIARY
or
INTELLIGENCE SUMMARY.
(Erase heading not required.)

Instructions regarding War Diaries and Intelligence Summaries are contained in F. S. Regs., Part II. and the Staff Manual respectively. Title pages will be prepared in manuscript.

Place	Date	Hour	Summary of Events and Information	Remarks and references to Appendices
DOMART FRESNOY	7/1/18	11 am	Whole Coy marched out of DOMART & were billeted at FRESNOY at 1 pm. Coy Strength 8 O.R. 189	//
FRESNOY	8/1/18	-	Transport work. - do -	//
FRESNOY BILLANCOURT	9/1/18		Coy left FRESNOY at 8 am & marched to Billets in BILLANCOURT arriving at 3.30 pm. Coy Strength 8 O.R. 189	//
BILLANCOURT	10/1/18		Lt. FERRIER proceeded with 2 N.C.Os to G.D. SERAUCOURT to take over work from 3/52 French Coy. Coy on Canada & Transport. Coy Strength 8 O.R. 189	//
B-OLLEZY to FRESNOY	11/1/18	9 am	Whole Coy marched to OLLEZY. - do -	//
	12/1/18		Coy training at OLLEZY. - do -	//
	13/1/18		2/Lt STAPYLTON-SMITH 2/Lt BRUNYATE & Two Setting Nos 3 & 4 marched by Lt H/15 forward billets at J.6 a.9.7 m railway cutting East of grand SERAUCOURT. Coy Strength 8 O.R. 189	//

WAR DIARY
or
INTELLIGENCE SUMMARY.

Army Form C. 2118.

Place	Date	Hour	Summary of Events and Information	Remarks and references to Appendices
Outside GD SERAUCOURT G.8.a.30.35	14/1/18		Nos 1 & 2 Sections Coy HQ & transport marched to GD-SERAUCOURT & took over back billet from French 3/52 Field Coy at GD-SER AUCOURT at G.8.a.30.35. Nos 3 & 4 Sect ions commenced work on three deep dugouts Nos. B, C & D in intermediate line - taken over incomplete from the French. Coy Strength 8 OR 189	
	15/1/18		Forward work as before. Rear sections has 1 & 3 commenced work on (1) Causeway across marsh & foot bridge across R. Somme at approx. A.21.c. This was left about 20% completed by French. (2) Deep dug out (H.O.I.) at approx A.29 a.2.8 This has 2 shafts sunk about 15 feet below ground. Coy Strength 8 OR 189	
	16/1/18		Work as before. HQ Transport at two rear sections nos 1 & 2 moved then back billet at G.9.C.1.h near GD SERAUCOURT. Forward section as before. 8 OR Coy strength 189	

WAR DIARY
INTELLIGENCE SUMMARY

Army Form C. 2118.

Place	Date	Hour	Summary of Events and Information	Remarks and references to Appendices
G.D SERAUCOURT J.6.a.77	17/1/18		Work as before on Bridge Causeway & Dugouts. Coy. Strength 8. 189 O.R.	
"	18/1/18		Work as before. Coy Strength 8. 189	
"	19/1/18		Work as before. Except No 1 Section was taken off work on intakeworks & in forward area. Started opening entrances to Dugout in front line Right Bn Sector. Coy. Strength 8.O. 189. O.R.	
"	20/1/18		Work in Back area as before. Work as before in Back area & forward area. Coy. Strength 7.O. 190. O.R.	
"	21/1/18		No 1 Section working on repairing & revetting & screening on rd SERAUCOURT - ESSIGNY. Road work otherwise as before. Coy. Strength 7.O, 190. O.R.	
"	22/1/18		Work on Bridge & Causeway handed over to 121 Troop & intermediate three entries handed over to 201 Field Coy RE - other work as before - new Deep Dug out for M. Guns started at B.21.c.8.0 Screening for railway cutting at A.30.B.1.9 commenced. Coy. Strength 7. off. 191. O.R.	

Army Form C. 2118.

WAR DIARY
or
INTELLIGENCE SUMMARY.
(Erase heading not required.)

Instructions regarding War Diaries and Intelligence Summaries are contained in F. S. Regs., Part II. and the Staff Manual respectively. Title pages will be prepared in manuscript.

Place	Date	Hour	Summary of Events and Information	Remarks and references to Appendices
	23/1/19		Work as before in line on Dugouts. Back area on Levening. Coy. Strength 7 Off. 191. O.R.	#
	24/1/19		Work in line as before. Levening of 3D SERAUCOURT ROAD as before. Road Repair started at 3 D 5.5. Coy. Strength 7 Off. 201. O.R.	#
	25/1/19		Work in line as before - Back area Levening continued. Road Repair completed. Coy. Strength 7 Off. 201. O.R.	#
	26/1/19		Work as before in Both Areas. Coy. Strength 7 Off. 201. O.R.	#
	27/1/19		Work in line as before also repair twine was commenced - wire in front of T.Yule GOZET + T'DAURILLAE started on. Coy. Strength 7 Off. 201. O.R. Back Area Road Levening as before work commenced on Arians roof at Cinema Hall SD SERAUCOURT. Coy. Strength 7 Off. 201. O.R. 9/Lt. C. L. KNOX returned from 14 days leave to U.K.	#

WAR DIARY
or
INTELLIGENCE SUMMARY.

(Erase heading not required.)

Army Form C. 2118.

Place	Date	Hour	Summary of Events and Information	Remarks and references to Appendices
Back Area J.D. SERAUCOURT Billets. J.9.C.1.4.	28/1/18		All work as previous day. In addition Dugout at Bty J.85 started. Shelves constructed to clear totals area out as offices storm officers etc. Coy strength 7 Off. 2010 O.R.	
	29/1/18		All work as previous day. In addition work was started on building a Div Barber Shop in J.D. SERAUCOURT. Coy strength 7 Off. 202 O.R.	
Forward Area Billet 2 Lee's J.6.a.T.7	30/1/18		Work as on previous day. Coy strength 7 Off. 202 O.R.	
	31/1/18		Work as on previous day. Major J.H OTWAY left for 14 days leave to U.K. Coy strength 7 Off. 202 O.R.	

H. Forshaw
Major
O.C. 150th FIELD COY. R.E.

Army Form C. 2118.

WAR DIARY
or
INTELLIGENCE SUMMARY.

(Erase heading not required.)

Instructions regarding War Diaries and Intelligence Summaries are contained in F. S. Regs., Part II. and the Staff Manual respectively. Title pages will be prepared in manuscript.

Place	Date	Hour	Summary of Events and Information	Remarks and references to Appendices

A3834 Wt.W4973/M687 750,00c 8/16 D. D. & L. Ltd. Forms/C.2118/13.

Vol 29

Confidential

War Diary

of

150th Field Coy R.E.

February, 1918.

Army Form C. 2118.

WAR DIARY
or
INTELLIGENCE SUMMARY.

(Erase heading not required.)

Instructions regarding War Diaries and Intelligence Summaries are contained in F. S. Regs., Part II. and the Staff Manual respectively. Title pages will be prepared in manuscript.

Place	Date	Hour	Summary of Events and Information	Remarks and references to Appendices
G.D SERAUCOURT Gg. C.1.4 Forward Billet g.6.a.77	1-2-18		Work in Back Area — Divisional Officers Hairdressing Room at G.8.c.2.9 now about 50% complete Erection of small hut to take instrument for Cinema in an ADRIAN HUT. By le Theatre just commenced at G.D SERAUCOURT Repairs and Re-erection of Screening along G.D. SERAUCOURT — ESSIGNY ROAD about 60% completed Forward Area Restoring & Rebuilding entrances to Dugouts in front lines Construction of new deep dugouts for M.G at B 21. c.q.2 (about 50% complete) up to that Repair and Strengthening of all wire in front of Support line — It ⁂⁂⁂ is all wire in front of Trenches De BOURG — VILLE BOOZE LeJEUNE Line of the Resout line (8 T.5 ST ETIENNE & D'AVRILLAE Provision of gas Doors & Frames + blankets to all deep dugouts in Right Bgde Area. Company Strength 7 Off. 201 O.R.	#1 #2

Army Form C. 2118.

WAR DIARY
or
INTELLIGENCE SUMMARY.
(Erase heading not required.)

Instructions regarding War Diaries and Intelligence Summaries are contained in F. S. Regs., Part II. and the Staff Manual respectively. Title pages will be prepared in manuscript.

Place	Date	Hour	Summary of Events and Information	Remarks and references to Appendices
GD SERAUCOURT	2/2/18		Work as on previous day. Also. The front of LE JEUNE Trench from B.15.d.5 to Bn Headquarters being entirely without wire a start was made on wiring it. By Strength 7 Off. 201. O.R.	A/1 /2
	3/2/18		**Back Area** Cinema Hut at Col - SERAUCOURT completed. Conversion of a barn into a Cinema at ARTEMPS commenced. Other work as before. **Front Area** New machine gun dugout at B.14.c.3.9. Commenced - This to be a deep mined dugout to take 1 Off. + 20 men. - Other work as before. Coy. Strength 7 Off. 201. O.R.	A/1 /3 /2

A.5834 Wt. W4973/M687 750,000 8/16 D. D. & L. Ltd. Forms/C.2118/13.

Army Form C. 2118.

WAR DIARY
or
INTELLIGENCE SUMMARY.
(Erase heading not required.)

Instructions regarding War Diaries and Intelligence Summaries are contained in F. S. Regs., Part II. and the Staff Manual respectively. Title pages will be prepared in manuscript.

Place	Date	Hour	Summary of Events and Information	Remarks and references to Appendices
	4/2/18		All work as before. Coy. Strength 7 Off. 201 O.R.	
	5/2/18		Work as before. Testing site at ARTEMPS completed. Coy. Strength 7 Off. 201 O.R.	
	6/2/18		All work as before. Coy. Strength 7 Off. 201 O.R.	
	7/2/18		All work as before – "Lt. Potts tarp attached to Coy. Coy. Strength 7 Off. 205 O.R.	
	8/2/18		Work in Back areas as before. Div. Baths shift completed. Salvage shed commenced at G.D Beaumont. Work in Line. Relaying offset line dugouts in left By front at By de Poston Complete – Work commenced on extending & improving an existing deep dugout at left of dugout. Other line work as before. B.H.Q Qrs as now R.A.P & building a splinter proof killer to take present hunkers of Coy. Strength 7 Off. 205. O.R.	

B'n H.Qrs as now. A.5834 Wt. W4973/M687 750,000 8/16 D. D. & L. Ltd. Forms/C.2118/13.

Army Form C. 2118.

WAR DIARY
or
INTELLIGENCE SUMMARY.
(Erase heading not required.)

Instructions regarding War Diaries and Intelligence Summaries are contained in F. S. Regs., Part II. and the Staff Manual respectively. Title pages will be prepared in manuscript.

Place	Date	Hour	Summary of Events and Information	Remarks and references to Appendices
—	9/2/18		Work as before	MM
	10/2/18		Major W.M. FORDHAM R.E. left for course at 5th Army Infantry School. Lieut. S.B. Hoyston-Smith R.E. took over the command of the Company. Coy. Strength 7 Off. 205. O.R.	MM
			Work on Line as before.	
			Work in back Area. New Brigade Head Quarters in Gd. SERAUCOURT at G.82.2.5. commenced. Coy. Strength 7 Off. 205. O.R.	MM
	11/2/18		Work on Line - As Left Batt. H. Ars moved back to day into dugouts previously occupied by Brigade H.Q. the need for a splinter proof billet ceased - work on this was stopped accordingly.	
			Work in back Area. Salvage Shed completed. Coy. Strength 7 Off. 2070. O.R.	MM
	12/2/18		Work as before. Coy. Strength 7 Off. 2070. R.	MM
	13/2/18		Work on Line. Reclaiming & rebuilding entrances to dugouts in front Line completed. Other work as before.	MM
			Work in Back Area - as before. Coy. Strength 7 Off. 206. O.R.	
	14/2/18		Work on Line. Work on erecting new wire (apron fences) "Z" from B.15.C.35.45" to B.15.C.80.60 & B.15.C.55.50 to B.15.C.60.25 – "Y" B.15 a 10.10 to B.15 a 20.57. commenced. "Z" left finished same night. Each left about 300x in length.	MM
			Back Area - Work as before. Coy. Strength 7 Off. 206. O.R.	

Army Form C. 2118.

WAR DIARY
or
INTELLIGENCE SUMMARY.
(Erase heading not required.)

Place	Date	Hour	Summary of Events and Information	Remarks and references to Appendices
	15/2/18		Work in Line - Apron fence "Y" Belt completed. Other work as before. Work in Back Area as before. Capt J.H. King 170 R.C. U.S.A arrived to be attached for duty with Div. R.E. Companies. Coy. Strength 7 Off. 206 O.R.	SLM
	16/2/18		Work in Line. An Apron fence "I.F." from B.14.a.95.25. to B.14.d.22.50. was taken on & completed the same night. Total length about 400ˣ. Other work as before. Lt Bruyade & No 4 Section withdrawn from forward Billets to Coy. H.Qrs. to take on work on new Brigade H.Q. dugouts - back area. Back Area Work as before. Major J.H. Otway R.E. returned from leave & took over command of the Company. Coy. Strength 7 Off. 206 O.R.	SLM
	17/2/18		Situation as before. Deep Mined dugouts at G.9.c.14. and G.8.a.9.4. commenced. Other work as before. Coy. Strength 7 Off. 206 O.R.	Jno
	18/2/18		Company situated as before, and employed as before. Coy. Strength 7 Off. 206 O.R.	Jno

Army Form C. 2118.

WAR DIARY
or
INTELLIGENCE SUMMARY.
(Erase heading not required.)

Place	Date	Hour	Summary of Events and Information	Remarks and references to Appendices
Field	19/7/18		Company situated as before. Forward Area work as before. Back Area work as before. Field Brigade bivouac as before, but other back area Q work decreased and extra accommodation started in Company lines to accommodate Brigade Hqs and Artillery Group H.Qrs. Coy. Strength 7 Off. 206 O.R.	App A
	20/7/18		Company situated as before. Both back & forward area work as before. Coy Strength 7 Off. 206 O.R.	A/40
	21/7/18		HQs. moved forward & sections 2 & 4 moved from camp at G.9.c.4.4 to new billets at LE HAMEL G.1.b.7.5. work on present dugouts returned but all other Q work done by these sections now to 122nd Field Co. Sections 1 & 3 moved from billets at B.6.a.5.8 to new billets in BRAY St CHRISTOPHE L.7.d.7.5. handing over all their work	A/2

WAR DIARY
or
INTELLIGENCE SUMMARY.

Army Form C. 2118.

Place	Date	Hour	Summary of Events and Information	Remarks and references to Appendices
To 122nd Field Co. 122nd Field Co.	20/3		And Taking over work previously done by Coy. Strength 7 Off. 206.O.R.	Apx
			HQrs C. Kindred Services & Lewis's 2&4 quartered at Le Hamel in billets. Sections 1&3 quartered at BRAY. Chr. [...] at Stroytort-Smith R. Coy. Sections 2&4 employed in constructing Burial chapels for Brigade HQrs at G.9.c.2.4 — G.8.a.9.4. — G.6.a.1.7. Sections 1&4 employed constructing HQrs for M.G. Batt. and taking 2 large pillboxes [...] at HAPPENCOURT also Reconnaissance of work at ARTEMPS – ST SIMON – TUGNY – AIESNES. Section 3 employed as follows – (a) Repairs to bridge over the Canal at ST SIMON and TUGNY (b) Preparing bridges for demolition at ARTEMPS – ST SIMON and TUGNY.	Apx Apx Apx Apx
		Oc. 150	Made responsible as R.E. Officer in charge of all work in construction of Strong Points at B.20.C.O.O — A.18.C.1. A.19 Central Map grid. 65 N.V.W.	Apx
		1/10 am	Just over by to Adv[...] [...] Coy. Strength 7 Off. 210.O.R.	

Army Form C. 2118.

WAR DIARY
or
INTELLIGENCE SUMMARY.
(Erase heading not required.)

Instructions regarding War Diaries and Intelligence
Summaries are contained in F. S. Regs., Part II.
and the Staff Manual respectively. Title pages
will be prepared in manuscript.

Place	Date	Hour	Summary of Events and Information	Remarks and references to Appendices
	23/7/18		Co. worked and employed as in previous day. Coy strength 7 off. 211 O.R.	Appx
	24/7/18		Co. worked and employed as before. Coy strength 7 off. 211 O.R.	Appx
	25/7/18		Co. worked and employed as before. New Strong Pt. at B.16.6.8.7 Accident on. Coy strength 7 off. 211 O.R.	Appx
	26/7/18		Co. worked and employed as before. Coy strength 7 off. 213 O.R.	Appx
	27/7/18		Co. worked and employed as before. Coy strength 7 off. 213 O.R.	Appx
	28/7/18		Co. worked and employed as before. Coy strength 7 off. 212 O.R. Major R.E.	Appx

36th Divisional Engineers

150th FIELD COMPANY R. E.

MARCH 1918

Confidential

War Diary

of

150ᵗʰ Field Coy R.E.

March, 1918

Army Form C. 2118.

WAR DIARY
or
INTELLIGENCE SUMMARY.
(Erase heading not required.)

Place	Date	Hour	Summary of Events and Information	Remarks and references to Appendices
Field	1/3/18		H.Q. Co. Personnel & Sections 2 & 4 Quartered at LE HAMEL in billets. G.I. G.75. Sections 1 + 3 under Lt. STAPYLTON - Bruff. Quartered in billets at BRAY St CHRISTOPHE. L7. 9.7.5. — Took Sections 2 + 4 employed at dismantling Minenwerfer BRIGADE HQRs at G.9.c.2.4 — G.8.a.9.4. — G.G.a.1.7. Coy. Strength 7. Off. 212. O.R.	JM/1
	2/3/18		Company situated as before. No.1. Section strips during "D" work in ST SIMON L.ARTEMPS and Hutt Nos. 1 & 3 sections engaged on preparing bridges in ST SIMON & TUGNY for demolition. Preparation of ARTEMPS group of bridges for demolition handed over to No.4 Section. Nos 2 & 4 sections employed on this in addition to previous work. Company Strength Coy. Strength 7. Off. 212. O.R.	W.O.P.
	3/3/18		H.Qrs, M.O. personnel & Sections 2 & 4 situated as above. Nos 1 & 3 section moved from BRAY St CHRISTOPHE to ST SIMON L.34.d.1.9. Preparation of ARTEMPS group of bridges for demolition completed. Remainder of work as before. Coy. Strength 7 Off. 212. O.R.	D.A.D.S.

Army Form C. 2118.

WAR DIARY
or
INTELLIGENCE SUMMARY.
(Erase heading not required.)

Instructions regarding War Diaries and Intelligence Summaries are contained in F. S. Regs., Part II. and the Staff Manual respectively. Title pages will be prepared in manuscript.

Place	Date	Hour	Summary of Events and Information	Remarks and references to Appendices
	4.3.18		Coy situated as before. Work on Bde. H.Q dugouts at G.9.c.2.8. G.8.a.9.4 handed over to 122 Fd Coy. R.E. Remainder of work as before. Coy. Strength 7 off. 212 O.R.	WTWD
	5.3.18		Coy situated as before. Nos. 1 & 3 sections work continued as before. No 2 section continue work on Bde H.Q. dugout at G.6.d.17. The galleries of this dugout having met, work on the chambers to begun. No 4 section works on erection of extra officers accommodation in billets. Coy. Strength 7 off. 212. O.R.	WTWD
	6.3.18		Coy situated as before Nos 1 & 3 sections work as before with the addition that a part of the town hall in ST SIMON was demolished, as it was in danger of falling. This demolition was completed by evening. No.4 sect. started work on pontoon bridge across ST QUENTIN canal at map ref L.35.d.5.4. R.6.d.5.6. Coy. Strength 8 off. 212 O.R.	WTWD
	7.3.18		Situation & work as before. Pontoon bridge completed. Return to baths at ST SIMON also begun by Nos 1 & 3 sections. 2/Lt Pre.MERCIER joined company as reinforcement. Coy. Strength 8 off. 212 O.R.	WTWD

2353 Wt. W2544/1454 700,000 5/15 D. D. & L.   A.D.S.S. Forms/C. 2118.

Army Form C. 2118.

WAR DIARY
or
INTELLIGENCE SUMMARY.
(Erase heading not required.)

Instructions regarding War Diaries and Intelligence Summaries are contained in F. S. Regs., Part II. and the Staff Manual respectively. Title pages will be prepared in manuscript.

Place	Date	Hour	Summary of Events and Information	Remarks and references to Appendices
	8.3.18.		Company situated as before. Nos. 1, 2 & 3 Sections work as before. No 4 Sect work at various accomodation for Officers, at billet; and also on erecting splinterproof wall round mens' billets. Work on R.E. H.Q. at HAPPENCOURT completed by Nos. 1, 2, 3 Sections. Coy. Strength 8 Off. 212 O.R.	
	9.3.18		Company situated as before. Work as before. Coy. Strength 8 Off. 212 O.R.	
	10.3.18		Company situated as before. Work as before. Coy. Strength 8 Off. 211 O.R.	
	11.3.18		Company situated as before. With addition of repairs to a bridge in ST SIMON the work is also the same. Coy. Strength 8 Off. 211 O.R.	
	12.3.18		Situation & work as before. Repairs to above bridge completed also Ram's Douches at ST SIMON. No 4 Section released demolition of bridges. Coy Strength 8 Off 211 O.R.	

2353 Wt. W2544/1454 700,000 5/15 D. D. & L. A.D.S.S. Forms/C. 2118.

Army Form C. 2118.

WAR DIARY
or
INTELLIGENCE SUMMARY.
(Erase heading not required.)

Place	Date	Hour	Summary of Events and Information	Remarks and references to Appendices
Field	13.3.18		Work & location as before. Practice demolition of ST SIMON group of bridges by No 3 Section. Coy. strength 8 Off. 211 O.R.	
	14.3.18		Work & location as before. Practice demolition of ARTEMPS group of bridges by No 4 Section. Coy Strength 8 Off. 208 O.R.	
	15.3.18		Work & location as before. Coy. Strength 8 Off. 207 O.R.	
	16.3.18		Work & location as before. Coy. Strength 8 Off. 205 O.R.	
	17.3.18		Work & location as before. Major A.N. FORDHAM returned from 3rd Army Infantry School & assumed command of the Company. Coy. Strength 8 Off. 206 O.R.	
	18.3.18		Work & location as before, with addition of work on Neyanta paths in L34d, L33d by Nos 1 & 2 Section. Experimental demolition by No 4 Section. Practice demolition of Artemps TUGNY bridges by No 3 Sect. Coy strength 8 Off. 206 O.R.	

WAR DIARY
or
INTELLIGENCE SUMMARY.
(Erase heading not required.)

Army Form C. 2118.

Place	Date	Hour	Summary of Events and Information	Remarks and references to Appendices
	19/3/18		Work as before. Coy Strength 8 Off. 206 O.R.	#
	20/3/18		Work as before. — Also a trench dugout was commenced by a Williams the trench station at Col. SERAUCOURT — Special Party from No. 2 Butsey Sent. Dressing back to ST. SIMON for practice on Bridge Demolition. Coy Strength 8 Off. 206 O.R.	#
	21/3/18	4am	Coy to Ball Stations 18 hrs 1.3 Butsey & half hr Sec to Bridges at TOGNY & ST. SIMON. 2 ho 4 Sect to Bridges at ARTEMPS — All troops at once changed to immediate readiness for demolition. Between 4 to 5 am heavy shells	
		8am	HQ Transport No. 2 Butsey vacated to HAMEL where shelling was heavy and Horses to TUGNY as prearranged. At 9pm an order from CRE withdrew 2 & 4 Secs to MERCIER dularts to effect but Coy Strength 8 Off 296 O.R.	#
	22/3/18	9am	All bridges at ARTEMPS ST. SIMON & TUGNY demolished — No 1.3 & 4 Secs rejoined Coy at PITHON & GOLAN COURT during the day. 10am the Transport moved to GOLANCOURT Pontoon wagons and to dump shells & fish from HAMD and to OLLEZY. Artillery concentrated 5 hy fire at GOLANCOURT. Coy Strength 8 Off. 203 O.R.	#

Army Form C. 2118.

WAR DIARY
or
INTELLIGENCE SUMMARY.
(Erase heading not required.)

Place	Date	Hour	Summary of Events and Information	Remarks and references to Appendices
GOLANCOURT	23/3/18	9.30am	Coy Transport proceeded by road to FLAVY & across the whole divisional position & held GOLANCOURT with two companies R.E. &	//
		11.30am	Some M.G. attack the whole under orders of Major LOWE. M.G. Coys — R.E. Coys took up line Q.29b central Q.2A a 5.8 P.19 a central — 121m west. 150 kittens 122 Scott. Transport ousted to FRETOY under command of Major OTWAY R.E. Coy strength 8 off 208 O.R.	//
	24/3/18	1am	Under orders from Major LOWE fell back on position at BEAUMEL CHATEAU Page Jones found line we (?) in our afforties. Three tail Coy helpto mea with 30th French Division	
		9am		
	25/3/18	3am	Received orders to withdraw as Coy transport was taking over wheel	
		11am	withdrew entirely of road to BEAULIEU. Transport	
		6pm	Whole Coy & transport proceeded to WASFRY Coy strength 8 off 201 O.R.	

150ᵗʰ Fild Cⁿ. R.E.
Diary March 1918
23ʳᵈ March 11.30 a.m.
"P.19" is a mistake
for "Q.19"

HMStaines
16.12.25

WAR DIARY
or
INTELLIGENCE SUMMARY.

(Erase heading not required.)

Army Form C. 2118.

Place	Date	Hour	Summary of Events and Information	Remarks and references to Appendices
GOLANCOURT	23/3/18	9.30am	Coy Transport proceeded by road to FLAVY & billets in. Whole dismounted portion traction & held GOLANCOURT with the coy some M.G details the whole under orders of Major LOWE. M.G. Coy & R.E. Coys.	#
		11.30am	Took up line Q.29.b central P.24.a.5.8. P.19.a central 131st Inf. 150 inch. 122 Batt. Transport under N. FRETOY under command of Major OTWAY R.E. Coy Strength 8 off 208 O.R.	#
	24/3/18	1am	Under orders from Major LOWE fell back on positions at BEAUMEL CHATEAU coord 72.95. Coy's trench held in B on our left retiring. These held by R.E. for these with 30th Field Division.	
		9am		
	25/3/18	8am	Received orders to withdraw as enemy troops were taking up whole line. Withdraw acting forward to BEAULIEU. Transport to MARGNY. Whole Coy transport arrived MARGNY	#
		6pm	Coy Strength 8 off 201 O.R.	
			Coy Strength 8 off 201 O.R.	

WAR DIARY
or
INTELLIGENCE SUMMARY.
(Erase heading not required.)

Army Form C. 2118.

Place	Date	Hour	Summary of Events and Information	Remarks and references to Appendices
	26/3/18		Wagons drew to LA PELISSE – One Section No 3 to MARES MONTIERS to prepare bridges for demolition. Remaining three Sections filled in at BECQUIVILLE and prepared bridge there for demolition. Coy Strength 8 off. 199 O.R.	
	27/3/18	10am	All 3 Sections withdrawn to MARES MONTIERS leaving small party with Townson bridge at BECQUIGNY	
		5pm	All 3 Sections proceeded to assist French in holding the line South of BOUSSICOURT	
		7.30pm	Bridge at BECQUIGNY destroyed. Coy Strength 8 off. 199 O.R.	
	29/3/18	7am	A Section relieved & withdrawn from French line – bridge at M. Montiers demolished.	
		3pm	Coy Transport arrived at ERAGNY. Three filled 0"	
			Coy Strength 8 off. 199 O.R.	
	29/3/18	8pm	Coy & Transport proceed to VALAMMES crossing river 2k.	1/28/3

Army Form C. 2118.

WAR DIARY
or
INTELLIGENCE SUMMARY.
(Erase heading not required.)

Place	Date	Hour	Summary of Events and Information	Remarks and references to Appendices
	30/3/18	6pm	Coy marched to entrain at SALEUX. Transport starts forward by road to EMBREVILLE	###
		8pm		
		10pm	Coy arrived at SALEUX Station	
			Coy Strength 8 off. 199 O.R.	
	31/3/18	12 noon	Coy entrained for GAMACHES from SALEUX Station	###
		12.30pm	Coy arrived at GAMACHES	
		1.2pm	Coy went into Billets at EMBREVILLE	
		8.15pm	Coy Transport arrived by road to EMBREVILLE & parked there	
			Coy Strength 8 off. 199 O.R.	

H. Fordham
Maj R.E.
O.C. 150th Field Coy.

36th Divisional Engineers

----------- ----

150th FIELD COMPANY R.E. ::: APRIL 1918.

Vol 31

War Diary

of

O.C. 150th Field Company R.E.

for month of April, 1918.

Army Form C. 2118.

WAR DIARY
or
INTELLIGENCE SUMMARY.
(Erase heading not required.)

Place	Date	Hour	Summary of Events and Information	Remarks and references to Appendices
EMBREVILLE	1/4/18		Coy proceed to Halt at EMBREVILLE, near GAMACHES. Coy strength 5 Off. 198 O.R.	
	2/4/18		Coy as before. 1 Officer + party proceed to AULT to prepare to Disposal Bye Baths. Rest of Coy training. Coy strength 6 Off. 198 O.R.	
	3/4/18		Coy as before. Coy strength 6 Off. 198 O.R.	
	4/4/18	4 am	Coy entrained at WOINCOURT for YPRES. Coy strength 6 Off. 198 O.R.	
YPRES SALIENT	5/4/18	2 am	Coy detrained at ROUSBRUGGE. Dismounted portion to billets at DIRTY BUCKET CAMP near VLAMERTINGE. Transport to HOSPITAL FARM. Lt MERCIER	
		5 pm	sent to forward Billet of No 26 Field Coy 1st Div at KEMPTON PARK. N of NIELTJE Bike area. Coy strength 6 Off. 198 O.R.	
	6/4/18		Two Sections N.C.Os. moved up to KEMPTON PARK preparing for relief of 26th rifles Coy on night of 7/8th. Coy strength 6 Off. 198 O.R.	

Army Form C. 2118.

WAR DIARY
or
INTELLIGENCE SUMMARY.
(Erase heading not required.)

Instructions regarding War Diaries and Intelligence Summaries are contained in F. S. Regs., Part II. and the Staff Manual respectively. Title pages will be prepared in manuscript.

Place	Date	Hour	Summary of Events and Information	Remarks and references to Appendices
YPRES - SALIENT	7/4/18	2pm	Registration and Nos 2 & 4 Sections proceeded to new forward Billet at KEMPTON PARK	#
		3pm	Wiring of Strong Points DENYS HOUSE, BAVAROISE (commenced)	
			Coy Strength 7 Off. 198 O.R.	
	8/4/18		Work as before – Work also started on erection of shelter at Bn HQ. Norfolk house for HQ Personnel and on making extra entrance to Pill Box off T.M keep Norfolk house.	#
			Coy Strength 7 Off. 198 O.R.	
	9/4/18	"	Work as before.	#
			Coy Strength 7 Off. 198 O.R.	
	10/4/18	"		#
			Coy Strength 8 Off. 213 O.R.	
	11/4/18			#
			Coy Strength 8 Off. 213 O.R.	

WAR DIARY
or
INTELLIGENCE SUMMARY.
(Erase heading not required.)

Army Form C. 2118.

Place	Date	Hour	Summary of Events and Information	Remarks and references to Appendices
	12/4/18	2 pm	Relieved by 121 Fd Coy R.E. Coy H.Q. setts at Canal bank C.25 d.35. Two Sections commenced Nhorse Bridges 2A-3-3a-36- Causeway-4 2a-5-6 for Demolition. One Section commenced to wire in Bridge heads. Company Strength 7 off 212. O.R.	///
	13/4/18		Work on before. One Section also working on preparing & wiring of Tramway from MINTY FARM to STEENBECK. Coy. Strength 7 off 212. O.R.	///
	14/4/18		Work stopped on tramway. Two Sections wiring in front of bridges. Coy Strength 7 off 210. O.R.	///
	15/4/18		All bridges ready for demolition, wiring almost completed. Coy. Strength 7 off 210. O.R.	///
	16/4/18		Mounted Section and transport lines moved onto P.Downs farm journal camp C.A9.a.37 o.2 Coy. Strength 7 off 210. O.R.	///

Army Form C. 2118.

WAR DIARY
or
INTELLIGENCE SUMMARY.
(Erase heading not required.)

Place	Date	Hour	Summary of Events and Information	Remarks and references to Appendices
Canal Bank	17/4/18		Coy working on Salvage of hunts huts at Turco Farm & Camp & of huts huts on Rly Siding	
YPRES			Coy Strength 7 Off. 201 O.R.	
	18/4/18		Two Sections employed on Salvage & drawing of hutages at Turco Camp & huts and on CANAL BANK. Coy Strength 7 Off. 200 O.R.	
		2 p.m	Pl Zonne "A" mun & 1 No 2 & 4 section proceeded to Transport Lines 7718a 87. 1 & 3 Section on Canal Bank defences Wire Netting & partial 1 Coy 14th AIF (?) 1 Coy inf.	A.1.
			Two sections found billet as before.	
	19/4/18		No 2 and 4 sections employed on fatigues then dull weather action officers & reme. authorised to wear Badges of Baptism ranks. Coy Strength 7 Off. 202 O.R.	A.1
	20/4/18		Forward sections Walken before Canal Bank E defences to Reserve from 12th to by RE. Coy Strength M Off. 202 O.R.	A.1.
			Rear sections on dugs road wiring & reflected services	
	21/4/18		Work commenced on East Bank of Canal, digging reserve and reiring & of the new front and continuing wiring in front of them. Offe work was on Before trenches. 1 Coy Pioneers 3 coys Inf. Coy Strength. 7 Off. 202 O.R.	
			Rear section Church parade. Proceeded Section Reserve inspection	A.1

WAR DIARY
~~INTELLIGENCE SUMMARY~~
(Erase heading not required.)

Army Form C. 2118.

Instructions regarding War Diaries and Intelligence Summaries are contained in F.S. Regs., Part II, and the Staff Manual respectively. Title pages will be prepared in manuscript.

Place	Date	Hour	Summary of Events and Information	Remarks and references to Appendices
	22/4/18		No 2 & 4 Sections pulled. Then marched up to Canal bank under Lt Dennis RE to relieve No 1 & 3 sects.	
			"1" Pn men preceded them to take over from Lt Smith.	A.7.
			Work as before.	
			Coy Strength 7 Officers 20 O.R.	
	23/4/18		Capt Jenion to forward billets as new work. Nos 1 & 3 Section duck inspection	B.2.
			Work as before. No.1 Coy Pioneers relieved from CANAL BANK and put on to enlarge PITTSBURG	
			Camp. Rear sections drill. Coy Strength 7 Officers 106 O.R.	C.2.
	24/4/18		Work as before. 4 new platoon posts in East Bank of CANAL and Brown posts	
			on W bank to about 4 of 3 Bn Infantry camp. Rear sections training.	C.2.
			Coy Strength 4 Officers 197. O.R.	C.2.
	25/4/18		As before.	
	26.		As before. Lt Morris and 10 men to von Luven forward section moved to Canal	C.2.
			Camp. Coy Strength 7 oft. 197. O.R.	C.2.
	27.		Nos 2 & 4 Sections with Lt Dennis and Lt Burnyeate on W bank testing out guard	
			bridges. Rear sections standing to. Orders for relief received Coy Strength 7oft. 196. O.R.	C.2.
	28"		Transport and rear sections moved to HIRST CAMP. H.19.a.0.2.	
			Work on east & west banks of Canal as before.	
			Coy Strength 7 oft. 196 O.R.	

Army Form C. 2118.

WAR DIARY
or
INTELLIGENCE SUMMARY.
(Erase heading not required.)

Instructions regarding War Diaries and Intelligence Summaries are contained in F. S. Regs., Part II. and the Staff Manual respectively. Title pages will be prepared in manuscript.

Place	Date	Hour	Summary of Events and Information	Remarks and references to Appendices
	29/1/18		Work forward on Canal Bank defences as before. Work also commenced on hasty an Infantry track from road at C.19.d.3.2 to a ft. bridge across marsh & right to C.25.d.3.8. (as an alternative means of getting across canal at Bridge 3.B.) Rear lewis gun training. Coy Strength 2 Off. 106 OR	
	30/1/18		Work on Track & Canal Bank defences continued. Coy Strength 2 Off. 193 OR	

JH Fordham
Maj R.E.

150th FIELD COY. R.E.

Confidential
War Diary
of
150th Infantry Regt.
from April 1st to April 30/1918

WR 32

Confidential
War Diary
of
150th Field Coy R.E.

From May 1st to May 31st.
1918

Army Form C. 2118.

WAR DIARY
or
INTELLIGENCE SUMMARY.
(Erase heading not required.)

Place	Date	Hour	Summary of Events and Information	Remarks and references to Appendices
Forward Billet for 2 Section Canal Bank	1/5/18		Forward work Defences of East West bank of Canal in 100 m Bygge Creek from Railway Bridge C.25 a.5.0 to C.25 d.5.1 consisting	
YPRES C.25 a.8.2 Wagon lines and two Sections			of 8 Platoon Posts on each side — Posts have practically dug out and were revetted around. Company Strength Officers 1 O.R. 193 All bridges from Bridge 4 to 2A prepared for Demolition	
HURST CAMP A.10 A.02			Tracks in hand almost complete (for Infantry) from C.25 d and Bridges Reav Sections employed on transport work and making huts in Camp. Annouval Tubes also preparing Railway bridge over POPERINGHE Canal for small cov at C 22 2.7.9	
	2/5/18		Work as before Nos 1 – 5 Sections sent forward to relieve 2 C.M. who came back to wagon lines. Company Strength Officers 1 O.R. 193	
	3/5/18		Work as before in forward area. Infantry track line complete. Company Strength Officers 1 O.R. 193	

WAR DIARY or INTELLIGENCE SUMMARY

Army Form C. 2118.

Place	Date	Hour	Summary of Events and Information	Remarks and references to Appendices
as before	4/5/18		Work as before	
	5/5/18		Company Strength Officers 7 O.R. 193	
			Work on Railway Bridge nr POPERINGHE canal completed by No 2 Section. No 4 Section Training — No 1 & 3 Lecting at Forward billets working on Canal Bank defences as before. Company Strength Officers 7 O.R. 193	
	6/5/18		No 1 & 3 Sections as before No 2 & 4 training — do —	a.9
	7/5/18		No 1 & 3 Sections as before No 2 & 4 Training Company Strength Officers 7 O.R. 203	a.7
	8/5/18		No 1 as before. No 3 took over admin of left inclusive km WIEHT7 No 2 & 4 both Company Strength Officers 7 O.R. 203	a.7
	9/5/18		No 1 & 3 Sections as before No 2 & 4 as before — do —	a.7
	10/5/18		No 1 & 3 Sections relieved by No 2 & 4 & later Bugs to billets Two Bridges taken over from Division on Staffen clearance. Company Strength Officers 7 O.R. 204 a.7	

Army Form C. 2118.

WAR DIARY
or
INTELLIGENCE SUMMARY.
(Erase heading not required.)

Instructions regarding War Diaries and Intelligence Summaries are contained in F. S. Regs., Part II. and the Staff Manual respectively. Title pages will be prepared in manuscript.

Place	Date	Hour	Summary of Events and Information	Remarks and references to Appendices
As before	11/5/18		Troops as from 2.3.3. 91 coyRE on one Bn Front held a newly RE's 107th Bde who relieved B.W. 41st Div	
			Demolition of Band Bridge & Salvation Army & Gutting of W&J X rds taken over by new sector	
			Nº 1 & 3 Sect as before Continuing Bancourt Line R	Q.7
	12/5/18		Work commenced on new support line in KAR IE and YPRES DEFENCES. Jam Nº 2 bridge to DICKBUSH GATE	
			Work on Canal Bank N of Nº 2 bridge given up. Nº 1 & 3. as before Embankment Q.N.Y. OR.20.Y	Q.7
	13/5/18		Nº 1 & 3 Towing as before Nº 2 & 4 Work commenced in putting a line of L.P.	
			under Canvas near Nº 2 Ridge. Other work going on before	Q.7
	14/5/18		Nº 1 & 3 as before commenced in covering col. 15.6.6. — do —	Q.7
	15/5/18		Nº 1 & 3. as before Nº 2 & 4. Bridges 3.A. 3.B. 4. scavenging 4.A. 5.6. Rendel SW to 12.2 NW 6.4.	
			Other demolitions including "Mint take ine" from 41st Div. as before. Work on KNOLL R.15 Y.F.R.5	
			defence as before Contour Strength OR.4. OR.20.Y	Q.7
	16/5/18		Nº 1 & 3 as before. Nº 2 & 4. Work on KNOLL & YPRES defences as before. Work also starte on the	
			new siding on old Pru Gov entrenched nr C.27.d. 5.1 near ST JEAN Embankment OR.4. OR.20.Y	Q.7

Army Form C. 2118.

WAR DIARY
or
INTELLIGENCE SUMMARY.
(Erase heading not required.)

Place	Date	Hour	Summary of Events and Information	Remarks and references to Appendices
As before	17/5/18		No 1 & 2 As before. No 3 Coy to CANAL BANK to billets area west of from Pderina	a 7
			Work as before day	
			Company Strength Off 9 OR 206	
			No 1 & 2 As before. No 3 Coy to CANAL BANK	
		18/5/18	Work as before day	a 8
			Company Strength Off 9 OR 211	
		19/5/18	No 1 & 2 As before. No 3 commenced Railway up from Lock N°1 & 3 Setion also had	
			N° 264 & returned to HIRST CAMP.	a 9
			Company Strength Off 9 OR 211	
		20th	Work as before in front Eng. KRUL defences & S' JEAN R.E. Coy C37 & Sn Work commenced	
			wiring in line for Flank defence from Bow ends at C.27.d.7.4 along N°1 Front	
			Found Rly 2 to avoid at I.21.a. 20 Small rafts for use by infy in crossing	
			the ands. Back Section timing	at
			Company Strength Off 9 OR 211	
			— do —	
	21st		As before	
	22/5/18		Work as before. Saw traffic of Enge H.Q. in front hack moved	10
			Company Strength Off 9 OR 210	

WAR DIARY
or
INTELLIGENCE SUMMARY
(Erase heading not required.)

Army Form C. 2118.

Place	Date	Hour	Summary of Events and Information	Remarks and references to Appendices
in the	23/5/18		Work on KAAIE defences from the posts M.G. Pill boxes & for proof as before	
			Company strength Off. 4 O.R. 210	
	24/5/18		Work as previous day	
			Company strength Off. 4 O.R. 208	
	25/5/18		Work as before. All ranks & officers warned to be in readiness at 6.28 & at 9.25 to move forward to counter attack coys A&B a6298aa in front of counter attack coys A&B d.6.9 in front of counter attack coys A&B up will existing belt at I.2.T.T through Pagoda wood.	
			Company strength Off. 4 O.R. 208	
	26/5/18		All work on defences & back billet leaving drawing duty & three parties	
			Company strength Off. 4 O.R. 210	
	27/5/18		All work on defences in forward & back area	
			Company strength Off. 4 O.R. 210	

WAR DIARY
or
INTELLIGENCE SUMMARY.
(Erase heading not required.)

Army Form C. 2118.

Place	Date	Hour	Summary of Events and Information	Remarks and references to Appendices
Oulx	28/5/18		All work as previous day. Company Strength Officers 7 O.R. 210	
	29/5/18		Work as before. Men in line a KAMIE defences. A few details for details at lettering of camps. Siege Group other work in HIRST Camp as before. Men in forward area Ypres stands before as before. Salvation Camp at I.1. d.50-55. Company Strength Off. 7 O.R. 211.	
	30/5/18		Work in forward area as before. Suring Drawing Stores standing at HIRST CAMP Continued. Company Strength Off. 7 O.R. 211	

Army Form C. 2118.

WAR DIARY
or
INTELLIGENCE SUMMARY.
(Erase heading not required.)

Instructions regarding War Diaries and Intelligence Summaries are contained in F. S. Regs., Part II. and the Staff Manual respectively. Title pages will be prepared in manuscript.

Place	Date	Hour	Summary of Events and Information	Remarks and references to Appendices
YPRES Salient as before	3/5/18		Work in forward areas as before. Bridge repair at T.1.d.50.55 completed. Work in back areas as before.	
			Company transpt Orders y. O.R. 911	

JM Foshorn
Major RE
O.C. 130th Field Coy RE

31/5/18

WA 33

Confidential

War Diary

of

150th Field Coy. R.E.

June, 1918.

WAR DIARY
or
INTELLIGENCE SUMMARY.
(Erase heading not required.)

Army Form C. 2118.

Place	Date	Hour	Summary of Events and Information	Remarks and references to Appendices
Back billet	1/6/18		Major H.M. FORDHAM R.E. O.C Coy proceeded to UK on 14 days leave of absence	
Wagon lines			No 201 Lutons relieved No 1 & 3 at Harwood billet in Canal Bank	
HIRST CAMP				
A·10 A.O.2			Forward area work. Line off KAAIE Defences from Bridge 3 across	
Forward Billet			Canal at C 25 d 5.6 to DIXMUDE GATE (I 8 a 4.8) Continued	
2nd Canal			Resiting & improving of the line generally & wiring	
Bank dugouts			joining up of front line positions from WIELTJE to	
YPRES			PROWSE FARM (C.22 d.4.3) Continued	
C.25 a.8.2			Wiring a new belt from C.28 b.9.0 to C.28 d.6.9	
			to C.28 C.9.5 - 2.5 then through PAGODA WOOD to join up with	
			existing belt at I 4 a 7.7	
			Concreting a Pill Box near ST JEAN at G 27 d.6.5	
			Wiring a line from C.27 d.7.4 along to 6 Track to road	
			at I 2 a 3.0 Continued - Rifle Pits dug along this line	
			Gas proofing of M.G. dugouts in & round the KAAIE line commenced	

A 1043. Wt. W11422/M1160 350,000 12/16 D. D. & L. Form/C/2118/14.

WAR DIARY
or
INTELLIGENCE SUMMARY.

(Erase heading not required.)

Army Form C. 2118.

Place	Date	Hour	Summary of Events and Information	Remarks and references to Appendices
Back Area	1/6/18		at HIRST Camp [Proburgts & Kunjarmark V.C. & T/2 P.C. Kaaswhe]	
			Road Repair 36th Geo Order 1st June	
			Drainage Leving Stove Standings	
	2/4/18		Training of No 1 & 3 Sections generally. By group 208 SR	7.9.R
			No 1 & 3 section on before No 2 section on wire No 4 section Gas Defence as before	A2
	3/6/18		No 2 & 4 Section by CANAL BANK in afternoon all parades to HIRST CAMP by alright 7.07 & 20 P.W.R	
			Lt Steavens & Lt Brangate Reported for Duty	
			to 458 Coy RE and the demolitions and wiring by a platoon of infantry of 12th Belgian Division. Closed with usual work by P.R. in Hirst Camp	A2
	4/4/18		Coy left HIRST CAMP and proceeded by rail to BALL CAMP E 31.79.27 6.9.4.6.17 7/7 & "17 P.R."	
	5/6/18		Taking over pasts previously invested to Blue Line East POPERINGHE SUPPORT (Old - Gas Rooks) 2 section and GREEN LINE VLAMERTINGHE (1) 836 - Coys Generally 2 Section Reconnd of Coy in huts in camp. Cap Danis took over the CAE 338 & Lieut caftair Coutteril reported 20 7 o.8	
			Information re work Army Strength 7 off 207 OR	

WAR DIARY
or
INTELLIGENCE SUMMARY
(Erase heading not required.)

Army Form C. 2118.

Place	Date	Hour	Summary of Events and Information	Remarks and references to Appendices
BAPS CAMP	6/6/18		No 1 and 2 sections to work on GRENAPE ve setting No 3 S.B. on BAPS tram workings T.3	
	7/6/18		at ( ) 6th	By strength 7 off 207 O.R.	a.y
			on 6th		
	8/6/18		As on 6th. Party from B.3 tch to A.3d for work on Rail line	a.y
				By strength 7 off 207 O.R.	
	9/6/18		Church parade and inspection of units, conference C.O. C.R.E.	By strength 7 off 207 O.R.	a.y
	10/6/18		All four sections on VLAMERTINGHE line. Telephone construction attached No 2 Sec. to H.3b.4.6 to A.3d.1.5. front. No 1 sect A.3d.1.5 to H.14.a.3.8. No 4 on night school No 3 sec. N13	a.y
			cmpt behind No 1. Working pts 2 sergeants of infantry, by strength 7 off 207 O.R.	
	11/7/18		Working Plts. N sec. working	PARADE & REHEARSAL. By strength 7 off 207 O.R.	a.y
	12/6/18		Work on Elev. Cc. trench No. 3 sect of scaffolding. By strength 7 off 207 O.R.	a
	13/6/18		Work on Elev. Tel by	By strength 7 off 207 O.R.	a.y

Army Form C. 2118.

WAR DIARY
or
INTELLIGENCE SUMMARY.
(Erase heading not required.)

Instructions regarding War Diaries and Intelligence Summaries are contained in F. S. Regs., Part II. and the Staff Manual respectively. Title pages will be prepared in manuscript.

Place	Date	Hour	Summary of Events and Information	Remarks and references to Appendices
FRAMES	14/6/18		Coy played football match v C6. Coy strength 7 Off. 207 O.R.	A2
"	15/6/18		Coy employed in musketry training. Major H.M. FORDHAM R.E. returned from 14 days leave to U.K. & resumed command of the Coy. Coy strength 7 Off. 207 O.R.	#
	16/6/18		Church parade & Rifle Inspection. Coy strength 7 Off. 4138 O.R.	#
	17/6/18		Training & musketry Boyle range	#
	18/6/18		Training & musketry Coy strength 7 Off. 208 O.R.	#
	19/6/18		Training & musketry Coy strength 7 Off. 208 O.R.	#
	20/6/18		As before Coy strength 7 Off. 208 O.R.	#

Army Form C. 2118.

WAR DIARY
or
INTELLIGENCE SUMMARY.
(Erase heading not required.)

Instructions regarding War Diaries and Intelligence Summaries are contained in F. S. Regs., Part II. and the Staff Manual respectively. Title pages will be prepared in manuscript.

Place	Date	Hour	Summary of Events and Information	Remarks and references to Appendices
As before	21/6/18		Coy Training – Drill musketry & Bayonet fighting Coy Strength 7 Off. 209. O.R.	
	22/6/18		Coy Training as before – Reserve line south of POPERINGHE. VLAMERTINGHE Road to POPERINGHE. BUSSE BOM Road. Reconnoitred prior to taking over from 122 Coy – Coy Strength 7 Off. 209. O.R.	
	23/6/18		Coy Training & Church parade as before. Coy Strength 7 Off. 210. O.R.	
	24/6/18		WaR. on E. POPERINGHE Res line taken over & Sections working. Major H.M. Jadhum. M.C. R.E. handed over command of Coy to 2/Capt. H. Ferrier temporarily. Coy Strength 6 Off. 210. O.R. Major J.H. Otway R.E. took over command of the company. No 1 Section training in Trenches. 2, 3 & 4 Sections in E. POPERINGHE Res line.	
	25/6/18		Coy Strength 7 Officers 212. O.R.	a.2
	26/6/18		No 2 Section musketry with front of Wg. real. 1, 3, 4 work as usual Coy Strength 7 Officers 210. O.R.	a.2

A6945. Wt. W14422/M1160 350,000 12/16 D. D. & L. Forms/C/2118/14.

Army Form C. 2118.

WAR DIARY
or
INTELLIGENCE SUMMARY.
(Erase heading not required.)

Instructions regarding War Diaries and Intelligence Summaries are contained in F.S. Regs., Part II. and the Staff Manual respectively. Title pages will be prepared in manuscript.

Place	Date	Hour	Summary of Events and Information	Remarks and references to Appendices
PRAWET	14/6/18		Coy started General musketry, Rifle inspection etc. Coy strength 7 Off. 207 O.R.	A4
	15/6/18		Coy employed on musketry training. Major H.M. FORDHAM R.E. returned from 14 days leave to U.K. & resumed command of the Coy. Coy strength 7 Off. 208 O.R.	#
	16/6/18		Church parade & rifle inspection. Coy strength 7 Off. 208 O.R.	#
	17/6/18		Training musketry 30 yds range	#
	18/6/18		Training musketry — Coy strength 7 Off. 208 O.R.	#
	19/6/18		Training musketry — Coy strength 7 Off. 208 O.R.	#
	20/6/18		As before. Coy Strength 7 Off. 208 O.R.	#

WAR DIARY
or
INTELLIGENCE SUMMARY.

Army Form C. 2118.

Place	Date	Hour	Summary of Events and Information	Remarks and references to Appendices
As before	21/6/18		Coy Training - Drill including Bayonet fighting. Coy Strength 7 Off. 209 O.R.	
	22/6/18		Coy Training as before - Reserve line South of POPERINGHE - VLAMERTINGHE Road to POPERINGHE - BUSSEBOM ROAD reinforced prior to taking over from 122 Coy - Coy Strength 7 Off. 209 O.R.	
	23/6/18		Coy Training & Such parties as before. Coy Strength 7 Off. 210 O.R.	
	24/6/18		War on E. POPERINGHE Res line taken over & Sections working. Major H.M. Jadham M.C. R.E. Devoted over command of Coy to 2/Capt H Ferris temporarily.	
	25/6/18		Major J.H. Otway R.E. took over command of the company. No 1 Section training in Buseboom 2, 3 & 4 Sections on E POPERINGHE Res line. Coy Strength 7 Officers 210 O.R.	2d
	26/6/18		No 2 Section working with half of No 3 and 1, 3, 4 work as usual. Coy Strength 7 Officers 210 O.R.	ad

Army Form C. 2118.

WAR DIARY
or
INTELLIGENCE SUMMARY.
(Erase heading not required.)

Instructions regarding War Diaries and Intelligence Summaries are contained in F.S. Regs., Part II. and the Staff Manual respectively. Title pages will be prepared in manuscript.

Place	Date	Hour	Summary of Events and Information	Remarks and references to Appendices
PROVEN	27/8/18		Same as the N°3 Sect Inspection	A?
	28/8/18		Same as yesterday. N°4 Sect working on horse lines	A?
			Coy Strength 7 Officers 208 O.R.	
	29/8/18		Same as yesterday	A?
			Coy Strength 7 Officers 208 O.R.	
	30/8/18		Same as yesterday	A?
			Coy Strength 7 Officers 208 O.R.	
			Coy Strength 7 Officers 208 O.R.	

A Penn Capt RE
O.C. 150th FIELD COY. R.E.

30/1/8

YSL 34

Confidential

War Diary
- of -
150th Field Coy R.E.
July 1918.

Army Form C. 2118.

WAR DIARY
or
INTELLIGENCE SUMMARY.
(Erase heading not required.)

Instructions regarding War Diaries and Intelligence Summaries are contained in F. S. Regs., Part II. and the Staff Manual respectively. Title pages will be prepared in manuscript.

Place	Date	Hour	Summary of Events and Information	Remarks and references to Appendices
PROVEN	1/7/18		Divisional Horse Show. 150th Inf. 2nd in Leader class. 4th in 6 horse teams	O.2
ST JAN TER BIEZEN	2/7/18		Whole Coy. moved at 3.0 A.M. L. BALL gun. Coy Strength 7 Off. 208 O.R. at TRUITER BIEZEN	O.2
B.6.c.2.7 O.20.c.4.2	3/7/12		Whole Coy. moved & could bomb at S.P. & Rel 2706 Divisional O.20.c.4.2. Coy Strength 7 Off. 208.O.R.	34
"	4/7/18		Coy on leaving out tribunes Coy Strength 7 Off. 208.O.R.	O.2
"	5/7/18		As before grays tid buzy on tribunes at C.R.G.R. Coy Strength 7 Off. 208.O.R.	O.2
"	6/7/18		Do. Do. Coy Strength 7 Off. 208.O.R.	
EECKE	7/7/18		Whole Coy. moved. No.3 Sect under L.C.Odeer GOT LEWIS GUNS WET. Coy Strength 7 Off. 208.O.R.	O.2
EECKE				
"	8/7/18		Coy employed on drums drills and training No.2 Sect on days of Divisional Sports at ?. Coy Strength 7 Off. 208.O.R.	O.2

Army Form C. 2118.

WAR DIARY
or
INTELLIGENCE SUMMARY.
(Erase heading not required.)

Instructions regarding War Diaries and Intelligence Summaries are contained in F. S. Regs., Part II. and the Staff Manual respectively. Title pages will be prepared in manuscript.

Place	Date	Hour	Summary of Events and Information	Remarks and references to Appendices
EECKE (Nord)	9/7/18		As before	Coy strength 7 Off 209 O.R.	A.2.
	10/7/18		As before	Coy strength 7 Off 209 O.R.	A.2.
	11/7/18		As before	Coy strength 7 Off 209 O.R.	A.2.
	12/7/18		As before	Coy strength 7 Off 209 O.R.	A.2.
	13/7/18		As before	Coy strength 7 Off 209 O.R.	A.2.
	14/7/18		As before	Coy strength 7 Off 209 O.R.	A.2.
	15/7/18		As before	Coy strength 7 Off 209 O.R.	A.2.
	16/7/18		As before	Coy strength 7 Off 209 O.R.	A.2.

WAR DIARY
or
INTELLIGENCE SUMMARY.
(Erase heading not required.)

Army Form C. 2118.

Place	Date	Hour	Summary of Events and Information	Remarks and references to Appendices
EECKE	17/7/18	—	As before. Coy strength 7 Off 209 O.R.	A.1
	18/7/18		As before. Coy Strength 7 Off 209 O.R.	A.2
	19/7/18		As before. Coy Strength 7 Off 209 O.R.	A.1
	20/7/18		As before. No 1 Sect took over demolition of Railway lines in GODE EWOUT & Coy strength 200 O.R. 7 Off	A.R
	21/7/18		As before. No 4 Sect started work on Bank lines Coy strength 7 Off 206 O.R.	A.R
	22/7/18		Company relieved the 122nd/64 R.E. O.C. in N° 2 1 Sect in MONT DES CATS. N° 1 3 & 4 Sect & Coy Command out from Hdqrs remain at EECKE. Coy strength 7 Off 206 O.R.	
			MONT NOIR. 2nd i/c Compand out from Hdqrs remain at EECKE. Coy Strength 7 Off 206 O.R.	
			Work of Sections. Rest whole of N°2 Sect BLUE LINE R 36.6.7.9 - R 35.6.97. Group 4	
			Dug out at Coy H.Q. N°3 Sect. Visual reserves sta R 20.c.9.1.35 Work over ½ Ply.	
			Also B.C. Post R 22 d 10 9 2 Work into N° 2 also brewing BENTHIN Road	
			Left subsector N° 1 Sct. Left Batt H.Q. 9-3 pm M 3 6 d 40.95 emplacing	
			Shelter Screening Cap Post M 36 d 60.12 - R 36 a 78 40th Bde M.G.S	
			No 4 Sct. BLUE LINE W 26 d 60.12 = R 36 a 78 40th Bde M.G.S	
			a Batt. Infantry.	
	23/7/18		Same as before. W.O. N° 8 No 3 Sct Took over B.C.post D.153 R.F.A. R 26 C 80 34	A.2
			also No 1 Sct took W.O.N° 10 Screening area. R 16 d R.U.C. R 26.6.3 R 22.26.95 to R 16 d 20 12 Coy strength 7 O. 206. O.R.	

Army Form C. 2118.

WAR DIARY
or
INTELLIGENCE SUMMARY.
(Erase heading not required.)

Instructions regarding War Diaries and Intelligence Summaries are contained in F. S. Regs., Part II. and the Staff Manual respectively. Title pages will be prepared in manuscript.

Place	Date	Hour	Summary of Events and Information	Remarks and references to Appendices
EECKE	24/7/18	—	Coy Strength 7.O. 206.O.R.	O.?
	25/7/18	—	Same as before. Coy. Strength 7.O. 206.O.R.	O.?
	26/7/18	—	Same as before. Coy. Strength 7.O. 206.O.R.	O.?
	27/7/18	—	Same as before. Coy Strength 7.O. 204.O.R.	O.?
	28.7.18	—	Co Employed on trenches as before. Capt A Lewis proceeded on Short leave to Paris. Duties of 2nd in Command taken over by Lt. V.S. Denson. Coy Strength 7 Off & 204.O.R.	Appx
	29.7.18	—	As before. No. 3 Harvest and works Order No. 10 to 17/18. 2 Co 16 R.I.R. (P) for execution under Revesin OC there to No. 3 Section but one Lewis Gun. No. 11 - Signallers Post for 407 Batt RFA at R.21.c. 90.35. No. 1 Section took over Charge. Assumed Maintenance of C.T. through M.26.d. Coy Strength 7O. 204.O.R.	Appx

WAR DIARY
or
INTELLIGENCE SUMMARY

(Erase heading not required.)

Army Form C. 2118.

Place	Date	Hour	Summary of Events and Information	Remarks and references to Appendices
	30.7.18		Coy Return took in Cleaning, driving & Check Parades of F.C.T. to M 31.C.	Offrs
			Co-Strength 7.O.2O4.O.R.	Offrs
			As before. Co-Strength 7.O.2O4.O.R.	Offrs
	31.7.18		As before. Corpl & 1 Sapper took over Charge of x Corps Advanced Dump at R 22.C.7.5. Co-Strength 7.O.2O4.O.R.	

Signature
Major M.
O.C. 150 Field Co. M.

WR 35

Confidential

War Diary

of

150th Field Coy. R.E.

August 1918.

Place	Date	Hour	Summary of Events and Information	Remarks and references to Appendices
Field.	1/6/18		Oct. & No 3, 2 & 3 Sections filling in dugouts Mont Des Cats. R.19.c.37. No 3 1 & 4 Sections at Mont Noir. M.20.c.1.1. Huts 27 & 28. 2nd Lt. Crammond & horse Lines at EECKE Q.26.a.6.3. No 2 & 3 Sections employed on construction of BLUE LINE. R.36.a.7.9. R.35.c.9.9. Night work with Infantry Anonsby to 1 Battalion. Also various B.C. Posts for Artillery. Screening of roads & various Brigade works. No 1 & 4 Sections on BLUE LINE M.26.d. 60.12. — R36. a.7.9. working partys Anonsby to 2 Battalions. Also improvements to forward Communication trenches through M.26.d. and. M.31.6, Also Brigade work, gas proofing etc — also construction of 5.9 proof dug out in Quarry for the 2 sections to live in. Coy. Strength 7 Off. 206 O.R.	Gas
	2/6/18		Company worked work as before. Raining hard all day. Work stopped in consequence. Coy. Strength 7 Off. 206 O.R.	

Army Form C. 2118.

WAR DIARY
or
INTELLIGENCE SUMMARY

(Erase heading not required.)

Instructions regarding War Diaries and Intelligence Summaries are contained in F. S. Regs., Part II. and the Staff Manual respectively. Title Pages will be prepared in manuscript.

Place	Date	Hour	Summary of Events and Information	Remarks and references to Appendices
	3/6/18		Co. located & work as before. N° Digging Parties were able to work last night owing to rain. And very little work was done. 2nd Lt J.G. MAIR. R.E. Seriously wounded about 11pm on BLUE LINE from Shellfire. Coy. Strength 6 Off. 207. O.R.	JNO
	4/6/18		Company located & work as before. Two picked Sappers left Kirkland sent back to take stump to a Qreen in coordinates of Command out of road. Coy. Strength 6 Off. 207. O.R.	JNO
	5/6/18		Co. located & work as before. No working parties were available last night. Infantry being given a rest. Coy. Strength 6 Off. 207. O.R.	JNO
	6/6/18		Co. located & work as before. 2nd Lt C L KNOX V.C. was presented with the V.C. by H.M. the King. Coy. Strength 6 Off. 207. O.R.	JNO

WAR DIARY
or
INTELLIGENCE SUMMARY

Army Form C. 2118.

Place	Date	Hour	Summary of Events and Information	Remarks and references to Appendices
	7/5/18		C. tested work as before. 122nd Field Co. sent up Officers & N.C.O.s to reconnoitre work, then ord all details.	Apps
	8/5/18		Coy. strength 6 Off. 207. O.R. All work by then to be taken over by 122nd Field Co. R.E. and all work carried out by 122nd F'd Co. taken over by this Co. Nos 1 & 3 Sections moved from present billets to new billets in GODEWAERSVELDE & took charge of Divisional Dumps there. Under 2nd offr C. L. KNOX V.C. 2nd & No. 2 & 4 Sections moved back to their old billets by this O.C. & No. 2 & 4 Sections moved back to their old billets by this O.C. & No. 2 & 4 Sections took and manning of Saw Mill there. No. 1 Sec. at EECKE took and in billet work there Also all took billet work Coy. strength 6 O. 207 O.R.	Apps
	9/5/18		2 Sections at Dump at GODE. O/C. 2 Sections & more Sum at EECKE. Work as above. Coy. strength 6 O. 207 O.R.	Apps

Army Form C. 2118.

WAR DIARY
or
INTELLIGENCE SUMMARY

(Erase heading not required.)

Instructions regarding War Diaries and Intelligence Summaries are contained in F. S. Regs., Part II. and the Staff Manual respectively. Title Pages will be prepared in manuscript.

Place	Date	Hour	Summary of Events and Information	Remarks and references to Appendices
EECKE	10/3/18		Work on Pylon	a.1
	11/3/18		O.C. proceeded to Officers rest camp HOULGATE and 2nd in command returned from leave in France and took over.	a.2
			Coy. Strength 6 Off. 207 O.R.	
	12/3/18		Lieut V.P. Dennis proceeded to Sir John Jacksons for the course. Work on Pylon.	a.2
			Coy. Strength 6 Off. 207 O.R.	
	13/3/18		Work on Pylon.	
			Coy. Strength 6 Off. 207 O.R.	
	14/3/18		Lectures from instructors reported from 9th R Sussex Inst. Instructional work and grenade given. NCO's placed under instructor. System of carrying from C.R.E. to field a mess coals as disposed of L.O.S.C. 12th and 122nd Field Coys R.E. to take effect at their movements.	a.1
			Coy. Strength 6 Off. 207 O.R.	
	15/3/18		No's 2 and 4 Section relieved No's 1 and 3. 2/Lt Ch. Knox R.E. and 2 O.R. returned to work under O.C. 122nd Coy R.E. CRE's Btte E/14/53	a.2
			Coy. Strength 6 Off. 207 O.R.	
	16/3/18		Pt J.B. Stygalm Smith act relate JM 1 + 3 Cohen dated work for 12/17/14 45 down trees make main frames etc.	a.1
			Coy. Strength 6 Off. 207 O.R.	

2449 Wt. W14957/M90 750,000 1/16 J.B.C. & A. Forms/C.2118/12.

WAR DIARY or INTELLIGENCE SUMMARY

Army Form C. 2118.

Place	Date	Hour	Summary of Events and Information	Remarks and references to Appendices
EECKE (NORD)	17/8/18		Coy strength 6 Off. 207. O.R.	
	18/8/18		As before. Coy strength " 6 Off. 207. O.R.	
	19/8/18		As before. Coy strength " 6 Off. 207. O.R.	
	20/8/18		As before. Coy Strength 6 Off. 207. O.R.	
	21/8/18		No 1 Section moved to Belleh cut MONT DES CATS, to carry out work under O.C. 122nd Coy. Remainder as before. Coy Strength 6 Off. 207. O.R.	A.F.
	22/8/18		As Before. Lt J.B. Stapleton-Smith to see 171 Tun Coy R.E. re taking over demolitions at Q.22.C.7.0. and Q.18.a.6.2. Major J.H. Otway returned from IX Corps rest station and took over command of company. Coy Strength 6 Off. 207. O.R.	A.F.
	23/8/18		As before. Lt J.B. Stapleton-Smith M.C. R.E. took over demolitions at Q.22.C.7.0 and Q.18.a.6.2 from 171 Tun Coy R.E. Demolition of railway at Q.23.b.2.6 also taken over by Lt Brungate R.E. Coy Strength 6 Off. 207.O.R.	
	24/8/18		Brownthroop at Lt Brungate R.E. and 2 O.R. proceeded on detachment to Div H.Q. for work on IX Corps Stone throw grounds.	

Army Form C. 2118.

WAR DIARY
or
INTELLIGENCE SUMMARY
(Erase heading not required.)

Instructions regarding War Diaries and Intelligence Summaries are contained in F. S. Regs., Part II. and the Staff Manual respectively. Title Pages will be prepared in manuscript.

Place	Date	Hour	Summary of Events and Information	Remarks and references to Appendices
EECKE	24/8/13		As before. Lieut V.D. Dennis R.E. went down to GODEWAERSELDE DUMP to take charge. Coy Strength	a 7
	25/8/13		As before. Lieut V.D. Dennis R.E. admitted to N° 2 C.C.S. in evening. Coy Strength 5 Off. 298.O.R.	a 7
	26/8/13		As before. Lt J.B. Stapylton-Smith R.E. placed in charge of GODE DUMP Det. remains billeted at Coy H.Q. Coy Strength 6 Off. 266.O.R.	a 7
	27/8/13		As before.	a 7
	28/8/13		As before. Orders for relief of 122nd by R.E. received CRE 34th Div OO N°9. Coy strength 5 Off. 206.O.R.	a 7
	29/8/13		Major J.H. Olivey R.E. and Lt J.B.S-Smith M.C. R.E. to MONT NOIR to see work of 122nd Coy. also Disinfector house over charge of GODE DUMP stock sheets Pt Dennis etc returned from detachment. Coy strength 6 Off. 206.O.R.	a 7
	30/9/13		O.C. and Lt Y.B. Stapylton-Smith M.C.R.E. and 4 returns moved to MONT NOIR taking men up from 122nd Field Coy R.E. Lt Pt B.L. Knox V.C. R.E. i/c Coy H.Q. Coy strength 5 Off 266 OR	a 7
	31/8/13		Coy standing by at MONT NOIR. Position of Enemy not yet known Coy Strength 5 Off. 208.O.R	a 7

for O.C. 150th FIELD COY. R.E.
Capt R.E.

Confidential

War Diary
- of -
150th Field Coy. R.E.

September 1918.

Army Form C. 2118.

WAR DIARY
or
INTELLIGENCE SUMMARY.
(Erase heading not required.)

Place	Date	Hour	Summary of Events and Information	Remarks and references to Appendices
	1/9/18		OC and 4 Sections moved from Bolek at Mont Noir to his billets in Allouw at Bailleul Asylum. S.14 c.2.8. at Con. 4 Sections on fatigue party. Employed in repairing road. S.7.6.3.8 – Bailleul Square – S.14 d.3.8 – S.15. c.8.8. Transport Lines moved from Escke to Billet- at Berthen R.22.c.30.40. Company strength 7 off. 207 OR.	Apx
	2/9/18		Co employed as before: 12 men employed in Allouw stables & entrance accommodation. remainder of Co employed on repairing roads at Cleary on road. S.9 a.6.5 – S.9.6.3.3. – S.15 c.8.8. Company strength 7 off. 207 O.R.	Apx
	3/9/18		Co located & employed as yesterday. Company strength 7 off. 207 O.R.	Apx

2/Lieut C L Knox V.C.
Rest of above to N.W.

WAR DIARY
or
INTELLIGENCE SUMMARY.

Place	Date	Hour	Summary of Events and Information	Remarks and references to Appendices
	4/9/18		Co located as before. 4 Section's two fatigue parties of 12 the Employed in repairing forward roads in S.16.c.2.4 - S.17.6.6.1. - T.19.a.S.7 to T.13. Central and from S.12.c.4.4 to S.5.6.9.4. Company Strength 7 off. 207 O.R.	JKO
	5/9/18		O.C. & 4 Section's located as before. Transport two horses from BERTHEN to join remainder of Co. at BAILLEUL ASYLUM. 3 Section's Employed on forward roads as yesterday with addition of piece from T Central to NEUVE EGLISE. 1 Section Employed in clearing cellars & preparing dets for R.E. Dumps at BAILLEUL ASYLUM also in loading & stacking material. Company Strength 7 off. 207 O.R.	JKO

Army Form C. 2118.

Place	Date	Hour	Summary of Events and Information	Remarks and references to Appendices
	6/9/18		C worked as before. 2½ Sections on forward roads ie S.12.C.3.4. to DRANOUTRE. and T.13. Central to NEUVE EGLISE. This portion of road was badly shelled with gas shell last night. Then had to wear respirators whilst filling in gas shell holes. Night 5th/6th L/Cpl A. Greene (no. to H.Q.) 1¾r Section on billet & dump work. Company Strength 7 Off. 208 O.R.	Gas
	7/9/18		C worked as before. Only 20 men out out on bicycles to work on forward road NEUVE EGLISE to WULVERGHEM. They were unable to do much work owing to very heavy gas shelling. Shelly & had to tie in the shell head of the Rouenles to Co. Employed road dumps & billets. Company Strength 7 Off 208 O.R.	Gas

WAR DIARY
or
INTELLIGENCE SUMMARY

Army Form C. 2118.

Place	Date	Hour	Summary of Events and Information	Remarks and references to Appendices
			Heavy Allies + enemy shaking Gavil + Ronds + advance to the dumps	S.R.O
	8/9/18		Co trained as before. 1 Section employed on Brigade work in locality Road Screep in front of Brigade Hqrs. Improved nels to Brigade Hq. billets etc. Remainder of Co employed on Co billets work. Entry, forms + Salvage behind the Roads Road dumps. By Strength 6 off. 208 O.R	S.R.O
	9/9/18		Co located as before. About 9.50 men were inoculated. Co taking in horses. Co in Allison Ack. Typhoid carriers. By Strength 6 off. 208 O.R	S.R.O
	10/9/18		Co trained as before. Remainder of Co two inoculated 1 Section employed on trench work. Men employed as before. By Strength 6 off. 208 O.R	S.R.O

WAR DIARY
or
INTELLIGENCE SUMMARY.

(Erase heading not required.)

Army Form C. 2118.

Place	Date	Hour	Summary of Events and Information	Remarks and references to Appendices
	10/9/18		Co. Employed and located as before. Very heavy rain all wh'h makes tracks badly. Coy Strength 5 Off. 203 O.R.	SFO
	11/9/18		Co. located as before. Co. Employed as before. Commenced establishing a shell dump at R.E. dump at T.11.C. 35.15 for infantry in line to draw from. Coy Strength 6 Off. 209 O.R.	SFO
	12/9/18		Co. located and Employed as before. Coy Strength 6 Off. 202 O.R.	SFO
	14/9/18		Co. located and employed as before. Coy strength 6 Off. 209 O.R.	SFO
	15/9/18		Location & work as before. At 4.30 pm 2 sections under Section officers L.O.C. moved to camp at T.19.C.6.7. taking over forward line work from 121st Fd. Coy. R.E. 2 sections remaining at rear billet under Lt Bonnyat. Coy Strength 6 Off. 209 O.R.	WNW

WAR DIARY
INTELLIGENCE SUMMARY

Army Form C. 2118.

Place	Date	Hour	Summary of Events and Information	Remarks and references to Appendices
	16.9.18		2 Sections & Horse Lines located at rear billet. 2 sections 2.O.R. located at T.14.c.6.7. Work of forward sections as follows:- A.D.S. T.15.b.25.99. Bn. H.Q. T.10.c.9.9. Bn. H.Q. T.15.b+6. Bde H.Q. T.14.c.8.8 also wiring & maintenance of front line. Front line at present is entirely wired & Sappers attached to Support Coy and accommodated and rationed by them. Work:- assistance & erecting of accommodation. One section brought up from rear billet to work during day on Forward Billets T.20.9+8.8.7.	
	17.9.18		Work & location as before. Additional work screening NEUVE EGLISE — MESSINES road as fast forward as possible. Coy Strength 6 off. 209 O.R.	
	18.9.18		Work and location as before. Complete belt of wire finished across Divisional front. Coy Strength 6 off. 209. O.R.	

WAR DIARY
or
INTELLIGENCE SUMMARY.
(Erase heading not required.)

Army Form C. 2118.

Place	Date	Hour	Summary of Events and Information	Remarks and references to Appendices
	19.9.18		All work carried out to CRE. 30 O.R. arrived back to War Help: at BAILLEUL ASYLUM. Sections 3 & 4 & OC moved back to War Help: at BAILLEUL ASYLUM. Coy Strength 6 Off. 209 O.R.	JWB
	20.9.18		All Co located at BAILLEUL ASYLUM. Co moved at 9 p.m. from BAILLEUL ASYLUM with Brawn Boys to billets at EECKE. 27/9, 26, 6, 10. 60 arriving at EECKE. Coy Strength 6 Off 209 O.R.	JWB
	21.9.18		Co in billets at EECKE. Employed in cleaning up, kit inspections etc. Lt. BRUNYATE proceeded on leave. Capt FERRIER returned from leave. Coy Strength 6 Off 209 O.R.	JWB
	22.9.18		Co located as before. Employed in Gas House in Morning. Later 3 sections Afternoon Church service. Coy Strength 6 Off 205 O.R.	JWB

WAR DIARY or INTELLIGENCE SUMMARY

Army Form C. 2118.

Place	Date	Hour	Summary of Events and Information	Remarks and references to Appendices
PESEL HOEK	23/7/17		Company moved under command of CAPT. H. FERRIER to PESELHOEK AREA from OTWHY proceeded on Road Work. Sgt Scotty Stables and his fire Horse were left 2 was naturally damaged	
	24/7/17		Work started at 27/H 21.6.2.7 taken over by which Bn Bns 148th Inf Coy started in craters of old R. and R.E. works party to Coy Engrs II Kpls started work Coy Strength 6 Off 205 O.R.	at
	25/7/17		Work as before Coy Strength 6 Off 205 O.R.	at
	26/7/17		Work as before. Much trouble with suns. Lieut R. Charlesworth RE joined for duty. Last day of E.W.I. duty. Coy Strength 7 Off 205 O.R.	at
	27/7/17		Worked party of 1 O.E. working supplied by infantry Coy Strength 7 Off 205 O.R.	at
	28/7/17		Four Sections under command of Capt Ferrier RE moved to 28 NW/H 12.70.10 Transport under Lieut 113 Shapotham moved to R51665/3BPO CHATEAU area Coy Strength 7 Off 205 O R	Aff.
	29/7/17		Four Sections under Capt A Ferrier moved to 28/J 8.6.60.20 Coy Strength 7 Off 205 O R	Aff.
	30/7/17		Work started on planks (repairing + fitting on Shell Cratered Roads in area 28/J 7 + 8. Coy Strength 7 Off 205 O R	Aff.

For O.C. 150th Coy RE

Confidential

War Diary

of

150th Field Eng. Rg.

October, 1918

WAR DIARY
or
INTELLIGENCE SUMMARY.
(Erase heading not required.)

Army Form C. 2118.

Place	Date	Hour	Summary of Events and Information	Remarks and references to Appendices
WEST HOEK	1/10/18		Company employed on work at SECRUSPION ROAD. Lt. F.D Downie & 20 Sappers forwarded on BECELAERE attached to Div. Commander. Orders received in afternoon to work on BECELAERE BROODSEINDE road. Dismounted portion of company accordingly moved to billets in and round BECELAERE. Coy Strength 7 Off. 205.O.R.	A.7
BECELAERE	2/10/18		Work on before Lt. Downie and party employed also on road three Dumps removed up from HEIGHTS.S.E.AS of BECELAERE. Coy Strength 7 Off. 205.O.R.	A.2
	3/10/18		Company working on BECELAERE - MENIN road. more communication Coy Strength 7 Off. 205.O.R.	A.2
	4/10/18		Work on before Lt. Downie Pl. and party employed demt. Sapper ROMMER and MACGREGOR recommended for M.M. for gallantry in befor wounded much file Coy Strength 7 Off. 205.O.R.	A.2
	5/10/18		Work on before O.C.'s conference as evening. Coy Strength 7 Off. 202.O.R.	A.2
	6/10/18		Work in rennum as before afternoon spent in bridging recces and construction of foot bridges Coy Strength 7 Off. 202.O.R.	A.2

Army Form C. 2118.

WAR DIARY
or
INTELLIGENCE SUMMARY.
(Erase heading not required.)

Instructions regarding War Diaries and Intelligence Summaries are contained in F. S. Regs., Part II. and the Staff Manual respectively. Title pages will be prepared in manuscript.

Place	Date	Hour	Summary of Events and Information	Remarks and references to Appendices
BECELAERE	7/10/18		Work on road in Bghe Also construction of foot bridges. Pl. Desmas went for beer to U.K. Coy Strength 7 Off. 202 O.R.	A2
	8/10/18		As before. Coy Strength 7 Off. 202 O.R.	A2
	9/10/18		Two section on the Bridges. Two section on road. Coy Strength 7 Off. 202 O.R.	
	10/10/18		As before sections renewed. Coy Strength 7 Off. 208 O.R.	A2
	11/10/18		N°1 sent road patrol to look after TERHAND DADIZEELE road. N°3 Sect erecting Calais shelters Coy Strength 7 Off. 210 O.R. N°2 & 4 Ponton Bridges.	
	12/10/18		N°2 Section found road patrol for TERHAND — DADIZEELE road. N°4 Sect on Calais shelters to A.C. N°1 & 3 on Bridges. Coy Strength 7 Off. 208 O.R.	A2
	13/10/18		Coy employed preparing gear for action. Owing to Offr. having gone N°3 Section has been temporarily put under command N°1, 2 and 4 Section Coy Strength 7 Off. 208 O.R. Capt Jerram to see G.O.C. 109th Bde and C.R.E. N°1 Sect under Lieut Knox R.E. moved off in evening with 6 Ligth Bridges to join 1st Batn Royal Innis Fusrs to be up pontons off Ponton pn Ridges NEUVE BEEK in 28/ L 14 and 15.	A2
	14/10/18		N°2 and 4 Section sent hoffey transport 109 3 Ridge wagon and escort road parched at 3.0 am and Coy Strength 7 Off. 208 O.R.	A2

Army Form C. 2118.

WAR DIARY
or
INTELLIGENCE SUMMARY
(Erase heading not required.)

Place	Date	Hour	Summary of Events and Information	Remarks and references to Appendices
Field	13/10/18		Marched off 3.20 p.m. to concentration point ARKANGSEM 28/K.15. Capt Penier & 1st Bn Kincaid Smith moved to Bde HQ. at BASS FARM 28/K.13.C.26. Information re advance full Ops of MERCKEGEM received by runner Thomas 09.05 from III Bn KNOXVIC at Capt Penier & II Bn Kincaid Smith accompanied Bde HQ to	
			ASHMORE FARM L.15.d. Found in position at CUREW HOUSE L.16.a. N° 2 and 4 section and Patty transport moved to way to CUREW HOUSE and three Lewis to BASS FARM. Section (2) compliment at BIRKENEKE Kemales. 1 killed & wounded N° 3 Sect. Company standing by Capt P. & 2nd Lt G.O.C. sent N° 1 Sect over 2 Lewis guns to collect Bn B and sent over to N° 2 Sect by 6 Lt AE. for the work. Coy strength 7 off. 203 O.R.	A.F
CUREW HOUSE	15/10/18		Men to lines ordered to move to CREW FARM L.15.d. Capt Penier to see C.R.E. ordered to move to LEDEGHEM area. Arrived at 12.30. With company concentrated in area L.8.6 and L.9.1 and got Supplies Pots and ? bedding wagon. Coy strength 7 off. 203 O.R.	a.F
	16/10/18		Coy strength 7 off. 203 O.R.	a.F
LEDEGHEM	17/10/18		Coy employed on inspections cleaning Rifles etc. Coy strength 7 off. 203 O.R.	a.F

Army Form C. 2118.

WAR DIARY
or
INTELLIGENCE SUMMARY.
(Erase heading not required.)

Instructions regarding War Diaries and Intelligence Summaries are contained in F. S. Regs., Part II. and the Staff Manual respectively. Title pages will be prepared in manuscript.

Place	Date	Hour	Summary of Events and Information	Remarks and references to Appendices
LEDEGHEM	18/10/18	13.30	Company moved off at 13.30. Horse lines to WINKEL st E1.01 29/7.13 ok. dismounted party and bivying wagons of 122nd Coy RE all got each a mess cart to 29/B.15.a. Coyt Jones and Lt A Rosherough proceed to see 11th Belgian Infantry regiment at B.17a 76. Lt A Rosherough R.E. went forward to make what reconnaissance of River LYS in OYGHEM area. Coyt Jones to 109 Bec at VLUGEHY FARM 29/B.15.c. at 22.20 Lt J.B.S Smith MC RE and 1st Pl Rosherough RE and No 2 Sectn took this pontoon wagons and erected them at B.7a.6.3. with Boats. In preparation for crossing LYS at 01.00 news came that crossing of LYS was postponed.	A.7.
			Coy Strength 7 offr 20.3 O.R.	
A.B.Sul Vucht 29/B.15.a	19/9/18	07.30	At 07.30 Lieut. W.M. Buongate RE and party went out and carried out a reconnaissance of MVER LYS and its approaches in 29/C.16.a a/c. Coy remained in Lillo Capt Jones to see C.R.E at 10.9.4.86. Aujo 911 Obery required permit to collect Kit and proceeded to England for course in India. Coyt I.B. on 109 BC again in afternoon thence to C.R.E. at 17.00 Lt J.B.Smith MC RE and 1st Pl Rosherough and No 2 Sct to C7d.6.3. to collect boats and take them down to C.19.a.9.7 to be in reserve to 121st Cay Bde. Successfully carried out at 17.30 Coyt P. Hr D know VC RE Lt Buongate and No 1 and 4 Sectn accompanied G.R. Keith wagons moved to Town at C.13.a. 5.5. in	R.

(19175) Wt W2355/P360 600,000 12/7 D.D.& L. Sch.510. Forms/C.1718/15

WAR DIARY
INTELLIGENCE SUMMARY
(Erase heading not required.)

Army Form C. 2118.

Place	Date	Hour	Summary of Events and Information	Remarks and references to Appendices
ABSUL (cont.)	19/9/18		Machines to build medium bridge over 6 yds. 2 everywhere and boats from No 7 Pontoon Park also arrived under 150th Coy. Jumelon. Capt. J. on sight knocked down to river bank in 19 a. VC set in truck with the 12.13? Pd. by Action proceeding satisfactorily. Truck gained with the J.B.S. Smith and his party in A Knox back to his own setting. Shelly after midnight one pontoon taken up to 21 st Coy. & Pl J.B.S. Smith and with flooring with N°2 Section. Casualties. One driver (Palmiter) killed and 3 horses. Cpl. Strength 7 Off. 201 O.R.	
	20/9/18		Special book 2 Aug 1m 10th Repr. Show) at 02.32. Order sent out to Cpl. J. from C 19 a 5.3 to N°1 and 4 sections to start bridging party. One recy stalled Sept Hutton killed at 06 in orders sent out to cease bridging owing to situation and firing from on left. At 07.00 orders sent out to recommence bridging. Work done on the Reconnaissance Parties & Cpl. J. and J. J.B.S. Smith R.E. Previous bridge for traffic completed by 10.15. A great deal of trouble caused by lack of parts and unsuitability of Nelson trestles owing to width of river. CRE to see bridge at 18.00. Portion of bridge C 14. c 7.9 13.c 5.3 C troops P.C. Advanced base line moved up to C troops P.C. Advanced base line to ShntPIETERS KNOCK. Guards of join discords left for the advance base line to. Bridge every 4 hours. 1 Officer and ½ section mounted on bridge. Coy Strength 7 Off 201 O.R.	O.F.

WAR DIARY
or
INTELLIGENCE SUMMARY.

Army Form C. 2118.

Place	Date	Hour	Summary of Events and Information	Remarks and references to Appendices
19/C13C33	21/4/18		Company employed on maintenance of medium pontoon bridge and erection of light foot bridge	
			No 3 Cy 11 R.I.E (?) also working with company constructing approach road for C.19.6.3.5 to	
			Canal bank. Coy (2 platoons) 1 platoon working on approach to medium bridge & platoon collecting	
			materials during morning medium bridge was shelled with 5.9" how but was undamaged.	a.1
			Pontoon lines ordered to move up to C.13.a central. Light bridge completed	
			b. oy Strength 7 off. 201 O.R.	
"	22/4/18		Company employed as before. Barrel pier bridge two stands complete at C.20 a 36.	
			Pioneers to 6/yr. Rgm. A.P. Abbot 14c R.E. arrived and took over command of coy.	a.2
			b. oy Strength 7 off. 201 O.R.	
"	23/4/18		Company employed on light bridge and approaches b.oy Strength 7 off. 201 O.R.	
"	24/4/18		Coy on wooden road leading to No2 Pontoon bridge and on completed bridges. Bridge O.C.E	a.2
			one Brigade Company bathed in afternoon. b. oy Strength 7 off. 201 O.R.	
"	25/4/18		Coy on commenced dismantling No 1 Pontoon Bdg. moved in afternoon to billets	a.2
			in DESSEIGNEM. b. oy Strength 7 off. 201 O.R.	
"	26/4/18		No 1 Bridge dismantled 122nd Fd Coy wagons equipment returned. Moved to issue at	a.2
			b. oy Strength 7 off. 195 O.R.	

Army Form C. 2118.

WAR DIARY
or
INTELLIGENCE SUMMARY.
(Erase heading not required.)

Instructions regarding War Diaries and Intelligence Summaries are contained in F. S. Regs., Part II. and the Staff Manual respectively. Title pages will be prepared in manuscript.

Place	Date	Hour	Summary of Events and Information	Remarks and references to Appendices
LENDERLEDE	27/9/18		Clearing wagon lines etc. Proceed to LENDERLEDE	A1
			Coy Strength 7 Off. 195 O.R.	
	28/9/18		Clearing wagons packing stores etc.	A2
			Coy Strength 7 Off. 195 O.R.	
ST ANNES	29/9/18		Marched to own near ST ANNES 29/M arriving about 11.00.	A3
			Coy Strength 7 Off. 195 O.R.	
	30/9/18		Inspection of kits and harness cleaning etc	A4
			Coy Strength 7 Off. 195 O.R.	
	1/10/18		Inspection of men. Physical drill. Got to mend in transport	A5
			Coy Strength 7 Off. 195 O.R.	

O. Tarbitt. Major R.E.
O.C. 150th Field Coy R.E.

Narrative of Operations by 150th Field Coy., R.E., 15th Oct.-21st Oct.1918

In the operations carried out by the II Corps commencing on the 14th October, 1918, the 150th Field Coy., R.E. was attached to the 109th Infantry Brigade and the following special tasks were allotted to the unit:-

(1). To assist the assault waves to cross the HEULEBEEKE, between 28/L.15.b.3.6. and L.16.c.6.1., by placing light infantry bridges across.

(2). To carry out any necessary repairs on the roads in the area to be captured by the Brigade, with especial reference to the bridges over the HEULEBEEKE at MOORSEELE, GULLEGHEM and HEULE.

Preparations were completed by the afternoon of the 13th October, the Company being organised on the following basis:-

No.1 Section, under II Lieut. C.L.KNOX, V.C., R.E., and one wagon attached to 1st Batt. R. Innis. Fusiliers, for the purpose of carrying forward infantry bridges.

No.2 Section, under II Lieut. R. CHARLESWORTH, R.E.

No.4 Section, under Lieut. W.M.W. BRUNYATE, each with a specially loaded bridging wagon attached in readiness to repair any craters or other gaps in the MOORSEELE-HEULE road.

Fighting transport, consisting of above mentioned wagons, a trestle wagon loaded with 15 feet of superstructure and spare timber, and a double tool-cart were all under the general control of Lieut. J.B. STAPYLTON-SMITH, M.C., R.E.

At 19-00 hours on the 13th, II Lieut. C.L.KNOX, V.C., and No.1 Section moved off into battle position with the 1st R. Innis. Fusiliers at JAGO FARM, 28/L.13.c. At 03-30 on the 14th, Nos. 2 and 4 Sections and fighting transport moved into a reserve position at ARKMOELEN, 28/K.16.b., arriving about 05-00. Capt. A. FERRIER, R.E., and II Lieut. R. CHARLESWORTH, R.E. then went forward to 109 Brigade Headquarters at BASS FARM, 28/K.18.c.

II Lieut. C.L. KNOX, V.C., and No.1 Section successfully bridged the HEULEBEEKE with the first wave, but the infantry bridges proving somewhat short, other crossings were constructed with local materials. Casualties were, 1 killed, 1 died of wounds, 4 wounded.

As the enemy carried out no demolitions to roads in the area captured by the 109th Brigade, the remainder of the unit was not called on to go into action. The whole Company, less horse lines, was concentrated on the night of the 14th, at COHEN HOUSE, 28/L.16.a. and fighting transport at ORAM FARM at 28/L.15.d.

On the Company 15th, the Company stood by for orders. Two pontoons, with wagons and teams complete, were attached to the 122nd Field Company, R.E., taking subsequent part in the bridging operations carried out by that unit on the 16th October, at COURTRAI.

On the 16th October, the Company moved to LEDEGHEM, and remained there until 13-30 on the 18th, when it moved to ABSUL, 29/B.15.a., with horse lines at WINKEL St. ELOI. During the afternoon of the 18th, Capt. FERRIER and II Lieut CHARLESWORTH visited the H.Q. of the 11th Belgian Infantry Regiment, from whence II Lieut. CHARLESWORTH went forward with a guide to gain information about the approaches to the LYS near OYGHEM. Capt. FERRIER returned to VLUGERY FARM and remained there all night in close touch with 109th Brigade.

At 22-20 on the 18th October, Lieut. J.B. STAPYLTON-SMITH, M.C. and II Lieut. CHARLESWORTH with No.2 Section went forward with two pontoons and placed them in concealment in OYGHEM, in case an attack should be ordered at dawn of the 19th.

At 07-30 on the 19th, Lieut. W.M.W. BRUNYATE, R.E., went up to OYGHEM and made a most valuable daylight reconnaissance of the LYS and its approaches in 29/C.14.a. and c. The information he gained, decided, without a doubt, the site at which a bridge was subsequently placed.

Just before dusk on the 19th, Lieut. J.B. STAPYLTON-SMITH and II Lieut. CHARLESWORTH, with two teams of horses and No. 2 Section went to OYGHEM and collected the pontoons, and took them to a reserve position in the farm at C.19.a.9.7.

In the meanwhile, Nos. 1 and 4 Sections, II Lieut. KNOX, V.C., and Lieut. BRUNYATE, with 2 trestle wagons, followed later by 2 pontoons belonging to No.7 Pontoon Park, under Capt. FERRIER, moved into position at the farm at C.13.a. central. Having arrived at this position, Capt. FERRIER and II Lieut. KNOX went forward to gain touch with No.2 Section and the pontoons, and also the 121st Field Coy., R.E. on the river bank in C.19.a. Touch having been gained, II Lieut. KNOX returned to his Section. Capt. FERRIER remained in a house at C.19.a.5.3.

During the night, O.C. 121st Field Company, R.E. asked for another pontoon, and Lieut. J.B. STAPYLTON-SMITH, M.C., and II Lieut. CHARLESWORTH with No.2 Section brought the wagon down to the bridge at C.19.a.45.10. under heavy shell fire and unloaded the boat. At this stage, one driver and 5 horses were killed in the farm C.19.a.9.7.

Word was received from O.C. 121st Field Coy., R.E. at 02-50 on the morning of the 20th, that the 107th Infantry Brigade had completely passed over the LYS. Instructions were accordingly sent to Lieut. BRUNYATE and II Lieut. KNOX, with Nos. 1 and 4 Sections, to investigate the river bank and start bridging if possible. The material was all brought down to the site, when these two Sections came under shell fire and were forced to scatter, one man being killed. At this time, owing to the situation on the left flank not being clear, orders were issued to stop bridging until later.

Shortly after 08-00 on the 20th, the situation on the left was reported clear, and bridging operations were again ordered to start. Capt. FERRIER and Lieut. J.B. STAPYLTON-SMITH, having previously made a rough reconnaissance of approaches to the bank, a medium bridge was constructed at C.14.c.7.5., the first transport passing over at 14-15. A certain delay was caused in the construction of the bridge owing to the shortage of pontoons.

During the 21st October, the Company was employed on maintenance of the pontoon bridge, construction of roadways, and a light footbridge.

36th Division "G"
Chief Engineer, 2nd Corps.
War Diary.

Robert A. Mackenzie

Lt. Colonel, R.E.,
C.R.E., 36th Division.

23/10/18.

WB 38

Confidential

War Diary

- of -

150th Field Company R.E.

November, 1918.

WAR DIARY
or
INTELLIGENCE SUMMARY.
(Erase heading not required.)

Army Form C. 2118.

Place	Date	Hour	Summary of Events and Information	Remarks and references to Appendices
ST ANNES	1/11/18		2 Sections route marched. Reconnaissance employed on construction experimental bridges	AA
	2/11/18		As before	at
	3/11/18		Church parade	at
	4/11/18		As on 2nd inst	at
	5/11/18		As before	at
	6/11/18		Coy moved to MOUSCRON S22d central 1/29. Coy Strength 7 Off. 1040 OR	at
	7/11/18		Coy employed on cables and wagons. Coy Strength 7 Off. 1040 OR.	at
	8/11/18		B1 on wagon and construction of left hinges. Coy Strength 7 Off. 1040 OR.	A
	9/11/18		Division to return employed in civil and hospital billets. Wounded taken stretcher inspection. Orders to move to RUTSYVE to work under CE X Bde. arrived at 11.30am. marched at once. Coy Strength 7 Off. 193 OR.	

WAR DIARY
or
INTELLIGENCE SUMMARY.
(Erase heading not required.)

Army Form C. 2118.

Instructions regarding War Diaries and Intelligence Summaries are contained in F. S. Regs., Part II. and the Staff Manual respectively. Title pages will be prepared in manuscript.

Place	Date	Hour	Summary of Events and Information	Remarks and references to Appendices
MON SCRON	10/11/18		Coy paraded 05.15. Moved off & marched via to AUTNOYE at 05.30 consisting of destination about 13.00. Work started on a road down to river SCHELDT	
	11/11/18		ESCANAFFLES, the a heavy barrage from 6.45. at 19.00 Cutting work in Shelter location of work 29/V.10.C. Coy Strength 7 Off. 198.O.R. Company still employed on road. About this time no large work carried on all day and continued till	at
	12/11/18		02.00 when job was completed. At 06.30 coy arrived again for about work on a 60 foot gap in road at 29/V.2.b.2.3. Reconnaissance of temporary work out at 10.0ms to bridge at V.23.c. central. Work carried on a temporary bridge to take foot transport usable 16.00 extra bridge now completed	at
ESCANAFFLES	13/11/18		Company paraded at 06.00 and am.h new stretch from Coy Strength 7 Off. 198.O.R. to 3 twenty foot span to camp Tubes. Work resumed till 12.31 when 122nd labs. Coy took over to their abutment complete and work obtained 75% complete one tenth 75% complete.	at
			Coy Strength 7 Off. 198.O.R.	
	14/11/18		Work started at 06.00. Trouble caused to Bert foundation for welding fruits of central span. Decided to shutter and help. Welds with dry filling a.G.boot	at
			Coy Strength 7 Off. 198.O.R.	

Army Form C. 2118.

WAR DIARY
or
INTELLIGENCE SUMMARY.
(Erase heading not required.)

Instructions regarding War Diaries and Intelligence Summaries are contained in F. S. Regs., Part II. and the Staff Manual respectively. Title pages will be prepared in manuscript.

Place	Date	Hour	Summary of Events and Information	Remarks and references to Appendices
ESQUELBECQ	15/4/18		Coy. from 10.05.45 to work on Ridge. Steel posts all carried over to Ridge before landing caw at noon to 12.1 to 6 p.m. Transport proceeded. Being louaser & Two kar. ben sup. sent out to Regt Steel Bivouac. Coy Strength 7 off. 138 O.R.	at
	16/4/18		Coy employed as on Rolle which we cleared to half the length of wire. Coy Strength 7 off. 207 O.R.	at
	17/4/18		Coy employed working wagons et preparations for move. Coy Strength 7 off 207 O.R. De-sub on Rolle Demoti. & section cleaning and search. by Strength 7 off 207 O.R.	at
	18/4/18		Move off at 6.00 a.m and marched to NUDEN KORNE Steel 24 Roads about 12 noon Weather turned to rain. Coy Strength 7 off 207 O.R.	a.t
RON C.R.	19/4/18		Removed inaal at 8.00 a.m. to RONCQ Steel 13 Officers Transport had to go a different road to dismounted personnel arriving too late and and Coy Strength 7 off 207 O.R. Rifle and ammunition inspection. Quell and survey fatigues. Coy Strength 7 off. 205 O.R. inpantry	at
	20/4/18			at
	21/4/18		Quell and survey fatigues blows clothing & rest as per P.R.O. Coy Strength 7 off 205 O.R.	at
	22/4/18		10.10 C.S. shelling and suss & fall of P.R.Rose Ron the Wagon fatigues etc. Coy Strength 7 off. 205 O.R.	at

Army Form C. 2118.

WAR DIARY
or
INTELLIGENCE SUMMARY.
(Erase heading not required.)

Instructions regarding War Diaries and Intelligence Summaries are contained in F. S. Regs., Part II. and the Staff Manual respectively. Title pages will be prepared in manuscript.

Place	Date	Hour	Summary of Events and Information	Remarks and references to Appendices
RONCQ	23/11/18	—	Review about in chief and inspection of arms and equipment. Sports in afternoon.	A.2
			Coy strength 4 off. 204 O.R.	
	24/11/18		Church parades for the wounded. Free afternoon for all ranks.	A.2
			Coy strength 4 off. 204 O.R.	
	25/11/18		Inspection and shall also physical training. Received being in afternoon.	A.2
			Company teams played 9th R Scots Fus 1st XV 1-2. Rugby transport parties attending	
	26/11/18		No 4 Section employed in unloading a furniture & chandeliers chandler to bob in the barracks	A.2
			Coy Strength 4 off. 204 O.R.	
	27/11/18		Recing and recreational training.	A.2
			No 2 & 6 Section in furniture evacuation. No 1 & 3 Route march and antr transport.	
			Coy Strength 4 off. 202 O.R.	
	28/11/18		A D V S visited River lines.	A.2
			No 1 and 3 on Route march and section transport. No 2 and 4 on furniture evacuation.	
	28/11/18		Inverted section moved winters.	
			Coy Strength 4 off. 205 O.R	
	29/11/18		Whole company employed in moving French furniture to education scheme. Wagon employed hauling less cart fetching fuel. Relieve on Sergeant & Cpl Adams injury.	A.2
			Coy strength 4 off. 205 O.R.	
	30/11/18		Company employed on Repr. Depr. clear on afternoon to all ranks. Evacuated return enclosed.	A.2
			Coy Strength 4 off. 205 O.R.	

Army Form C. 2118.

Vol 39

Confidential

War Diary

- of -

150th Field Coy. R.E.

December 1918

Army Form C. 2118.

WAR DIARY
or
INTELLIGENCE SUMMARY.
(Erase heading not required.)

Instructions regarding War Diaries and Intelligence Summaries are contained in F. S. Regs., Part II. and the Staff Manual respectively. Title pages will be prepared in manuscript.

Place	Date	Hour	Summary of Events and Information	Remarks and references to Appendices
RONCQ	1/1/18		Whole Company employed all day in clearing up the Divisional camp. Two parties by Lieuts Toll. 205 O.R.	a.7
	2/1/18		Same as on the 1st. Snow afternoon a practice. Draw by Lieut Toll 205 O.R. Inspection parade cancelled. Sappers employed from out. Tablets	a.7
	3/1/18		Same as 3rd. By Lieut Toll 205 O.R.	a.7
	4/1/18		By Lieut Toll 205 O.R.	
	5/1/18		Same as 3rd No officers etc. Same as [?] of previous pension or 6th by Lieut Toll 205 O.R.	a.7
	6/1/18		Whole Company employed in clearing up March to Italian Residence & erecting tent roofs and linen [?] for Prisoners parade Returned in afternoon by [?] 205 O.R.	a.7
	7/1/18		Company employed on furniture workshops and frame up near bridge in factory. H.Q. and mounted orderlies Horses and mounted orderlies moved to Lille belge in Factory by Lieut Toll 205 O.R.	a.7
	8/1/18		Church parade etc. Small pass of N.C.O.s to Lille for 1/2 of Company Captain George to off 205 O.R.	a.7
	9/1/18		Lt Stapleton-Smith M.C. RE and 23 men drawn from all sections attended work under Capt Allen RE at Pridge over Lys between WARNINGHEM Captain George to off 205 O.R.	a.7
			Remainder working on furniture & clothes	a.7

Army Form C. 2118

WAR DIARY
or
INTELLIGENCE SUMMARY
(Erase heading not required.)

Place	Date	Hour	Summary of Events and Information	Remarks and references to Appendices
RONCQ	10/12/18		As before. Coy. Strength 7 Off. 205 O.R.	A.7
	11/12/18		As before. Afternoon spent in preparing for Divisional parade. Coy Strength 7 Off. 205 O.R.	A.7
	12/12/18		Div. Parade cancelled. Work as before. Coy Strength 7 Off. 205 O.R.	
	13/12/18		Work as before. Coy Strength 7 Off. 205 O.R.	
	14/12/18		As before. Coy Strength 7 Off. 205 O.R.	
	15/12/18		Men employed in constructing permanent latrines and preparing for Inspection by Corps Commander. Coy. Strength 7 Off. 208 O.R.	AA
	16/12/18		Parade at HALLUIN aerodrome. Reviewed by XV Corps Commander. Coy. Strength 7 Off. 208 O.R.	
	17/12/18		Lt. Knox V.C. constructing Bowsing ring for 109th Bde. Bowsing saw now running. W.O.L. on 14th. Coy. Strength 7 Off. 208 O.R.	A.7.
	18/12/18		Work on Bde Bowsing ring completed to day. Div. Commander visited the unit. Work on tables and forms as before. Coy. Strength 7 Off. 208 O.R.	A.7
	19/12/18		Work as before. Coy. Strength 7 Off. 208 O.R.	A.7
	20/12/18		Detachment working on bridge between HALLUIN and MENIN furnished to day. Coy. Strength 7 Off. 208 O.R.	A.7
	21/12/18		Whole company on construction of forms and tables for Bde. P/L 7B Stopford-Smith MC proceeded for leave to U.K. Coy. Strength 7 Off. 202 O.R.	

Army Form C. 2118.

WAR DIARY
or
INTELLIGENCE SUMMARY

(Erase heading not required.)

Instructions regarding War Diaries and Intelligence Summaries are contained in F. S. Regs., Part II. and the Staff Manual respectively. Title Pages will be prepared in manuscript.

Place	Date	Hour	Summary of Events and Information	Remarks and references to Appendices
RONCQ	22/12/13		Company employed on construction of dug-outs. Coy. Strength 7 off. 202 O.R.	A.1
	23/12/13		Coy. reform. Coy. Strength 7 off. 202 O.R.	A.1
	24/12/13		Company given the day to decorate their billets for Xmas day. Coy. Strength 7 off. 202 O.R.	A.1
	25/12/13		Maj. A.L. ABBOTT M.C., R.E. and 6 officers moved to visit men at Xmas dinner. Holiday. Coy. Strength 7 off. 202 O.R.	A.1
	26/12/13		Holiday. Coy. Strength 7 off. 202 O.R.	
	27/12/13		Companies employed on the repair & reception of own dug-outs. Re technical instruction. Clearing up billets etc. Coy. Strength 7 off. 202 O.R.	A.1
	28/12/13		W.O.R. carried on as before. Preparation of a carpenters and joiners shop. Also a machine shop being got into running order. Coy. Strength 7 off. 202 O.R.	A.1
	29/12/13		General Offensive no work. Coy. Strength 7 off. 202 O.R.	
	29/12/13		W.O.R. carried on as on 28/12/13 Coy. Strength 7 off. 202 O.R.	A.1
	30/12/13		Coy. Strength 7 off. 203 O.R.	
	31/12/13		W.O.R. as on 30th.	A.1

A. Fewer. Capt. R.E.
for O.C. 150th FIELD COY. R.E.

Confidential

War Diary

-of-

150th Field Coy. R.E.

January, 1919.

WAR DIARY or INTELLIGENCE SUMMARY

Army Form C. 2118.

Place	Date	Hour	Summary of Events and Information	Remarks and references to Appendices
RONCQ	1 Jan 1919		Dismounted forbe working in conjunction with men in lines. Coys filling up tables and benches for future educational classes. Also filling up new engine and lamp lathes mounted. Half day exercising and set work from Officers Room.	a.1
	2/1/19		Same as 1st. 30 men (1 hour) to Mouscron for army group Information re by strength 7 officers 203 O.R.	a.1
	3/1/19		Same as before. Coy strength 7 officers 7 203 O.R.	a.1
	4/1/19		Morning as usual. Bonjour proper closed in afternoon. Coy strength 7 officers 199 O.R.	a.1
	5/1/19		Fatigue cleaning up, billets &c. Church parade in afternoon. Coy strength 7 officers 199 O.R.	a.1
	6/1/19		Work in workshops as before. Coy out for run at 3.0 p.m. Hour increased as usual. Coy strength 7 officers 199 O.R.	a.3
	7/1/19		Same as on 6th. Coy strength 7 officers 199 O.R.	
	8/1/19		Party of men from infantry for education reported. Work in shops and lectures from 7 officers 199 R as usual. Coy strength 7 officers 199 O.R.	a.3
	9/1/19		As on 8th. Coy strength 7 officers 199 O.R.	
	10/1/19		As on 9th.	
	11/1/19		As on 10th except half day off. Fetes in aid of Pakanday Fund in Mouscron. Coy strength 7 officers 203 O.R.	a.4

2449 Wt. W14957/M90 750,000 1/16 J.B.C. & A. Forms/C.2118/12.

WAR DIARY
or
INTELLIGENCE SUMMARY

Army Form C. 2118.

(Erase heading not required.)

Place	Date	Hour	Summary of Events and Information	Remarks and references to Appendices
Ron Cq.	12/1/19		Sections rifle inspection. Scrubbing down billets. Shovel parades. Coy Strength 7 Officers 203 O.R.	A.A.
	13/1/19		Work in shops as usual. Firing table. Lewis rifle ranks etc. Coy Strength 7 Officers 203 O.R.	a.a.
	14/1/19		As in 13th. Coy Strength 7 Officers 203 O.R.	a.a.
	15/1/19		As before. Coy Strength 7 Officers 203 O.R.	a.a.
	16/1/19		As before. Coy Strength 7 Officers 203 O.R.	a.a.
	17/1/19		As before. Coy Strength 7 Officers 203 O.R.	a.a.
	18/1/19		As before. Coy Strength 7 Officers 203 O.R.	a.a.
	19/1/19		Washing down billets etc. 6 men demobilized. Coy Strength 7 Officers 197 O.R.	a.a.
	20/1/19		Work in shops as usual. 5 more men demobilized. Coy Strength 7 Officers 192 O.R.	a.a.
	21/1/19		Work in shops as usual. Lieut Dunn & 10 O.R. & Lieut Harrison & 1 O.R. left for demobilization. Coy Strength 5 Officers 175 O.R.	a.a.a
	22/1/19	" " " " " Coy Strength 5 Officers 175 O.R.	a.a.a
	23/1/19	" " " " " Company Strength 5 Officers 175 O.R.	a.a.a
	24/1/19	" " " " " 3 O.R. left for demobilization. Coy Strength 5 Officers 172 O.R.	a.a.a
	25/1/19	" " " " " Working down billets inspection etc. Lieut J.B.S. Smith left with 3 O.R. for demobilization. Coy Strength 4 Officers 176 O.R.	a.a.a
	26/1/19			a.a.a

WAR DIARY or INTELLIGENCE SUMMARY

Army Form C. 2118.

Place	Date	Hour	Summary of Events and Information	Remarks and references to Appendices
RONCQ	27/1/19		Work & ships as usual. 9 O.R. left for demobilization. Coy strength 4 Off. 87 O.R.	AAA
	28/1/19		" " " " 6 " " " " " " Coy strength 4 Off. 81 O.R.	AAA
	29/1/19		" " " " " " 3 O.R. attached from 2nd R.I.R's Coy Strength 4 Off. 84 O.R. called out unexpected chaps	AAA
			G.O.C and C.R.E called out unexpected chaps. Company Strength 4 Off. 80 O.R.	AAA
	30/1/19		1 O.R. left for demobilization. Company Strength 4 Off. 80 O.R. Work as before.	AAA
	31/1/19		C.R.E. called. H.R.H. The Prince of Wales with the G.O.C. inspected the works during the afternoon. Coy Strength 4 Off. 157 O.R.	AAA

[signature]
Royal R.E.
O.C. 150th FIELD COY. R.E.

Vol 4

Confidential

War Diary

-of-

150th Field Coy. R.E.

February 1919.

WAR DIARY
INTELLIGENCE SUMMARY

Army Form C. 2118.

(Erase heading not required.)

Instructions regarding War Diaries and Intelligence Summaries are contained in F.S. Regs., Part II. and the Staff Manual respectively. Title Pages will be prepared in manuscript.

Place	Date	Hour	Summary of Events and Information	Remarks and references to Appendices
RONCQ	1/2/19		Dismounted portion of Coy. and attached Infantry working half day in wood and metal shops under instructor. 2 O.R. left for demobilisation. Coy Strength 4 officers 155 O.R. All.	
	2/2/19		Rifle Inspection 9 am. Washing down billets and Divine Service. 2 O.R. left for demobilisation. Coy strength 4 officers 153 O.R. All.	
	3/2/19		Work continued in School of Instruction. 7 O.R. left for demobilisation. Coy strength 4 officers 146 O.R. Lieut O'Hagan of 121 Coy attached for work on old German Anti-Aircraft. All.	
	4/2/19		Work as above, also 4 Sappers with Infantry working party under Lieut O'Hagan working to dismantle old German Huts. Coy strength 146 O.R. 4 officers. All.	
	5/2/19		Work as above. Ten trestle wagons and Trans. attached from 116 2 pontoon Park for carting wood from Rain Dump. Coy strength 4 officers 146 O.R. All.	
	6/2/19		Work as above. Lieut O'Hagan returned to his Unit. Started carting wood from Rain, cut on circular saw, and carried and stacked by 10 German prisoners. 4 O.R. left for demobilisation. Coy strength 4 officers 142 D.R. All.	
	7/2/19		Work as above. Rode over to 6 Pk. re demobilisation. 7 O.R. left for demobilisation. 1 O.R. evacuated sick. Coy Strength 4 officers 144 O.R. All. (13+ ? O.R.O.S.)	
	8/2/19		Work as above for half day. Strength as for 7. All.	

WAR DIARY or INTELLIGENCE SUMMARY

Army Form C. 2118.

Place	Date	Hour	Summary of Events and Information	Remarks and references to Appendices
Ronc Q.	9/2/19		Rifle inspection, working down billets, divine service. Coy strength 4 officers 144 O.R. a/a.	
	10/2/19		Work in school of instructors as before. 1 O.R. left for demobilization. 8 L.D. horses demobilised. Coy strength 4 officers 143 O.R. a/a.	
	11/12/2/19		Work as above, strength as above. a/a.	
	13/2/19		Work as above, 20 German prisoners employed. 7 O.R. left for demobilization. Coy strength 4 officers 136 O.R. a/a.	
	14/2/19		Work as above. 6 L.D. horses demobilised. a/a.	
	15/2/19		Work as above for half day. 1 O.R. demobilised while on leave U.K. and 2 more from Coy. Coy Strength 4 officers 110 O.R.	B.M.O.S
	16/2/19		Inspection. Divine Service. Cleaning billets. 3 O.R. demobilised from unit. Coy Strength 4 Officers, 107 O.R?	B.M.O.S WT/WS
	17/2/19		Work in schools as before. 3 O.R. demobilised. Strength 4 officers, 104 O.R.	
	18/2/19.		Maj A.L. Abbott went on leave to U.K. Work in schools as before Strength as before	WT/WS
	19/2/19		Work as before, also strength. Carpenter shop & metal shop practically closed down	WT/WS
	20/2/19		Work as before Coy strength as before.	WT/WS
	21/2/19		Work as before Coy strength ditto. For lack of men. Cutting firewood & a certain amount of other work continuing	WT/WS

Army Form C. 2118.

WAR DIARY
or
INTELLIGENCE SUMMARY

(Erase heading not required.)

Place	Date	Hour	Summary of Events and Information	Remarks and references to Appendices
RONCQ	22.2.19		Work as before for half a day. 3 men demobilised. Strength 4 officers 101 O.R. D.17.J.S.	
	23.2.19		Rifle inspection. Church Service. Cleaning billets. 3 O.R. demob. Strength 4 off. 98 O.R. D.17.J.S.	
	24.2.19		Work as before. 1 man demobilised with Knitting Company on 15.2.19. Attempt made by Provisional civilians(?) on the Factory containing our horses & stores, billets etc. A hole was cut in one gate way and an attempt made to raise the latch, another locked up entrance way knocked down. Nothing missed. Strength 97 O.R. D.17.J.S.	
	25.2.19		Work as before Strength as before D.17.J.S.	
	26.2.19		Work as before also strength D.17.J.S.	
	27.2.19		Work as before & strength D.17.J.S.	
	28.2.19		Work as before. 25 horses (Class Z) demobilised D.17.J.S.	

www.ingramcontent.com/pod-product-compliance
Lightning Source LLC
Chambersburg PA
CBHW080809010526
44113CB00013B/2352